NATURE
WALKS
in & around
SEATTLE

NATURE WALKS in & around SEATTLE

All-Season Exploring in Parks, Forests, and Wetlands

2nd edition

Cathy M. McDonald and Stephen R. Whitney

Photographs by James R. Hendrickson

THE
MOUNTAINEERS

Published by
The Mountaineers
1001 SW Klickitat Way, Suite 201
Seattle, WA 98134

© 1987 by The Mountaineers
© 1997 by Cathy M. McDonald and Stephen R. Whitney

All rights reserved

First edition 1987. Second edition: first printing 1997, second printing 1998

No part of this book may be reproduced in any form, or by any electronic, mechanical, or other means, without permission in writing from the publisher.

Published simultaneously in Great Britain by Cordee, 3a DeMontfort Street, Leicester, England, LE1 7HD

Manufactured in the United States of America

Edited by Susan Hodges
Maps by Debbie Newell
Cover design by Ani Rucki
Book design by Alice C. Merrill
Book layout by Hargrave Design
Cover photograph: Washington Park Arboretum
Frontispiece: Japanese Garden, Bloedel Reserve

Library of Congress Cataloging-in-Publication Data

McDonald, Cathy M.
  Nature walks in & around Seattle: all-season exploring in parks, forests, and wetlands / Cathy M. McDonald and Stephen R. Whitney; photographs by James R. Hendrickson.—2nd ed.
    p.   cm.
  Rev. ed. of: Nature walks in and around Seattle/Stephen R. Whitney. c1987.
  Includes bibliographical references and index.
  ISBN 0-89886-525-5
  1. Natural trails—Washington (State)—Seattle Region—Guidebooks.
  2. Natural history—Washington (State)—Seattle Region—Guidebooks.
  3. Parks—Washington (State)—Seattle Region—Guidebooks.
  4. Seattle Region (Wash.)—Guidebooks. I. Whitney, Stephen, 1942– . II. Whitney, Stephen, 1942– Nature walks in and around Seattle. III. Title.
QH105.W4M34 1997   97-25271
508.797'77—dc21   CIP

♻ Printed on recycled paper

Contents

Introduction / 9

Part I: The Natural Setting / 13
Climate / 14
Geology / 14
Habitats / 15
Human Impact / 20
The Present and Future / 22

Part II: Nature Walks / 23
Seattle
1. Seward Park / 24
2. Camp Long / 28
3. Schmitz Reserve / 32
4. Washington Park Arboretum / 36
5. Union Bay Natural Areas / 41
6. Ravenna Park / 45
7. Discovery Park / 50
8. Carkeek Park / 56

North of Seattle
9. Meadowdale County Beach Park / 61
10. North Creek Park / 64

Eastside
11. Saint Edward State Park / 67
12. O. O. Denny County Park / 72
13. Juanita Bay Park / 76
14. Farrel-McWhirter Park / 80
15. Marymoor Regional Park / 84
16. Bridle Trails State Park / 89
17. Mercer Slough/Bellefields Nature Park / 92
18. Bellevue Botanical Gardens at Wilburton Hill Park / 99
19. Kelsey Creek Farm and Community Park / 102
20. Lake Hills Greenbelt / 107
21. Lakemont Trail System / 110

22. Cougar Mountain Regional Wildland Park / 115
23. Coal Creek Canyon Park / 120
24. Pioneer Park / 125

South King County
25. Ed Munro/Seahurst Park / 129
26. Soos Creek County Park / 133
27. Lake Fenwick Park / 136
28. Saltwater State Park / 141
29. West Hylebos State Park / 144
30. Rhododendron Species Botanical Garden and Pacific Rim
    Bonsai Collection / 148

Vashon and Bainbridge Islands
31. Burton Acres / 154
32. The Grand Forest / 158
33. Bloedel Reserve / 162

Part III: Plants and Animals / 167

Plants
    Trees / 168
    Shrubs / 175
    Flowering Plants / 184
    Nonflowering Plants / 193
Animals
    Birds / 197
    Amphibians and Mammals / 208

Appendix A: Selected Reading / 213
Appendix B: Useful Telephone Numbers / 216
Index / 219

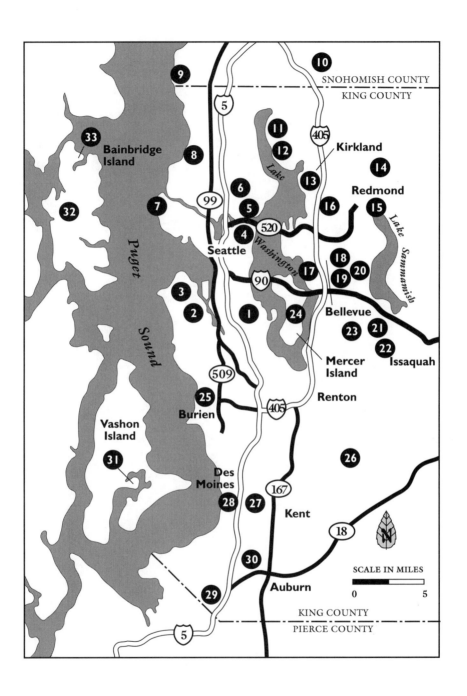

SCALE IN MILES

0   5

Introduction

John Muir once said, "The clearest way into the universe is through a forest wilderness." While our local parks are perhaps not wilderness, they are oases in the urban or suburban world where most of us live or work. Nestled among mountain ranges, a vast inland sea, and two long, glacier-gouged lakes, there are many pockets of wildness tucked away within the greater Seattle area. They offer nearby windows into the natural universe.

This second edition of *Nature Walks In and Around Seattle* describes thirty-three nature parks from Seattle to Edmonds to Redmond to Federal Way, including three parks on Vashon and Bainbridge Islands. An additional four small parks are discussed briefly. The first edition provided self-guided walks along trails of interest, with particular plants and natural features described in detail. Because such features may change from one year to the next, this edition has been revised to provide a more enduring general discussion of each park's terrain, with added information on the natural and cultural history of the region. The book has also been expanded to include eleven additional parks.

The parks featured in this book are all within an hour's drive of downtown Seattle. Most have an area of at least 50 acres, offering a sense of wilderness within the metropolitan area. The trails through these local forests and wetlands are not strenuous; the walks are ideal for families with young children and others seeking an easy outdoor excursion.

How to Use This Book

Within these pages, you will discover a newly-established park to explore, or a piece of history about your favorite haunt. Longtime residents, recent arrivals, and vacationers will all find this book a handy introduction to the natural history of the Seattle area.

This book is divided into three sections. Section I offers an overview of the natural setting of the Puget Sound region.

Section II provides descriptions of thirty-three Seattle-area parks. Each park chapter begins with a list of pertinent information, including park highlights, trail length and terrain, the best season for visiting, facilities, hours, wheelchair access, and special regulations. Directions are given for reaching the park by car and, whenever applicable, by bus. (Because bus routes and schedules are subject to change, call the appropriate transit provider to verify information. See Appendix B for phone numbers.) A brief overview of each park describes its highlights, and a section on trail logistics provides additional details about the surface and condition of the trails and the type of terrain. A human history section discusses the land and its former occupants, and a natural history section describes the ecology and geology of the park land. Each park chapter concludes with a listing of some of the more common plants and animals found in the area, grouped by habitat.

Section III contains brief descriptions of some of the most common flora and fauna found in Seattle-area parks. Not intended to take the place of a field guide, this section includes information on habitats and how indigenous peoples made use of the plants native to our area.

What to Take

Running shoes are sufficient for any of the walks in this book, but hiking boots will provide better support on longer hikes or on uneven ground. On wet or muddy trails, boots will always be appreciated. Choose clothing appropriate for the weather conditions. Wear adequate rain gear to prevent hypothermia, and take along extra layers of clothing in case the weather changes. Water is always recommended on walks, and a snack will help you keep up your energy.

Binoculars are recommended for bird-watching; a tripod-mounted spotting scope is useful in parks where birding is a highlight. A small magnifying hand lens is helpful for examining the intricacies of flowers and insects. If plant or animal identification is your intention, take along a field guide. Refer to Appendix A for a list of field guides and other useful publications.

Maps

The overall map shows the location of each of the thirty-three walks in this book. Refer to the description of each park for directions on how to reach the site from downtown Seattle. (Bring along a current street map for a visual guide.) A map of each park outlines its major trails and marks the location of facilities and important natural features. More detailed trail maps may be available for some of the parks; inquire at the park visitor center, or call the appropriate administrative office (see Appendix B for phone numbers).

Safety

Generally, few urban pastimes are safer than walking the trails of our local city, county, and state parks. However, it is best to exercise common sense and caution when walking on these or any trails. Boardwalks and bridges can be slick when wet; take care when walking on planks and logs. In some parks, cliffs or ravines may pose a hazard, especially for unattended children. Be aware of weather conditions; stay out of the forest during windstorms, and use discretion when walking on bluff trails prone to landslides after heavy rains.

Although incidents of crime in public parks are rare, it is wise to take precautions. Whenever possible, bring a companion on walks in secluded areas. If you do visit a park alone, consider letting someone know where you are going and when you expect to return. Most parks are closed after sunset; do not attempt these walks at night. Any suspicious or threatening behavior should be reported to the police.

Of the thirty-three parks described in this book, Cougar Mountain Regional Wildland Park is the only one where there is real danger of getting lost. Visitors hiking that park are advised to carry the Ten Essentials: map, compass, extra food, extra clothing, rain gear, matches in a waterproof case, flashlight, first-aid kit, pocketknife, and sunglasses.

Plant identification is challenging, even for experts, and many poisonous plants resemble edible species. Unless you have some knowledge of edible plants, it is best to avoid sampling the berries, mushrooms, and other plants you encounter in the wild. Although Section III describes some of the ways that local Indian tribes used native plants for food and medicine, this information is presented in a historical context only and should not be construed as endorsing the edibility or efficacy of particular plants.

Be vigilant when exploring the outdoors with young children, who tend to be curious about plants and are particularly susceptible to their poisonous effects. Among the most common hazards you may encounter in area parks is stinging nettle. Although the discomfort it causes is minor and only temporary, it is a good idea for both children and adults to learn to identify and avoid this plant. (See Section III for more information on nettles and other plants.)

Stinging nettle: memorize its leaves, then avoid!

Etiquette

Because our public parks are so heavily used, their woods and wetlands are especially vulnerable. A few trails and streambanks are in places badly eroded and stripped of vegetation. To help protect these areas from further erosion, stay on trails and avoid taking shortcuts through switchbacks. Stay away from the edges of streams—collapsed banks dump soil into the water, eroding streambanks and destroying animal habitat. Salmon runs in urban areas are particularly delicate. Pets are not permitted to eat salmon, even dead ones. The carcasses provide food for wild animals and add nutrients to the stream and soil.

Picking, collecting, uprooting or otherwise damaging plants for any purpose is forbidden in all the parks. Please respect this prohibition so that wild plants may be left for others to enjoy.

Do not disturb or collect wildlife, especially nesting birds and animals that live in the intertidal zone on beaches. If you turn over a rock to examine the creatures that live on its underside, replace it the way you found it. Shells, rocks, wood, and other natural material should also be left in place. Remember the saying, "take nothing but garbage from the park."

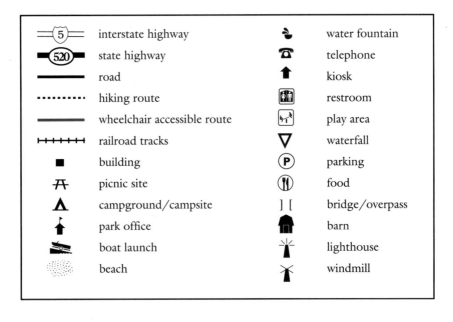

⬭5⬭	interstate highway	water fountain	
520	state highway	☎	telephone
	road	⬆	kiosk
·········	hiking route	restroom	
	wheelchair accessible route	play area	
⊦⊦⊦⊦⊦⊦	railroad tracks	▽	waterfall
■	building	Ⓟ	parking
🜊	picnic site	🅨	food
Λ	campground/campsite	] [	bridge/overpass
⬆	park office		barn
	boat launch		lighthouse
	beach		windmill

Part I
The Natural Setting

The climate, geology, botany, and biology of our region are inexorably intertwined. The Northwest's geographical location and topography affect the climate, while drastic climate changes in the past have helped to shape its geology. Soil types, along with climate, affect what types of plants grow here, which in turn determines the types of animals that live here.

Climate

The prevailing southwestern winds that blow during the winter months pick up moisture as they travel over the Pacific Ocean to give the Puget Sound region a moderate marine climate. The Olympic Mountains lie directly in the path of these wet winds and usually protect the region from the brunt of major storms and even larger amounts of precipitation. As the airflow comes up from the southwest, it splits around the Olympic Mountains and joins up again north of Seattle near the Snohomish County line in the famous "convergence zone." This area usually gets more rainfall than the rest of the Seattle area.

The Cascade Mountains to the east help shield the area from the temperature extremes of the dry continental air of eastern Washington and interior Canada. However, on occasion, pressure distributions do force continental air into the area. Dramatic ice- and snowstorms occur when warm rainy air coming up from the south collides with a cold front coming down from the north.

Geology

The area now occupied by Puget Sound was once a broad, flat coastal plain, crossed by meandering streams that flowed north to the Straits of Juan de Fuca. Large variations in the climate led to at least four periods of glaciation in the Puget Sound lowlands. Great continental glaciers periodically moved southward from Canada during the ice ages of the Pleistocene era (2 million to about 13,500 years ago). The region's present topography was shaped by the last glacial advance, known as the Vashon Ice Sheet.

As the climate cooled, the Vashon Ice Sheet advanced from Canada and eventually covered the Seattle area with a layer of ice, at least 3,000 feet thick, that extended to just south of Olympia. When the ice sheet retreated, it carved out Puget Sound and the Hood Canal, along with Lake Washington and Lake Sammamish. The melting glacier dumped huge piles of rock debris, or till, which form most of the bluffs and hills of the region. (The major exception is the range of high hills on the Eastside known as the Issaquah Alps, which are part of an ancient mountain range that was formed before the Cascades. These hills contain volcanic and sedimentary rocks, including coal.)

Since most of the hills and bluffs in the Seattle area consist of loose sand and gravel rather than solid rock, they are prone to landslides. Plants anchor the top layers of soil; however, slides can occur even on well-forested slopes on these rock piles. When vegetation is removed and the soil becomes saturated

Sword ferns are the most common type of fern seen in area forests.

with groundwater, slides are inevitable. Heavy winter rains saturate the soil and lubricate soil particles, causing them to slide past one another more easily. The resulting soil creep causes trees on steep slopes to lean outward at increasingly precarious angles until they finally topple. When a tree's root ball is torn out of the ground, the exposed soil erodes more quickly, and runoff channeled into the depression begins to cut away a gully. Landslides have caused considerable damage to residential areas in recent years.

The area's most recent soil layers can often be seen in roadcuts or bluffs, and result from the retreat of the Vashon Ice Sheet. A layer called the Vashon Till is made up of jumbled rock material of different sizes and shapes that was carried in the glacier, then dumped on the ground when the glacier retreated. As the Vashon Ice Sheet melted, streams of water flowed out from the glacier and reworked the previously dumped material into a layer called the Vashon Outwash. This layer was laid on top of the till layer, and is made of sorted sand and gravel. The soil layer above this outwash layer is called alluvium. It consists of material deposited after the glaciers by rivers, landslides, and other forces.

Habitats

Soil type, climate, and human impact have helped shape the ecology of the Puget Sound region. The soils on the glacially dumped ridges, called moraines, are generally poor and do not hold moisture, while the rich sediments in the river valleys are more conducive to the growth of a variety of plant species.

The rainfall is concentrated in most years from October through April, and this climate favors the growth of conifers. These evergreen trees are able to store moisture and temporarily shut down during the dry summer months and remain active during the cool, moist winter months.

The parks highlighted in this book feature forested or wetland areas. The vegetation of the Seattle region is a blend of native and exotic plants, a legacy of more than a hundred years of continuous human habitation. Most of the introduced plants were unable to compete with native ones, but some were successful, especially in areas where there had been disturbances and the original plants had been removed.

Forests

When the first white settlement was established at Alki Point in 1851, almost all the land was covered by a luxuriant conifer forest that mantled western Washington from the Cascades to the Pacific Ocean. Giant western red cedars dominated the old-growth forests. These early trees reached up to 12 feet in diameter and over 200 feet high. Deciduous trees, so common today, were rare and mostly restricted to the banks of lakes and streams. Only after early settlers cleared the land for farming and commercial loggers finished clearing the conifers did deciduous trees take over.

Today's second-growth woods consist mostly of bigleaf maples and red alders, with some Douglas-firs, western hemlocks, and western red cedars. Learn to identify these five trees, and you will know most of the trees in the local parks. Forests allow the development of several layers of plants, such as trees, shrubs, ferns, and herbaceous plants. Each layer provides a niche for particular types of animals.

The dominant plants in the forest are trees. By blocking the sun and hogging water and nutrients, they place constraints on which plants will live below in the understory. Since deciduous leaves decompose faster to add nutrients to the soil, rich soils—and therefore more lush, more varied arrays of understory shrubs and herbs—tend to develop more rapidly beneath deciduous trees.

Tall, standing dead trees, called snags, provide wildlife habitat within a forest. Large numbers of snags are characteristic of old-growth forests. Raptors perch on snags, and woodpeckers excavate nesting holes, which are later used by many other birds and mammals like squirrels, raccoons and owls for nesting, overwintering, and shelter.

Fallen logs are also essential to the health of the forest; they provide nutrients that support a host of plants and animals. The vast majority of successful tree seedlings in area forests grow on fallen logs known as nurse logs.

Layers of trees, shrubs and herbaceous plants share space within a forest.

Fungi are the principal agents of decomposition in conifer forests. (Mushrooms are the spore-producing organs of fungi.) They break down complex organic compounds found in dead wood into carbon dioxide, water, and other simple substances, which liberates nutrients bound up in these molecules and returns them to the forest. Mosses and lichens on the stump or log benefit from the water liberated during decomposition. Mosses do not contribute directly to the decomposition of wood. However, by retaining water, they help maintain a moist environment, which accelerates the decomposition process.

Bracket fungi cling to a tree trunk.

Wetlands

To be classified as a wetland, an area must have certain types of soils that are at least periodically saturated with or covered by water; it must support water-loving vegetation at least periodically; and it must be inundated or saturated by water for at least two weeks during the growing season. Wetlands have water tables that are at or near the surface.

Why are wetlands important? These areas filter out pollutants and convert harmful chemicals into less harmful ones. Wetlands act like a giant sponge, absorbing, then gradually releasing, large amounts of water that would normally be quickly carried off downstream. By regulating the release of water, wetlands prevent flooding and help maintain streams during dry periods. This, in turn, provides a more stable source of water for plants and animals that live in or near these streams. Also, water moves down through wetlands and recharges groundwater supplies, and wetland vegetation reduces shoreline erosion. Finally, wetlands provide valuable habitat for a wide variety of insects, fish, birds and other animals.

In natural watersheds, runoff is filtered through the soil, which removes most or all of any pollutants it may contain. In urban and suburban areas, however, extensive areas of pavement not only increase the rate of runoff and prevent the water from soaking into the soil, but also contribute large amounts of surface pollutants from road oil, garden and lawn chemicals, pet waste, and other sources. Several programs in local parks educate the public to reduce these effects of development.

You can identify different types of wetlands by observing which plant species grow together in a zone. Although many wetland classification systems exist, the following is taken from the King County classification system.

Open-water wetlands contain water averaging over 3 feet deep. Submerged and floating-leaved plants such as European water milfoil, pondweed, duckweed, pond lily, bladderwort and liverwort are characteristic of these types of wetlands.

Deep marshes have water depths of 1 to 3 feet and the dominant plants are emergent species such as cattail, yellow iris, marsh cinquefoil and bur-reed. Pond lily, duckweed, bladderwort, and liverwort are also found here.

Shallow marshes average less than 1 foot of water, and the soil may be exposed during dry seasons. Characteristic plants are cattail, yellow iris, bur-reed, water parsley, reed canary grass, marsh speedwell, sedges, and rushes.

Wet meadows may have up to 6 inches of standing water except during the growing season. Then, although the soil is saturated, water remains only in depressions and small channels. The dominant plants are reed canary grass, spike-rushes, bulrushes, and sedges. Scattered among these may be horsetail, yellow monkey flower, and marsh speedwell; bur-reed or cattail may grow in standing water within the meadow. Pockets of shrubs and small trees, such as hardhack, willow, or red alder may also exist.

Shrub-scrub wetlands have shrubs and small trees that grow in soil that

Different wetland plants prefer varying depths of water.

is seasonally or always flooded. These may be a single species or a combination of hardhack, willow, red-osier dogwood, Pacific crabapple, red alder, and cascara. If open spaces exist between the shrub layers, emergent plants such as water parsley, marsh speedwell, and Labrador tea may arise.

Forested or wooded wetlands have many layers of plants. The upper canopy consists of deciduous or evergreen trees such as black cottonwood, red alder, Oregon ash, bigleaf maple, western red cedar, western hemlock, and Sitka spruce. A shrub/small tree layer usually consists of salmonberry, devil's club, red elderberry, vine maple, or cascara. Underneath the shrub layer, a layer of plants such as lady fern, skunk cabbage, and water parsley may occur, along with deer fern, foamflower, and wild lily-of-the-valley.

Bogs eventually fill in small lakes, and are indicated by a floating mat of sphagnum moss, upon which wild cranberry and sundew may grow. Labrador tea and bog laurel form a shrub layer above the moss, and western hemlock or Sitka spruce trees may be scattered throughout the bog.

Human Impact

Native Peoples

The ecology of the Puget Sound lowlands has changed dramatically in the last 150 years. Before the coming of the white settlers to the Seattle area in the 1850s, most of the region was covered by a dense coniferous forest.

Areas were burnt by the Indians to produce meadows and open forests for deer and elk, which they hunted, as well as bear, cougar, and beaver. The salmon were so plentiful that it was said one could practically walk across the streams on their backs. In the summer, the native peoples went to salt-water beaches to dig clams, which they dried for use in the winter, and to catch fish such as halibut, sole, skate, and flounder. Summer was also a time for gathering the abundant huckleberries, cranberries, and salmonberries.

Smallpox decimated the Indian population during the 1820s and 30s, so the burning of meadows declined and dense stands of young trees filled in previously open areas. The Indian survivors trapped beavers, and the loss of beaver dams greatly affected local wetlands.

White Settlement and Deforestation

When the white settlers moved into the region, they cleared the forests to farm. Logging destroyed huge areas of first-growth forest, which had a dramatic effect on wildlife. Larger animals could travel to new areas, but less mobile animals were trapped. Opened to the sun, the land dried out, killing creatures such as insects, slugs, newts, and salamanders. The reptiles, birds, and mammals that relied on these creatures suffered a loss of food. Native orchids like the Calypso borealis, along with native insect-eating plants, went extinct. Deforestation increased soil erosion, which clogged streams with silt and destroyed salmon spawning grounds.

Non-native plants were introduced, either accidentally or intentionally. The first English holly farms were established on Yarrow Point on the Eastside in 1900. Seeds spread by bird droppings have made holly an invader in many area parks. Rumor has it that the Himalayan blackberry, which now grows in clearings everywhere, originated locally at Luther Burbank's nursery on Mercer Island.

The Ship Canal

In 1916–1917, the creation of the Lake Washington Ship Canal lowered the level of the lake by about 9 feet, which greatly affected the shoreline environment. Shallow spawning grounds for sockeye salmon and other types of fish were destroyed. Marshes, now left standing above water, dried up, eliminating feeding and nesting sites for thousands of resident and migratory birds. The wapato, a shallow-water plant that the Indians had gathered for food, disappeared from the lake.

However, with time, the plants and animals adjusted to the changes. Logged areas allowed the growth of trees and other plants that require a lot of sunlight, which provided food for animals. Within two years of the lowering of Lake Washington, a forest of willows and cottonwoods grew on the new shorelines, which helped beaver and muskrats recover. Marshes gradually reestablished themselves along the lowered shoreline, and the marsh birds returned.

The Present and Future

In recent years, there has been an increase in some animal populations. More black bears and cougars have been sighted, sometimes moving down the wildlife corridor from the Cascades to the Issaquah Alps down through Cougar Mountain and Coal Creek Parks. The pileated woodpecker, a bird that requires large trees, was thought to be going extinct twenty years ago, but as trees in towns and suburbs mature, its numbers are increasing. Salmon are being reintroduced to local streams as streambeds are being restored.

Park management and local community groups are working to create habitats to increase biodiversity in local parks. Isolated parks can support only a limited number of animals, but corridors of preserved land offer a chance for animals to move within a larger range, or among several environments. For example, bald eagles use large snags or living trees in mature forests for nesting and roosting, and require a nearby expanse of water for hunting. There are park efforts to encourage wildlife habitats on farms and suburban areas; for instance, Lake Hills Community Park in Bellevue offers programs on organic gardening and creating backyard habitats.

Part II

Nature Walks

Seattle

1 · Seattle
Seward Park

Highlights: Mature upland forest with large western red cedars and Douglas-firs; wide variety of birds; views of Lake Washington, Seattle skyline, I-90 bridge, Mercer Island, and Mount Rainier

Size: 277 acres (including 70 acres of shorelands); 2.5-mile loop pedestrian path around park perimeter and several miles of forest trails

Ownership: Seattle Department of Parks and Recreation

Season: Year-round

Terrain: Flat to moderately sloping

Facilities: Restrooms, phone, and water fountain at art studio/bathhouse and on entry loop drive; restrooms also at northern end of park and on upper loop road; picnic tables, grills, and playground in southern third of park and on upper loop road; fishing pier; swimming area

Hours: Dawn to dusk

Interpretive Programs: Bird walks conducted by naturalists from Camp Long (see Appendix B for phone number); an environmental center is being completed near park entrance

Wheelchair Accessibility: Level perimeter pedestrian road has asphalt surface (a bit bumpy in places)

Pets: Leash (crucial to wildlife) and scoop; not allowed on beach

Horses: No

Bikes: Allowed on shoreline road and upper loop road; not on forest trails

Bus: Metro 39

Driving Directions: From downtown Seattle, take I-5 south to exit 163, South Columbian Way, and go south on South Columbian Way. Take a right (south) on Beacon Avenue South, then take a left (east) on South Orcas Street. At the bottom of the hill, where South Orcas Street intersects with Lake Washington Boulevard South, turn right into the park. Parking areas are to the left, by the art studio/bathhouse, or all along the southern shore of the park.

Park Overview   This forest oasis is located on a peninsula that juts out from the western shore of Lake Washington. The park is popular with walkers, joggers, dog walkers, and birders, but most activity occurs in the developed southern third of the park and on the shoreline road. The interior hill of

The old road along the perimeter of the peninsula offers views of wetland vegetation along Lake Washington.

the park features an upland forest that harbors large Douglas-firs and western red cedars. The park is quiet, with little noise from local traffic in the interior forest, although passing motorboats can be heard in season.

Trail Layout   A perimeter road (closed to motor vehicles) encircles the park and offers a flat paved surface for walkers, joggers, cyclists, and disabled visitors. An interior road (also closed to motor vehicles) and numerous dirt/gravel trails offer passage through the forested park interior. The trails are fairly well drained, although some parts are muddy after rains. The uplands in the park's southern third have flat-to-sloping lawn areas with trees. A few benches are sprinkled throughout the park, offering a welcome rest. The fish hatchery (closed to the public) was constructed by the Works Progress Administration (WPA) during the Depression and raises trout to stock local lakes.

Human History   Before Lake Washington was lowered, the peninsula was almost an island during rainy seasons. Native Americans probably utilized the area for fishing and hunting. William Bailey, the owner of the *Press Time* newspaper (now the *Seattle Times*) bought the Seward Park tract in 1889, and the area became known as Baileys Peninsula. In 1911, the city bought the peninsula and named it for U.S. Secretary of State William H. Seward, who had negotiated the nation's purchase of Alaska in 1867. After the city acquired the park land, it began filling in the marshy neck of the peninsula to prevent it from becoming an island during seasonal rises in the lake level. The park land expanded again in 1916–17, when, with the construction of the ship canal, the Lake Washington water level dropped about 9 feet, exposing the perimeter road area and the wide grassy meadow that now leads to the swimming beach.

In the late 1920s, a suspension bridge was proposed across the narrowest part of Lake Washington. This bridge would have connected Seward Park to the south end of Mercer Island. The construction of this bridge would have required a 1,700-foot earth fill across Seward Park. The idea was revived again in 1931, then later dropped.

Natural History   This peaceful forest preserve features large Douglas-fir and western red cedar trees, some reaching 6 feet in diameter, as well as one of the best collections of large, healthy western hemlocks in the area. Of a handful of big trees left on Seattle public lands, these are the only ones found on an upland rather than in a ravine. Other native trees include bigleaf maple, red alder, Pacific madrone, cascara, Pacific crabapple, grand fir, Garry oak, vine maple, bitter cherry, and Pacific yew.

Sword, lady, licorice, and bracken ferns blanket the forest floor. A native plant interpretive garden adjacent to the environmental center educates visitors about park species. Shrubs such as salmonberry, thimbleberry, coast red elderberry, Indian plum, California hazelnut, black twinberry, snowberry, and

Huge western red cedars evoke a second glance in the upland forest at Seward Park.

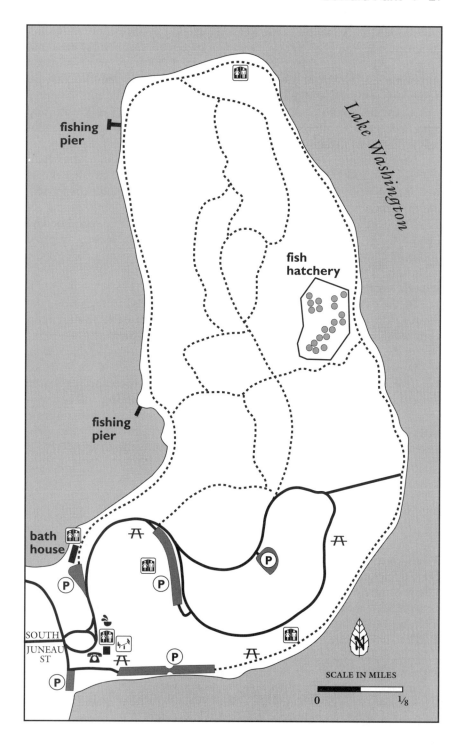

fishing
pier

fishing
pier

Lake Washington

fish
hatchery

bath
house

SOUTH
JUNEAU
ST

SCALE IN MILES

0   1/8

red huckleberry are found in the forest. Flowering plants include fringecup, stinging nettle, youth-on-age, and creeping buttercup. Ocean spray, salal, and Oregon grape occupy drier sites. English holly, English ivy, and Himalayan and evergreen blackberry are invasives that need constant removal. Stay on designated trails to avoid poison oak.

Along the lakeshore, look for black cottonwood, poplar, Oregon ash, and Sitka and weeping willows. The lake marsh on the western side of the peninsula is filled with cattails.

Non-native trees (mostly in the southern end of the park or by the hatchery) include European birch, sawara cypress, veitch fir, Washington hawthorn, weeping juniper, and several species of pines and poplars. Japanese cherry trees put on a show at the park entrance in the spring.

The park's variety of habitats, which include freshwater shoreline and upland forest, attract many different species of birds in season. Ospreys and bald eagles occasionally nest on the steep northwestern slope of the peninsula. Year-round, the forest on top of the hill may harbor western-screech, great-horned, and northern saw-whet owls.

In the water, look for resident American coots, mallards, and double-crested cormorants, joined in fall and winter by canvasbacks, buffleheads, common goldeneyes, common loons, and western and eared grebes.

In the forest, spot resident black-capped and chestnut-backed chickadees, red-breasted nuthatches, spotted towhees, Hutton's vireos, golden-crowned kinglets, winter and Bewick's wrens, bushtits, brown creepers, pileated woodpeckers, cedar waxwings, and purple finches. In spring and summer, look for several species of warblers, western tanagers, black-headed grosbeaks and olive-sided flycatchers. In fall and winter, ruby-crowned kinglets, golden-crowned sparrows, fox sparrows, and varied thrushes come to visit.

---

2 ♦ West Seattle
Camp Long

Highlights: Forest, stream, pond wetland, educational programs
Size: 68 acres; approximately 5 miles of trails
Ownership: Seattle Department of Parks and Recreation
Season: Best spring through fall
Terrain: Flat to moderately sloping
Facilities: Restrooms, water fountain, and phone at visitor center; picnic shelters, cabins, and meeting rooms available for rental
Hours: 8:30 A.M. to 5 P.M. Tuesday through Sunday, closed Sundays in January (see Appendix B for lodge phone number)
Interpretive Programs: Saturday nature walks, interpretive classes for organized groups (preregistration required; see Appendix B for phone number)

An observer records plant species along the Animal Tracks Nature Trail.

Wheelchair Accessibility: Rolling Hills Trail and several cabins
Pets: Leash and scoop; prohibited on Animal Tracks Nature Trail and in pond
Horses: No
Bikes: No
Bus: Metro 21
Driving Directions: From downtown Seattle, take I-5 south to exit 163A, South Spokane Street/West Seattle Freeway, which eventually turns into Fauntleroy Way Southwest. Turn left at the light on 35th Avenue Southwest, and in approximately 0.5 mile, turn left on Southwest Dawson Street. The visitor center is the stone building directly ahead through the gates (which are locked after hours). Turn right into the parking area. If the lot is full, park along 35th Avenue Southwest.

Park Overview   This pleasant park of red alders, bigleaf maples, and young western red cedars is tucked away just south and west of the West Seattle Golf Course. The park offers a variety of easy-terrain trails, and on-site naturalists lead free nature walks. Walk topics vary with the season, but include programs on animals, plants, and forest, pond, and watershed ecology, with all ages from five and up welcome. There are also many natural history programs for children in preschool through sixth grade, and rock climbing and rappelling classes for those ages seven and older. The camp has facilities for rent year-round, including meeting rooms, rustic cabins, picnic shelters, a climbing rock, and a simulated glacier.

Trail Layout Trail maps are available at the park lodge. Wire grids on bridges and boardwalks give good traction on rainy days.

The Rolling Hills Trail is wheelchair-accessible and begins at the south end of the parking lot. It provides access to the parade ground, restrooms, and several wheelchair-accessible cabins. The first part of the trail is gently sloping with a handrail, its surface composed of hard-packed fine gravel, while the flat portion along the edge of the parade ground is paved.

The Animal Tracks Nature Trail (0.5 mile) is a dirt/gravel loop over gently sloping forest terrain. This trail has three short sets of stairs.

The Ridge Trail is a flat dirt/gravel trail along a forested ridge. Access from the south end is along a gentle grade off the park access road, while the northern end is moderately steep. The Midwood Loop consists of several dirt/gravel forest trails, which are flat to gently sloping.

A trail leading to Longfellow Creek branches off from the Midwood Trail through a grove of young cedars over several small boardwalks to come out through a back gate at Southwest Brandon Street and 29th Avenue Southwest (check with ranger beforehand to make sure gate is open). Cross the road and turn left to find a narrow dirt and wood-chip trail (muddy after a rain), which heads north for a few blocks along the east side of 29th Avenue Southwest, then view the creek from either side of the road.

Camp Long is the home of the Longfellow Creek Watershed Action Project, a cooperative effort between Seattle Parks and the Seattle Public Utilities Department. As part of this program, local schoolchildren plant trees and shrubs along the creek to provide shade and shelter for coho salmon and other wildlife and replace non-native plants with native species. The program also encourages homeowners to protect delicate stream ecology by limiting their use of pesticides and fertilizers, by wise landscaping, and by composting.

Human History   The park land was originally slated to become part of the West Seattle Golf Course, which was being constructed during the Depression, but the land was too wet. Through the efforts of Superior Court Judge William G. Long and county commissioner Archie Phelps, Camp Long was established to serve scouting troops. Clark Schurman, a camping and mountaineering expert, helped design the park, as well as the climbing structure that bears his name. The park buildings were built during the Depression by the Works Progress Administration (WPA), and the park was dedicated in 1941. For many years, the park was available only to organized groups, but it has been open to the public since the mid-1980s.

Natural History   Deciduous red alders are the most common trees in this moist park, although over a hundred years ago, before the area was logged, the original forest in this area probably consisted of cedars. There are also bigleaf maples, western red cedars, western hemlocks, and Douglas-firs on the park's hillsides. Other native trees in the park include black cottonwood, California hazelnut, cascara, Scouler's willow, Pacific madrone, Pacific dogwood, Pacific crabapple, and Pacific yew.

Most of the non-native trees in the park were acquired from local nurseries that went bankrupt during the Depression. These include Lombardy and Cathay poplars, horsechestnuts, paper birches, incense cedars, Japanese larches, piñon pines, European hornbeams, and balsam, hybrid, and Nikko firs.

Native ferns include sword, licorice, and lady fern. Stinging nettle, common horsetail, red huckleberry, ocean spray, salmonberry, and snowberry are among the native plants in the park, with salal and Oregon grape growing in the higher, drier sections. Little Polliwog Pond has native yellow pond lilies and duckweed on its surface. Non-native plants in the park include the three aggressive invaders English holly, English ivy, and Himalayan blackberry.

A native plant interpretive path and plaza is located at the front entry of the park lodge. Interpretive signs offer a way to familiarize yourself with some of the many native forest plants in the park before striking out onto the trails.

The park attracts an array of wildlife; animal species include Townsend's chipmunk, mouse, eastern gray squirrel, opossum, shrew, coast mole, coyote, red fox, raccoon, and mountain beaver. Amphibians such as the Pacific chorus frog, the ensantina, and northwestern, long-toed, and western redbacked salamanders are also found.

Many species of birds can be seen in the park year-round, including great blue heron, red-tailed hawk, belted kingfisher, band-tailed pigeon, brown creeper, golden-crowned kinglet, spotted towhee, song sparrow, dark-eyed junco, bushtit, red-breasted nuthatch, Hutton's vireo, mallard, black-capped and chestnut-backed chickadee, western-screech and great-horned owl, and several types of finch, wren, and warbler.

Cedar waxwings enjoy the red berries of the park's madrones. Resident downy and pileated woodpeckers, as well as red-shafted flickers, drill holes in trunks year-round, while red-breasted sapsuckers visit in winter. In fall and winter, sharp-shinned and Cooper's hawks, red-winged blackbirds, and ruby-crowned kinglets may be spotted. In spring and summer, visitors include killdeer, western tanagers, rufous hummingbirds, Swainson's thrushes, and several varieties of swallows and flycatchers.

---

3 ◆ West Seattle
Schmitz Reserve

Highlights: Large old-growth trees, stream
Size: 50 acres; several miles of trails
Ownership: Seattle Department of Parks and Recreation
Season: Year-round
Terrain: Flat to moderately steep
Facilities: None; restrooms and water fountain at Alki Community Center west of park
Hours: Dawn to 11 P.M.
Interpretive Programs: Occasional naturalist walks arranged through Camp Long (see Appendix B for phone number)
Wheelchair Accessibility: Paved pedestrian road leads from Alki Community Center into park

Pets: Leash and scoop
Horses: No
Bikes: No
Bus: Metro 56
Driving Directions: From downtown Seattle, take I-5 south to exit 163A, South Spokane Street/West Seattle Freeway. Bear right off West Seattle Freeway onto Southwest Admiral Way. Follow Southwest Admiral Way uphill through the business district, and then downhill. Watch for the rainbow-colored park sign on the left, just before Southwest Admiral Way crosses a bridge over the ravine, and take a left on Schmitz Park Drive. Keep right and follow the road down to the parking area.

Park Overview This wonderfully quiet preserve is one of the last bits of modified old-growth forest around Seattle. Even knowing this information, prepare to be astonished at the amazing forest thriving in this lush ravine. In this hidden grove of magnificent trees, with giant nurse logs swathed in mosses and fungi, you may question if you are really this close to Seattle. In town for a quick visit? Come here to get a glimpse of the Seattle forest of the nineteenth century.

Trail Layout A dirt trail loop leads up one side of the stream and down the other. Other trails climb up hillsides to exit on neighborhood streets, and a

A fallen cedar will serve as a nurse log for future generations of plants.

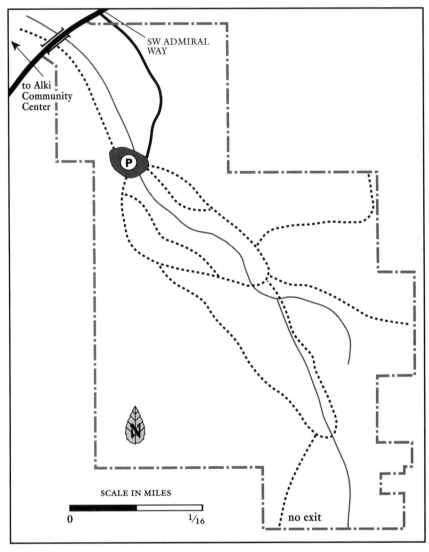

SW ADMIRAL WAY

to Alki Community Center

P

SCALE IN MILES

0   ¹⁄₁₆

no exit

wide, flat paved path at the bottom of the ravine leads to the Alki Community Center. Higher parts of the trail offer a glimpse into the treetops—keep a lookout for pileated woodpecker holes.

Human History The city acquired the park land in two separate parcels, most of it in 1908, with the remainder given in 1912. The land was donated by Park Commissioner Ferdinand Schmitz, a German immigrant who came to Seattle in 1887. A restaurateur, Schmitz profited from some shrewd real-estate investments after the financial panic of 1893, and later enjoyed a successful career in banking.

Natural History The largest trees in the park area were removed by loggers by the early part of the twentieth century. Many stumps still show evidence of logging activity. Blackened trunks record past forest fires. Trees native to the park include western hemlock, Douglas-fir, bigleaf maple, red alder, California hazelnut, Pacific yew, and willow.

Mushrooms common to older-growth forests grow here. Sword, deer, and lady ferns cover the hillsides and licorice ferns decorate the trunks of bigleaf maples. Red huckleberry, evergreen huckleberry, coast red elderberry, salmonberry, and thimbleberry are among the berries that grow here. Herbaceous plants include Cooley's hedgenettle and trillium. Salal can be found on higher, drier hillsides, while skunk cabbage and water parsley thrive in the wet ground near the stream. Invasive plants like English holly are being replaced with Douglas-fir, western red cedar, and western hemlock.

The reserve attracts birds that prefer mature coniferous forests. Year-round residents include Steller's jays, spotted towhees, brown creepers, song sparrows, pileated woodpeckers, red-breasted nuthatches, black-capped and chestnut-backed chickadees, and great-horned and western-screech owls. Swainson's thrushes, black-throated gray warblers, and western tanagers are among the visitors in spring and summer. Varied thrushes may be spotted in fall and winter.

The trails of Schmitz Park offer a glimpse of the vast forest that once occupied the region.

4 ◆ Seattle
Washington Park Arboretum

Highlights: Native and non-native trees, waterfront marsh trail on Union Bay
Size: 200 acres; several miles of trails
Ownership: Seattle Department of Parks and Recreation and University of Washington
Season: Year-round
Terrain: Flat to moderate
Facilities: Restrooms, water fountain, and phone at Donald G. Graham Visitor Center and Museum of History and Industry; boat rental at University of Washington Waterfront Activity Center (see Appendix B for phone numbers)
Hours: Dawn to dusk; visitor center open 8:30 A.M. to 4:30 P.M. weekdays, 10 A.M. to 4 P.M. weekends, April to October
Interpretive Programs: Free guided tour most Saturdays and Sundays leaves from visitor center at 1 P.M.; hour-long group hikes for small fee; marsh trail pamphlet available at west trailhead, visitor center, or the Museum of History and Industry
Wheelchair Accessibility: Visitor center and a few paved trails
Pets: Leash and scoop; allowed only on established trails; prohibited in Japanese Garden and on Waterfront Trail
Horses: No

Great blue herons frequent the marshes along the Waterfront Trail.

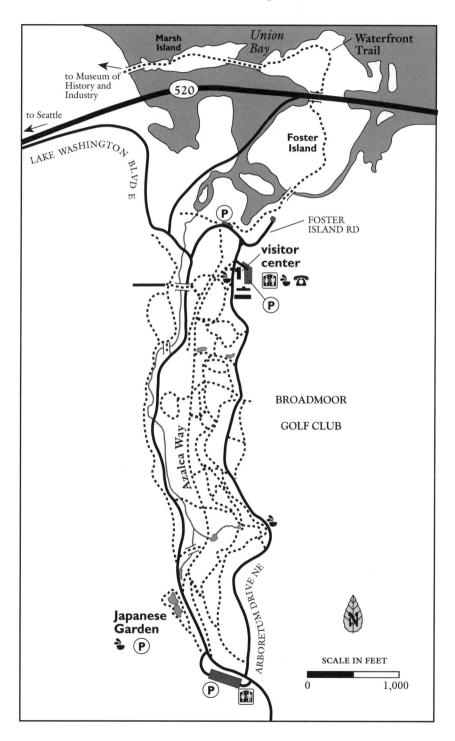

Bikes: Limited to paved roads
Bus: Metro 11, 43, 48
Driving Directions: From downtown Seattle, take I-5 north to Highway 520. Follow Highway 520 east and take the Montlake Boulevard exit. At the stoplight, go straight across Montlake Boulevard to Lake Washington Boulevard East. In a block, turn left on Park Drive, cross over the freeway, and enter the parking lot of the Museum of History and Industry. Park at the far end of the parking lot and follow the wood-chip path to the west entry of the Waterfront Trail.

To drive directly to the arboretum, continue on Lake Washington Boulevard East, take a left on Foster Island Road, and then turn right on Arboretum Drive Northeast. The visitor center and parking lot are on the left. Parking is also available at the intersection of Arboretum Drive and Foster Island Road. To reach the east entry of the Waterfront Trail from the corner of Foster Island Road and Arboretum Drive, follow the pedestrian road between the arboretum duck pond and the Broadmoor Golf Club onto Foster Island. Go through the Highway 520 underpass, and follow the path to the east trailhead.

Park Overview   This living museum of plants offers a variety of nature experiences, from wetland birding in the rain to sunny strolls viewing spring cherry blossoms and rhododendrons. The arboretum is the second largest plant collection of exotic woody shrubs, trees, and vines in North America. An estimated 10,000 native trees are displayed. A waterfront trail takes you into the heart of the fragile wetland on Foster Island, the largest wetland left in Seattle. From fall through spring, there are waterfowl here in abundance. To get a blackbird's-eye view of the marshes, rent a canoe from the University of Washington Waterfront Activity Center.

Trail Layout   The dirt/gravel trails within the arboretum are fairly well-drained, though they can be muddy in spots after a rain. The Azalea Way lawn area is often mucky fall through spring. Benches are scattered throughout the park. The flat to gently sloping Waterfront Trail (0.5 mile) takes you over floating walkways, and bridges, and up to an elevated platform that overlooks the marshes and open waters of Union Bay.

Human History   The Indian name for Foster Island meant "Tiny Island," and they laid their dead in burial boxes in trees here.

When the land for the Territorial University (later the University of Washington) was acquired between 1890 and 1893, Edmond S. Meany appealed to timberman legislators by pointing out the advantages in establishing a campuswide arboretum as a laboratory for studying timber resources. Selected

Boardwalks and bridges lead to a closer look at wildlife in the marshes of Union Bay.

native trees were spared from logging, and imported trees were planted. However, the construction of buildings led to continual movement of the arboretum.

The city acquired the park area in 1934. A working relationship was developed between the Seattle Parks Department and the University of Washington. The famous Olmsted Brothers designed the basic layout of the park, and Works Progress Administration (WPA) crews sculpted the grounds during the Depression. The waterfront lands of the park emerged from the waters of Lake Washington in 1916–17, when the Hiram M. Chittenden Locks were completed and the lake level was lowered around 9 feet.

Natural History   The size and scope of the arboretum can be overwhelming—take advantage of tours offered by guides to focus on individual parts of the collection. The park is a spectacular place to walk at any time of year, but for maximum glory, visit in April and May for spring flowers or in October for fall foliage. Although the arboretum is a large, tended study garden rather than a wilderness area, it is a fine place to get acquainted with a variety of native plants.

The grounds west of the visitor center display many labeled native plants of the Pacific Northwest. A clump of large conifers offers a valuable opportunity to compare the bark and needles of a western red cedar, a Douglas-fir, and a western hemlock side by side. Other native plants include grand fir, vine maple, bigleaf maple, Scouler's willow, red alder, Pacific dogwood, Oregon ash, Pacific madrone, Pacific crabapple, California hazelnut, Indian plum, red huckleberry, evergreen huckleberry, thimbleberry, Oregon grape, salal, snowberry, salmonberry, and sword fern.

Among the trees in the arboretum, you may see resident band-tailed pigeons, Steller's jays, woodpeckers, chickadees, red-breasted nuthatches, kinglets, bushtits, peregrine falcons, and several species of owls.

The lakeside marshes around Foster Island provide a rich habitat for waterfowl and other animals. White water lilies cover the open water, their lovely blooms appearing in early summer. The view across Union Bay encompasses the Montlake Cut and the University of Washington, the fields and marshes of the Union Bay Natural Areas, and the Laurelhurst neighborhood. On clear days, the Cascade Mountains are visible to the east.

Marsh Island is a floating mat consisting mostly of peat that has built up as generation after generation of marsh plants has died and accumulated on the shallow lake bottom. Island habitats include willow and birch thickets, and bulrush and cattail marshes. Black cottonwood, red alder, Pacific and Scouler's willow, and swamp and European white birch trees grow in the area. Other plants include rushes, horsetail, hardhack, creeping buttercup, European yellow iris, and invasive purple loosestrife and reed canary grass. European water milfoil, a particularly invasive plant that first appeared in Lake Washington in 1975, hangs suspended just below the surface of the water.

Massive erosion occurs along the arboretum shoreline due to human and animal activity.

An array of fish, birds, and other animals reside in the area at various times of the year. Chinook (king), coho, and sockeye salmon, along with steelhead and ocean-going cutthroat trout, migrate up the ship canal and through Lake Washington as they return to their streambed spawning grounds. In the warmer, shallower margins of the lake are freshwater fish which feed off the plankton, insect larvae, and algae abundant in the water. These include largemouth bass, carp, and pumpkinseed sunfish.

The combination of marsh and open water makes Foster Island one of Seattle's prime wintering grounds for ducks. Nearly a dozen species can be expected, including gadwall, American and Eurasian wigeons, northern shoveler, teal, goldeneye, scaup, and merganser.

Other open-water birds include resident double-crested cormorants, belted kingfishers, American coots, pied-billed grebes, Canada geese, and bald eagles, while ospreys visit in spring and summer. Among the marsh plants, look for resident red-winged blackbirds, marsh wrens, American bitterns, Virginia rails, and green and great blue herons.

Higher sections of the marsh support shrubs not found in the wetter portions, which attract bushtits, American goldfinches, and song sparrows. Bullock's orioles and yellow warblers are spring and summer visitors.

---

5 ◆ Seattle
Union Bay Natural Areas

Highlights: Union Bay marsh and ponds with excellent bird-watching
Size: Approximately 12 acres; approximately 1 mile of trails
Ownership: University of Washington
Season: Best fall through spring
Terrain: Flat
Facilities: Restrooms at the Center for Urban Horticulture weekdays during business hours; picnic table at parking lot
Hours: Dawn to dusk
Interpretive Programs: None
Wheelchair Accessibility: None
Pets: No
Horses: No
Bikes: No
Bus: Metro 25, 30
Driving Directions: From downtown Seattle, take I-5 north, then go east on Highway 520. Take the first exit, Montlake Boulevard, and at the light turn left onto Montlake Boulevard Northeast. In approximately 1 mile,

keep right as the road curves to merge with Northeast 45th Street. Pass the University Village Shopping Center on your left, then take a right on Mary Gates Memorial Drive Northeast. In a few blocks, turn right into the parking lot for the University of Washington Center for Urban Horticulture.

Park Overview   This broad field dotted with ponds and fringed with marsh is one of Seattle's birding hot spots, so bring binoculars. The area has gone from lakebed to lakeshore to garbage dump to bird sanctuary, all within the twentieth century. The park's location makes it moderately noisy—you can hear a constant whoosh of traffic from the 520 bridge just south across the bay. It also offers an excellent vantage point for watching passing boats, with views west to the University of Washington, south across Union Bay to the Arboretum marshes, and east to the Laurelhurst neighborhood.

Trail Layout   The Montlake Fill, now known as the Union Bay Natural Areas, lies between the University of Washington parking lots along Montlake Boulevard Northeast and the Center for Urban Horticulture at the corner of Mary Gates Memorial Drive and Northeast 41st Street. Connecting the two areas is a broad flat gravel path dubbed Wahkiakum Lane. South of the lane lies a maze of narrow dirt, bark, and grassy paths that poke about ponds, marshes, and the lakeshore. The fill is like a saturated sponge; most of the area dries out by midsummer, but some portions are soggy year-round, so wear boots or shoes fit for tromping through muck.

Human History   This area was submerged beneath the waters of Union Bay until the 1916–17 completion of the Lake Washington Ship Canal lowered the water level. The bay formerly extended from the present site of Husky Stadium northward to just beyond University Village and east over to Laurelhurst. The idea of a canal to improve access from Lake Washington to Puget Sound had been suggested since the 1860s.

In 1861, Harvey Pike, a carpenter and a contractor, moved to Seattle to build Seattle's new Territorial University. Pike had wanted to build canals all his life, and he decided to attempt one in this area, essentially by himself. He bought land near the university site and began excavating a 200 foot-wide strip of marsh for a canal that would cross from Portage Bay to Lake Union along the route of the present Evergreen Point Bridge approach. The project was suspended several times until, in 1884, a small ditch was completed near Pike's original proposed route, just large enough to allow logs to pass through to Lake Union.

When the lake level dropped, over 600 acres of exposed land was gained, and gradually, marsh plants invaded the new ground. After World War II, much

Meadows in the Union Bay Natural Areas attract ring-necked pheasants.

of the area was filled in for real-estate development, and the land immediately north of Wahkiakum Lane was used for dumping garbage. Later, additional areas were filled in as parking lots and athletic fields. Husky Stadium, Hec Edmundson Pavilion, and campus housing near Laurelhurst were all erected on fill land once covered by Union Bay.

Natural History The wildlife area is managed by the Center for Urban Horticulture as an ecological research center. The center is the first institution in the country to combine research, university teaching, and public outreach on plants in urban environments. The Elisabeth C. Miller library, located on site, includes the archives of the Washington Park Arboretum. The library is open to the public for horticultural research, and occasional signs in the fields describe current research projects.

Trees in the fill area include black cottonwood, red alder, European white

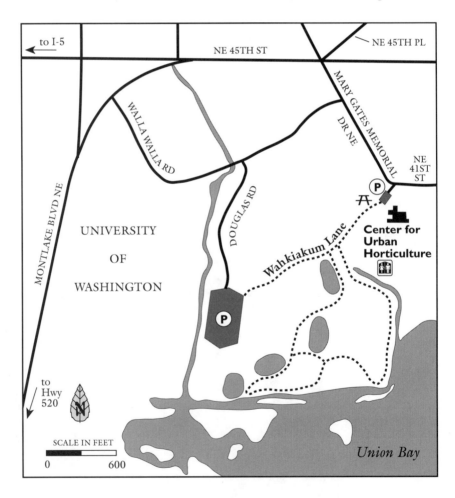

birch, and Scouler's willow. Queen Anne's lace, chicory, Scot's broom, and Himalayan blackberry grow in the fields, and cattail and purple loosestrife flourish in the marsh.

Muskrats, raccoons, and beavers are among the marsh's animal residents. Look near the shoreline for chewed black cottonwood stumps and feel the broad grooves made by the beaver's big teeth.

Marsh and shoreline birds include resident Virginia rails, marsh wrens, red-winged blackbirds, pied-billed grebes, American bitterns, killdeer, spotted sandpipers, and green and great blue herons. Sora and common yellowthroats arrive in the spring.

Among the birds seen in the fields are resident ring-necked pheasants, song sparrows, common snipes, and California quail. Savannah sparrows and tree swallows visit in spring and summer, and water pipits pass through in spring and fall.

On the open water, you will find resident American coots, mallards, Canada geese, and cormorants. Ruddy ducks and buffleheads visit in fall and winter. Raptors spotted in the area include red-tailed hawks, northern harriers, bald eagles, and short-eared and snowy owls.

The ponds of the Montlake Fill attract a remarkable variety of shorebirds and waterfowl, including species rarely seen elsewhere in the region. In late summer and early fall, numerous migrating shorebirds frequent the ponds. As autumn progresses, waterfowl arrive with the rains, and by winter the greatly enlarged ponds may be thronged with ducks of many kinds. Resident mallards and gadwalls are joined by northern shovelers, hooded mergansers, and wigeons in fall and winter. Spring brings migrating swallows and green-winged, blue-winged, and cinnamon teals.

---

6 ◆ Seattle
Ravenna Park

Highlights: Forest, stream, redwoods
Size: 52 acres; several miles of trail
Ownership: Seattle Department of Parks and Recreation
Season: Year-round
Terrain: Moderately steep descent from top of bluff into ravine, flat along stream, gently sloping from Cowen Park and Northeast 55th Street entrances
Facilities: Restrooms, water fountain, picnic shelter and tables at 20th Avenue Northeast parking lot; picnic tables by Northeast 55th Street playing fields; nearest phone on Northeast Ravenna Boulevard, 1 block from 20th Avenue Northeast entrance
Hours: Dawn to dusk

Douglas-firs display a shallow root system.

Interpretive Programs: None
Wheelchair Accessibility: Gravel trail at eastern entrance near Northeast 55th
    Street playing fields.
Pets: Leash and scoop
Horses: No
Bikes: Yes, on main trail only (not permitted on trails less than 5 feet wide)
Bus: Metro 71, 72, 73 (Cowen Park entrance), 74 (Northeast 55th Street
    playing field entrance)
Driving Directions: From downtown Seattle, take I-5 north. Get off at exit
    170, Northeast Ravenna Boulevard. At the light, turn right on Northeast
    Ravenna Boulevard, and drive east. After about 0.75 mile, turn left on 20th
    Avenue Northeast. The street dead-ends in 1 block at the bridge over
    Ravenna Park, and the park entrance is on the right. From the parking lot,
    walk north past the restrooms to the trailhead kiosk at the edge of the ra-
    vine. Northeast Ravenna Boulevard also accesses additional park entrances
    and parking areas to the west, at Cowen Park, and further east, at the
    Northeast 55th Street playing fields.

Park Overview This wooded ravine offers a lush haven in the midst of the
northern part of the University District. The park is popular with students,
local joggers and dog owners, while cyclists use it to traverse the area. The
ravine holds a wide variety of trees, including two small but startling groves
of redwoods. The park is generally quiet, with street noise limited to local

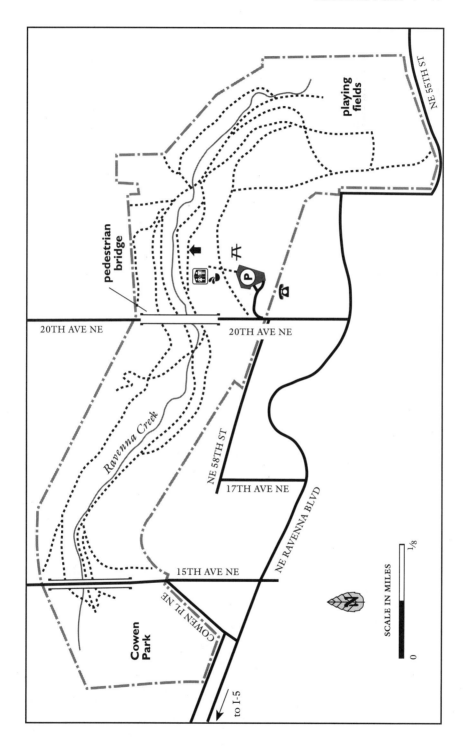

NE 55TH ST

playing fields

pedestrian bridge

20TH AVE NE

20TH AVE NE

Ravenna Creek

NE 58TH ST

17TH AVE NE

NE RAVENNA BLVD

15TH AVE NE

COWEN PL NE

Cowen Park

to I-5

SCALE IN MILES

0   1/8

traffic. Two graceful old bridges frame the ravine, and enhance rather than detract from the views: the 15th Avenue bridge still carries traffic, while the 20th Avenue bridge was closed to vehicles in 1975.

Trail Layout   The hard-packed gravel trails that flank Ravenna Creek are broad and flat, while steeper dirt paths climb up the sides of the ravine. The lower trails are generally well drained, while the upper ones can be muddy after a rain. A very gradual entry into the ravine can be made either from the east side of the park at the playing fields off Northeast 55th Street, or from Cowen Park to the west. A few benches scattered throughout the park provide welcome resting spots.

Human History   Originally, Ravenna Creek was the outlet for Green Lake. The stream flowed through the ravine in Ravenna Park and emptied into Union Bay through a large marshy delta, where Native Americans found good fishing.

When the Seattle, Lake Shore, and Eastern Railroad reached this area in 1887, Reverend William W. Beck, a German immigrant, purchased land along the stream and made 60 acres into a private park which he named after the seacoast town of Ravenna in Italy. Beck installed pavilions, benches, and pathways, and operated the Ravenna Springs Park, charging a small fee to view the ravine's extremely large trees, which grew tall due to the moisture and

The 15th Avenue bridge spans the trail which leads from Ravenna Park west to Cowen Park.

wind protection of the steep ravine. The popular park was known as the place to see the "trees that swept the stars," with some specimens reaching from 50 to 60 feet in circumference and up to 400 feet in height.

In 1911, Beck sold a portion of his land to Seattle for a park. The lowering of Green Lake that year forced the city to create an underground drainage system for Ravenna Creek to flow into Union Bay. The creek delta was filled in the 1920s for real estate and is the current site of University Village shopping center.

Timber crews began clearing away felled timber in the park for cordwood and eventually the great trees began to disappear under mysterious circumstances. By 1930, the last great tree had been cut. The word from the city was that the huge trees were a threat to public safety, but unconfirmed reports suggested that a corrupt member of the park board profited from their sale.

Natural History   Ravenna Creek flows through a glacial ridge of rock debris. On the southern side of the stream, an attractive little boardwalk skirts a huge boulder that has traveled far from its original home in British Columbia. This glacial erratic was dropped here by the retreat of the Vashon Ice Sheet around 14,000 years ago.

Streambed reconstruction and revegetation projects combat present-day stream erosion. These projects are a community effort and enlist the help of schoolchildren. Ravenna Creek Alliance is attempting to daylight the creek and route it once again to Union Bay.

The park's habitats include forest, stream, and open meadow. The ravine's original forest was dominated by Douglas-fir, western red cedar, and western hemlock trees. Today, the forest consists of a mixture of these conifers and deciduous trees. Bigleaf maple and red alder are the dominant species of deciduous trees, with some Pacific madrone, bitter cherry, Pacific dogwood, and Pacific yew. Ponderosa pine and western larch, rare west of the Cascades, also grow here.

Over the years, many non-native ornamental trees have been planted in the park. The most spectacular ones are the coast redwoods found in two small groves in the middle of the park south of the creek. Other non-native trees include Norway spruce, horsechestnut, black walnut, incense cedar, London planetree, European white birch, bald cypress, Nikko fir, and several varieties of cherry, pine, and poplar trees.

The ravine's hillsides are sheathed in sword ferns, while licorice ferns cover the trunks of bigleaf maples. Birds enjoy the fruit of snowberry and red huckleberry shrubs, and California hazelnut and Indian plum form tall thickets. Salal and Oregon grape grow on the drier upper hillsides, while salmonberry thickets and creeping buttercup grow in wetter areas near the stream. Tiny green leaves of watercress dot the waters of the stream—do not eat these greens! High levels of fecal coliform bacteria in the stream (probably from pet waste) render these plants unfit for human consumption.

Poison water-hemlock, which resembles watercress, is also common in the stream.

Several non-native invaders threaten the forest's native plants, including English holly and English ivy. Along the stream, forest openings are choked by dense thickets of Himalayan and evergreen blackberry. The blackberries crowd out native tree seedlings, hindering the growth of new trees. Local volunteers periodically remove the invasive plants and replace them with native species. However, eradication is difficult.

Park animals include the usual local forest assemblage. Evening grosbeaks visit the area in spring to eat budding bigleaf maple seeds. Resident red-breasted sapsuckers drill holes in white pine and spruce trees. Three ponds were constructed in 1996 near the 15th Avenue bridge to reintroduce the Pacific treefrog.

---

7 ◆ Seattle
Discovery Park

Highlights: Forests, streams, meadows, saltwater beaches, lighthouse, wild-life observation, views of Puget Sound, Olympic Mountains, and Mount Rainier; excellent interpretive programs

Size: 534 acres; over 7 miles of trails

Ownership: Seattle Department of Parks and Recreation

Season: Year-round

Terrain: Flat to moderately steep

Facilities: Visitor center with full-time staff and exhibits; restrooms and water fountain at visitor center, North Bluff, South Meadow, and West Point; picnic tables near visitor center, North parking lot, South parking lot, and South Meadow; play area and phone near visitor center

Hours: Dawn to dusk; visitor center open daily 8:30 A.M. to 5 P.M.

Interpretive Programs: Visitor center offers free Saturday nature walks, plus classes for the public and schools; maps and pamphlets for sale

Wheelchair Accessibility: Paved roads throughout the upper parts of the park (off limits to cars); wheelchair-accessible road to South Beach and several other accessible trails

Pets: Leash and scoop; prohibited on beach and Wolf Tree Nature Trail

Horses: No

Bikes: On paved surfaces; must be walked on unpaved trails

Bus: Metro 19, 33

Driving Directions: From downtown Seattle, follow Elliott Avenue (which becomes 15th Avenue West) to the West Dravus Street exit and turn left at the stop sign. Turn right on 20th Avenue West (which becomes Gilman

Staircases along the South Beach Trail descend the bluff to the beach.

Avenue West, then West Government Way) and follow it to the park entrance. The visitor center is to the left; park here, or at the park's north parking lot, near Commodore Way. The South Parking Lot is located off West Emerson Street.

Park Overview   This huge park on Magnolia Bluff boasts some of the best bird-watching and tidal-pool exploration in the region; spectacular views of Puget Sound, the Olympics, and Mount Rainier; and a Coast Guard lighthouse. The park's visitor education center offers numerous programs on the natural history of the region.

Trail Layout   Maps of the park are posted at several kiosks in this large park, but it is wise to stop first at the visitor education center and buy your own. The dirt/gravel trails are fairly well-drained, even in wet areas, with old asphalt roads throughout the park available to walkers, joggers, and cyclists. There are occasional benches, including some wonderful log ones overlooking the South Bluff. Stay behind barriers on the steep cliffs—there are often landslides here. A section of the North Bluff road began sliding down the cliff during the winter of 1996.

The Wolf Tree Nature Trail (0.5 mile) offers a flat to moderately sloping walk through a forested wetland. At the trailhead near the North Parking Lot, borrow a pamphlet that describes plants found along the trail. Trails run west

The Coast Guard lighthouse at the tip of West Point attracts admirers by land and sea.

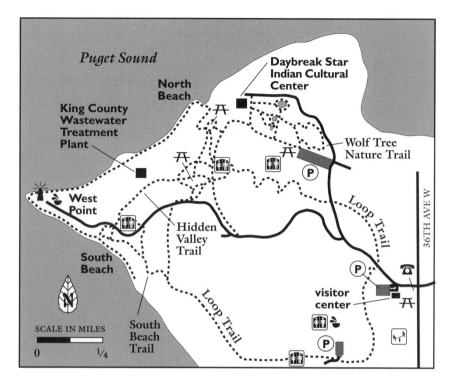

to three ponds, then on to the Daybreak Star Indian Cultural Center.

The Loop Trail (2.8 miles) winds through the forest, passes by the visitor center, skirts the South Meadow, and is the starting point for trails leading down to the beach. The South Beach trail follows a staircase down to the beach area. Several incredible overlooks offer eagle-eye views of the driftwood-festooned beach. The lighthouse at West Point (not open to the public) was built in 1881, and is owned by the U.S. Coast Guard. For a more gradual descent to the beach, follow the Hidden Valley Trail, or the road that leads to the wastewater treatment facility.

Human History The Magnolia Bluff is an area rich in Native American history. Many Puget Sound tribes used the beach area below the bluff, including the Shilshoh, Duwamish, Suquamish, Tulalip, and the White and Green River groups (tribes now living on the Muckleshoot Reservation).

The construction of additional facilities at the King County Wastewater Treatment Plant in 1992 gave archeologists a rare opportunity to learn more about the area's earliest residents. Radiocarbon tests on evidence gathered at the site suggested that the beaches and low bluffs were first used as campsites and for food gathering from 4,250 to 3,550 years ago. Then, as now, the instability of the bluffs affected land use. From 3,550 to 2,700 years ago, the inhabitants moved their camp slightly to the north, partly in response to land-

An observation platform along the South Beach Trail gives a bird's-eye view of the beach.

slide activity. Around 1,000 years ago, an earthquake along the Seattle Fault caused the beach area to drop about a meter, which decreased its acreage but does not seem to have affected its use. Archeologists found that different areas of the beach were used for village sites, fishing stations, shellfish gathering, hunting, and plant gathering places. Clam midden areas, with fire pits for clam drying and fish processing, were uncovered, as were numerous stone and bone tools, including choppers, scrapers, and projectile points. Petrified wood from the Columbia River drainage and artifacts crafted from Oregon obsidian provided clues to outside trade activity.

Discovery Park is named for the ship of Captain George Vancouver who, in 1792, was dispatched to the Northwest to negotiate an agreement between the English and Spanish over claims of ownership. In trying to find the Northwest Passage, Vancouver discovered and explored Puget Sound. Farmers settled the land in the 1870s, including Christian Scheuerman, for whom the creek along the Wolf Creek Nature Trail was named.

In 1897, the city of Seattle donated 700 acres of Magnolia Bluff land to the U.S. government for the construction of the Fort Lawton army post. In 1964, the Army surplused most of the site and in 1970, Congress passed a bill allowing surplused federal property to be given to cities for parks at no cost. Discovery Park was dedicated in 1972, and the city leases 17 acres to the United Tribes for a cultural and education center.

Natural History   The layers of sediment in the South Bluff tell the recent geologic history of the area. The Kitsap Formation, a 70-foot-thick layer of sands and clays at the base of the cliff, consists of sediments formed by streams and lakes on the broad, marshy floodplain that existed before the last glacial advance. As the climate cooled, the Vashon Ice Sheet advanced from the north and dammed the north-flowing streams, creating a huge freshwater lake. Sediments formed in that lake are seen in the 80-foot-thick, dark gray layer of clay and silt called the Lawton Clay, which lies above the Kitsap Formation. Above that layer, a hundred feet of yellowish sand marks deposits made by streams flowing off the advancing glacier. A 30-foot-thick jumbled layer of rock debris (till) lies higher still, dropped by the glacier as it retreated.

Discovery Park holds a wide variety of habitats, including meadows, forests, ponds, and saltwater beaches. A land survey in 1855 documented a forest of mature Douglas-fir, western red cedar and western hemlock trees, with a few bigleaf maples and red alders. Other trees noted were vine maple, cascara, Pacific yew, and Pacific dogwood. Surveyors also described ferns and shrubs such as red huckleberry, Oregon grape, California hazelnut, native blackberry, and snowberry. Pacific madrone was mistaken for magnolia, and the area was named Magnolia Bluff. The bluff was logged beginning in the 1860s, with the last wave of old-growth logging carried out by the Army in 1907.

Today, the mainly deciduous forest consists of red alder and bigleaf maple trees, with some Douglas-firs, western red cedars, and western hemlocks. The same plants noted by the early surveyors are still found here, along with bitter cherry, black hawthorn, Sitka spruce, Pacific crabapple, and Pacific and Scouler's willow trees.

Non-native trees include European mountain ash, horsechestnut, English hawthorn, white fir, shortleaf pine, white poplar, English holly, golden weeping willow, and European white birch.

Shrubs include Indian plum, salal, swamp gooseberry, salmonberry, coast red elderberry, and baldhip rose. Herbaceous plants include youth-on-age, fireweed, Cooley's hedgenettle, water parsley, skunk cabbage, common horsetail, cattail, creeping buttercup, bedstraw, western bleeding heart, enchanter's nightshade, fringecup, foamflower, large-leaved avens, candyflower, yellow violet, starflower, stinging nettle, sweet cicely, twinflower, Pacific waterleaf, bulrush, trillium, and sedges. Fern varieties include sword, lady, deer, licorice, maidenhair, wood, and bracken.

Himalayan blackberry, Portuguese laurel, and Scot's broom are among the non-native plants removed by volunteer efforts in the park. A clever program in December invites visitors to remove the park's non-native invasive English holly and English ivy to festoon their houses for the holidays. After they remove the plants, helpers gather in the visitor education center for hot drinks and tips on decorating.

The spit was formed by currents that transported sand along South Beach from the crumbling base of Magnolia Bluff. North Beach's rocky shoreline is less exposed to waves from the south and shelters intertidal life. At low tide, you may find crabs, sea stars, sea anemones, sea urchins, mussels, limpets, and periwinkles. (Take care not to disturb or remove the intertidal animals.)

Thirty-two species of mammals have been spotted in the park, including long-tailed weasel, red fox, mountain beaver, coyote, muskrat, raccoon, opossum, Townsend's chipmunk, rabbit, shrew, shrew-mole, mouse, vole, squirrel, and numerous types of moles and bats. River otters, harbor seals, sea lions, Dall's porpoises, pilot whales, and orcas have been seen offshore.

Discovery Park is renowned among birders as perhaps the best place in Seattle for viewing birds. Bird sightings number over 253 species—half the species recorded in the state have been seen at least once in the park, and more than 50 species nest here, including bald eagle. The greatest numbers and variety of birds can be found in late fall through early spring, and the bluffs and beach zones are important nesting and feeding areas for migratory species. The woods of mixed conifers and deciduous trees within the park also harbor many species of resident and migratory forest birds, and the park's meadows, thickets and ponds are home to numerous other birds. Purchase a species list at the visitor center to learn more.

---

8 ◆ Seattle
Carkeek Park

Highlights: Forest, stream with spawning salmon; saltwater beach, Olympic Mountain and Puget Sound views; old skid road
Size: 223 acres (including 23 acres of tidelands) approximately 6 miles of trails
Ownership: Seattle Department of Parks and Recreation
Season: Best spring through fall; winter good for watching birds and storms
Terrain: Flat to moderately steep
Facilities: Restrooms, water fountain, picnic tables and shelters, grills, and

A bridge over Pipers Creek leads to hillside trails.

play area at Puget Sound overlook; portable toilet and picnic tables at lower parking lot; phone outside Environmental Education Center; water fountain, picnic tables and grills at 6th Avenue Northwest (MacAbee) trailhead

Hours: Dawn to dusk

Interpretive Programs: The park's Environmental Education Center offers free nature walks and low-cost classes on topics such as streams, beaches, animals, and plants, with group programs for schoolchildren (see Appendix B for phone number)

Wheelchair Accessibility: Paved walkways at overlook area

Pets: Leash and scoop; prohibited on beach

Horses: No

Bikes: Allowed only on paved surfaces and gravel Pipers Creek Trail

Bus: Metro 28 (Get off at Northwest 100th Place and 3rd Avenue Northwest and walk to the northern end of 6th Avenue Northwest to access the northeastern end of the Pipers Creek Trail; walk 0.5 mile to the ravine parking lot.)

Driving Directions: From downtown Seattle, take I-5 north to exit 173. At the bottom of the exit ramp, take a left onto 1st Avenue Northeast, then another left on Northgate Way. Go west on North Northgate Way, cross Aurora, and take a right on Greenwood Avenue. Turn left on Northwest 110th Street at the first stoplight. This road crosses 3rd Avenue Northwest and becomes Northwest Carkeek Park Road down to the park; in just over

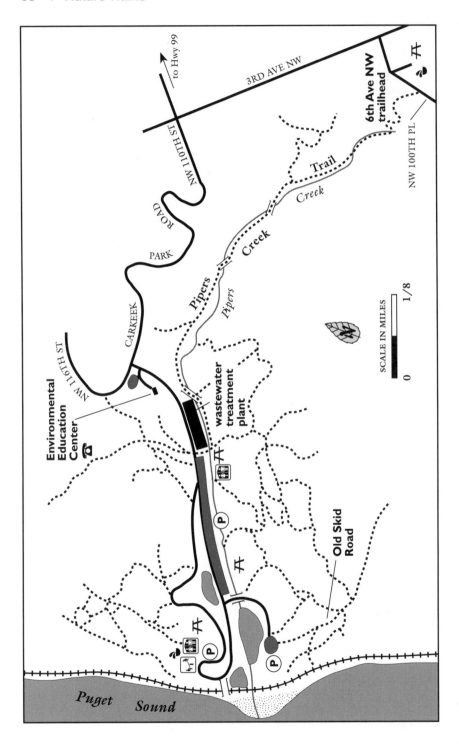

0.5 mile, turn left into the park. The Carkeek Park Environmental Learning Center will be on your right. Drive another 0.2 mile to a parking lot on the left near the wastewater treatment plant. To park closer to the beach, pass the first parking lot and continue up a hill to the overlook loop.

Park Overview   The high bluff of Carkeek Park overlooks Puget Sound, the Olympic Mountains, Bainbridge Island, and the Kitsap Peninsula. A rocky glacial-till beach below is home to shorebirds and intertidal animals. Forest and stream trails wind through a lush second-growth forest. The bluff playground features a whimsical salmon slide, where kids enter the mouth and are "spawned" out near the tail.

Trail Layout   The Pipers Creek Trail is a flat, easy walk that switchbacks down the ravine from the MacAbee park entrance at Northwest 100th Place and 6th Avenue Northwest. The path empties out into a flat, wide, dirt/gravel trail (muddy in a few spots after rains) that follows the creek. An occasional bench offers a spot to rest. The trail passes the wastewater treatment plant and reaches the lower parking lot approximately 0.5 mile later.

The tangle of southern hillside trails is accessed by a footbridge that crosses Pipers Creek across the lawn from the lower parking lot. Stay on the main trails to lessen impact on wildlife. While it is difficult to get really lost in this maze of dirt/gravel trails, keep your ear attuned to the trains and the voices in the ravine and be sure to return before twilight. These trails can be muddy after a rain. If you walk down to the beach, use the pedestrian overpass to cross the railroad tracks—there have been fatalities here.

Human History   Several Northwest tribes camped along the beach in summer, where they came to fish and gather clams, then headed inland to permanent settlements. The creek and ravine are named for Andrew W. Piper, who purchased 40 acres in the canyon between 1884 and 1891 from the timber companies that had logged off its old-growth western red cedar trees. The Piper family lived in the old lumber-camp house and had a large vegetable garden where the wastewater treatment plant now stands. Piper and his wife, Minna, an orchardist, sold fruit, produce, and flowers downtown at the Pike Place Market. Their old orchard was rediscovered along the Pipers Creek Trail in a thicket of blackberries and red alders, and is being restored.

An old skid road heads downhill from the forest to the model airplane field. The old-growth western red cedars and western hemlocks that once grew on this slope were skidded down this road to a sawmill below. Half-buried logs laid at intervals across the road served as skids to keep the tree ends from nosing into the mud on their way down the hill. The mill closed in the 1920s, when the last old-growth red cedars and hemlocks were cut down.

The city of Seattle purchased Pipers Canyon in 1927, with the help of a

$25,000 gift from Morgan J. Carkeek, an English-born building contractor. This is actually Seattle's second Carkeek park—in 1918, Carkeek deeded 23 acres on the north side of Sand Point to the city for a park, but in 1926 the land was converted into an airbase. The Carkeeks' gift was returned in the form of $25,000, which went toward the purchase of the Carkeek Park here. The new park was dedicated in 1929, and was first used to grow vegetables for animals in the Woodland Park Zoo. Work projects during the Depression created the trails and shelters, and the U.S. Army camped here briefly during World War II.

Natural History The forest consists mostly of good-sized bigleaf maple and red alder trees, along with some western red cedars, Douglas-firs, and western hemlocks. Cedars once dominated this moist slope—look for large stumps that remain from the days of logging. As the red alders reach maturity and die off, the western hemlocks will eventually take over. Other native trees in the forest include Pacific crabapple and grand fir. Pacific willows, red alders, and black cottonwoods grow on the banks along the stream.

Thickets of salmonberry and stinging nettle indicate abundant moisture on the slope. Other plants include Indian plum, coast red elderberry, Pacific waterleaf, fringecup, candyflower, Pacific bleeding heart, youth-on-age, and creeping buttercup. Sword, lady, wood, and licorice ferns grow in the park, and Oregon grape and ocean spray thrive on the drier parts of the hillside. Non-native invasive vegetation includes English ivy, English holly, false bamboo, and Himalayan and evergreen blackberry.

The forest is home to abundant wildlife. Forest animals include raccoons, squirrels, coyotes, mountain beavers, shrew-moles, and toads. Resident woodpeckers, owls, song sparrows, spotted towhees, American dippers, and Bewick's wrens live in the forest, with Wilson's warblers visiting in the spring and summer months. On the shoreline, look for loons, grebes, brants, diving ducks, gulls, terns, alcids, and spotted sandpipers in season.

In 1993, released chum salmon fry began returning in the fall to spawn in Pipers Creek for the first time since 1927. You will find a great salmon-viewing spot at the eastern end of the parking lot—look for the display sign west of the wastewater-treatment plant. The bridge that crosses over to the hillside trails also offers a good overhead vantage point. Stay off the streambanks (eroded banks add silt to the stream) and be aware that it is illegal to disturb the salmon, dead or alive. Dead carcasses feed park wildlife and fertilize the stream and nearby plants. Volunteer salmon stewards host interpretive talks along the stream near the lower parking lot in the late fall when the salmon are running. The park-based Salmon Restoration Project is an effort to improve local water quality. The program seeks to protect the watershed from sources of waste, and to restore stream habitat by planting vegetation and combating bank erosion.

North of Seattle

9 · Edmonds
Meadowdale County Beach Park

Highlights: Forest, stream, Puget Sound beach
Size: 105 acres, 1.25-mile trail
Ownership: Snohomish County Parks and Recreation Department
Season: Year-round
Terrain: Flat to moderately steep
Facilities: Portable toilets and picnic tables at upper parking lot and at beach; water fountain, picnic shelter, outdoor sink, and grills near beach; emergency phone at ranger's residence near beach
Hours: 6 A.M. to dusk
Interpretive Programs: Available for school and scout groups (call to schedule)
Wheelchair Accessibility: Level, paved 0.25-mile loop on lawn near beach; contact the on-site ranger or administrative office for access to lower parking lot (see Appendix B for phone numbers)
Pets: Leash and scoop
Bikes: Yes
Bus: Community Transit (see Appendix B for phone number)
Driving Directions: From downtown Seattle, take I-5 north to exit 183. Turn left at the end of the exit ramp and go west on 164th Street Southwest, which will curve into 168th Southwest. Turn right onto Highway 99, then turn left soon onto 164th Street Southwest. Turn right onto 52nd Avenue

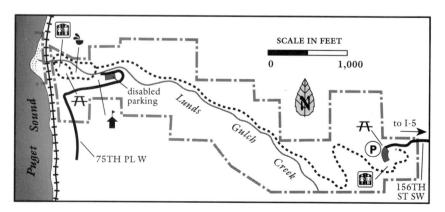

West, and take a left onto 160th Street Southwest. Turn right onto 56th Avenue West, and then turn left onto 156th Street Southwest. The park entrance is at the end of the road.

Park Overview The park trail descends westward from the parking lot down forested Lunds Gulch to a gravel beach that extends 200 yards along Puget Sound. The beach features spectacular views of the Sound and the Olympic Mountains. (Visitors with disabilities can call to arrange direct beach entry.) The ravine is very quiet, with light filtering through the largely deciduous forest, and the secluded shoreline recalls a time when the region was less populated.

Trail Layout The wide dirt, gravel, and bark trail is well designed and well drained; muddy spots are few, even in the rainy season. Along the lower portions of the path, culverts under the trail divert the many rivulets that drain the moist hillside after a rain. The path runs close to the north side of the stream once it descends into the ravine. A long set of steps climbs the steepest portion of the trail, and a few benches offer places to rest.

Human History Native Americans probably visited the area to gather clams, but no evidence of permanent villages has been found. Unfortunately, any existing middens were probably destroyed in 1890, when the shoreline railroad track was constructed.

John Lund was the first resident of the ravine that now bears his name. Lund, a Norwegian immigrant, built a shanty near the beach about 1878. He lived on the land for four years and proved up his claim, receiving his land patent in 1882. Lund cleared some of his land himself, and planted an orchard along the creek. Later, he worked for local loggers to clear more of the area. The creeks of the region were excellent trout streams, but old-timers said that none of the streams supported salmon. Fish traps were built out into the Sound to snare salmon heading for streams in the vicinity of Everett or Seattle.

Several others owned the ravine after Lund, including the last private owner, Meadowdale Community Club. Snohomish County acquired the land in 1971, and in 1988 the park was constructed.

Natural History The saltwater beach is covered with an assemblage of multicolored pebbles, remnants of glacial rocks scraped southward from Canada. A huge blue glacial erratic once lay on the south slope of Lunds Gulch. It originally weighed several thousand tons, but a previous owner quarried most of it away to use for landscaping.

The original forest of western red cedar, Douglas-fir, and western hemlock trees, protected in the lush gulch, was said to resemble the rainforests of Olympic National Park. Cascaras were once very common along the early logging roads. The bark was stripped and sold for use in the drug trade, while the berries were made into pies by the logging camp cooks.

Today, the forest consists mostly of deciduous red alders and bigleaf maples, with black cottonwoods and willows growing close to the stream. Douglas-firs, western red cedars, hemlocks, and Sitka and Norway spruce grow in the park, and huge cedar stumps along the trail near the stream show the size of the former trees. Several signs placed by scouts identify individual species of trees.

Salal and Oregon grape grow on higher, drier parts of the park, lush sword ferns drape the hillsides, and plants such as thimbleberry, salmonberry, youth-on-age, and creeping buttercup indicate moister ground farther down the slopes. Himalayan blackberry, English holly, and English ivy are among the non-native invaders.

The park's varied habitats attract many kinds of birds. Resident pileated and hairy woodpeckers and red-shafted flickers live in the forest, along with golden crowned kinglets, American dippers, owls, red-tailed hawks, and bald eagles. Shorebirds include resident belted kingfishers, spotted sandpipers, great blue herons, and migrating wigeons.

It was noted that in the early days, sheep raising in Lunds Gulch was unsuccessful because of the bear population in the canyon. No bears inhabit

The Meadowdale forest trail and beach are a favorite for family outings.

the ravine now, but many forest animals, including coyote, deer, and mountain beaver, live in this park. Otters are seen occasionally in the lower parts of the stream, and seals swim off the beach. Coho and chum salmon have been introduced into the Lunds Gulch Creek. Look for postings of salmon sightings on the bulletin board near the ranger station.

---

10 ◆ Bothell
North Creek Park

Highlights: Wetlands
Size: 96 acres; approximately 1 mile of trail
Ownership: Snohomish County Parks and Recreation Department
Season: Year-round
Terrain: Flat
Facilities: Portable toilets and picnic tables at parking lot
Hours: Dawn to dusk
Interpretive Programs: Signs
Wheelchair Accessibility: Sand path leads evenly onto boardwalk trail
Pets: No
Horses: No
Bikes: No
Bus: Community Transit (see Appendix B for phone number)
Driving Directions: From downtown Seattle, take I-90 east to I-405, and head north. Take exit 26, and take a right off the exit ramp to head north on Highway 527 (the Bothell-Everett Highway). Turn left on 183rd Street Southeast. The park entrance is on the right in 0.5 mile. There is

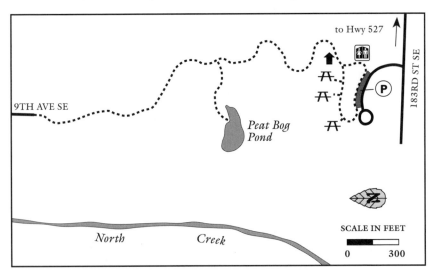

also parking at the north end of the park: continue north on Highway 527 and turn left on 164th Street Southeast. Take a left at 9th Avenue, and then drive south to the end of the road.

Park Overview   A sinuous boardwalk trail winds through restored wetlands in a peaceful bowl-shaped valley surrounded by upland forests and crowned by a huge expanse of open sky. Interpretive signs explain the purpose of wetlands and the history of the region, and the chirps, quacks, and trills of marsh birds mask the noise of a nearby highway.

Trail Layout   A fine sand path slopes gently down into the marsh from a grassy picnic area dotted with several large western red cedars and other conifers. A long boardwalk with off-shooting spurs curves among the hardhack shrubs, offering privacy for people and fauna. Benches at boardwalk junctions or at the ends of sections provide resting places. The boardwalk may be slippery under dewy or rainy conditions, and cold air can settle in the low, bowl-shaped marsh, so dress accordingly.

Human History   White settlers came to the North Creek valley around 1880. John C. Bailey, originally from Canada, homesteaded 160 acres on what is now the park land. The property was used for trapping, logging, peat mining, and agriculture. Most of the land has remained in the Bailey family through five generations until the 1980s, when all but 27 acres was sold to a development company. By 1996, the company had sold 84 acres to Snohomish County. The wetlands park, dedicated in late 1996, was built as part of a water detention facility, in a partnership between Snohomish County Parks and Surface Water Management. A box culvert at the southwest end of the park will control downstream flooding after heavy rains. Large volumes of stormwater will be stored in the wetlands and released slowly through this gate.

Loggers began felling trees in the valley during the late nineteenth century, and landowners were known as shingle-bolt farmers, because they logged cedars for roof and siding shingles.

The town of Bothell might not have survived the great depression of the 1890s, were it not for the industriousness of Gerhard Ericksen, a Norwegian immigrant. Ericksen diked and straightened meandering North Creek into a 7-mile-long flume, enabling the cedar logs harvested in the North Creek valley to be floated down to the Sammamish River, then on to Lake Washington and its shingle mills. By the 1930s, most of the timber on hills surrounding the valley had been harvested. Once the valley floor was cleared, it was used for raising dairy cattle and crops.

Natural History   North Creek's original channel is now being restored. Beavers are breaching the eroding flume dike, allowing the creek to return to its meandering course across the valley and restore the wetlands. Coho salmon and cutthroat trout spawn in Nickel Creek, a tributary, due largely to the efforts of local schoolchildren at the Lively Environmental Center.

Trees in and surrounding the wetlands include Douglas-fir, western red cedar, Sitka spruce, red alder, bigleaf maple, vine maple, willow, cascara, and Pacific yew. To help restore the wetlands, Pacific ninebarks, red-osier dogwoods, and Sitka willows have been planted. Tall fields of hardhack flourish in the marsh, along with creeping buttercup, sedges, rushes, cattails, and grasses.

The valley's metamorphosis from farmlands back to marsh is luring wildlife back to the area. Wetlands maintain water quality by filtering out pollution before it reaches streams, making them livable for animals. Coyotes, muskrats, beavers, creeping voles, black-tailed deer, Northwestern salamanders, western pond turtles, frogs, and brown bats have been spotted in the marsh, and signs of black bear have frequently been found. Red-tailed hawks, great-horned owls, and eagles nest in the Douglas-firs and western red cedars on the hills and hunt in the wetlands. Other resident birds include swallows, belted kingfishers, marsh wrens, red-winged blackbirds, great blue herons, red-shafted flickers, barn owls, and various species of ducks and geese.

Several ponds in the marsh are magnets for wildlife, and are important breeding grounds for insects and amphibians. Peat Bog Pond was dug in the early 1900s, probably for drainage purposes. Stickleback fish and sunfish snack on shrimp-like crustaceans in the pond.

A curving boardwalk entices explorers into the marsh adjacent to North Creek.

Eastside

11 ◆ Kirkland
Saint Edward State Park

Highlights: Forest, wild Lake Washington lakefront
Size: 316 acres with 3,000 feet of freshwater shoreline; over 7 miles of trails
Ownership: Washington State Parks and Recreation Commission
Season: Year-round
Terrain: Flat to moderately steep
Facilities: Restrooms, portable toilets, and water near parking areas; portable toilets at beach; picnic tables (bottles and cans allowed in picnic areas, but not on trails); indoor heated 25-yard swimming pool
Hours: Dawn to dusk
Interpretive Programs: Environmental education classes for local school groups in spring and fall
Wheelchair Accessibility: On park road and at some picnic tables
Pets: Leash and scoop
Bikes: Yes, on designated trails
Horses: No
Bus: Metro 234 (0.5-mile walk to trailhead)
Driving Directions: From downtown Seattle, take I-90 or Highway 520 east to I-405. Drive north on I-405 to exit 20A, Northeast 116th Street. Turn left (west) at the bottom of the exit ramp, and follow Northeast 116th Street to 98th Avenue Northeast. Continue straight through the intersection; the road becomes Northeast Juanita Drive, then Juanita Drive Northeast. In about 3.5 miles, turn left into the park. Take the first right to the state park parking lot. (The driveway continues to Bastyr University.)

Park Overview   Located on the grounds of a former seminary on the outskirts of Kirkland, this beautiful quiet forest of fern-covered ravines sweeps down to the largest remaining undeveloped area on the Lake Washington shoreline. Three thousand feet of prime low-bank shoreline are protected forever, accessible only by trails.

Trail Layout   Five dirt/gravel trails, which can be muddy in the rainy season, lead down the hillside, all meeting up at the shoreline by a small grassy beach. Take your pick of moderate to steep inclines. The beach is great for

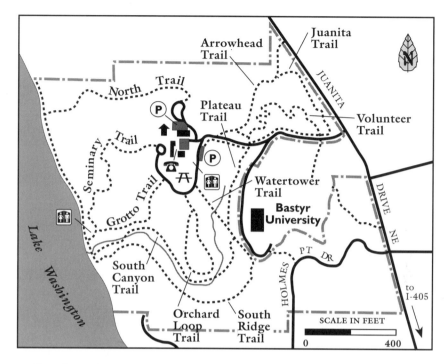

wading, but swimming is not advised, because the water becomes quite deep about 30 feet out from the shoreline. Several other trails traverse the upper part of the park.

The North Trail (0.6 mile) starts at the edge of the parking lot behind the gym. The trail initially heads north, then heads west down the side of a steep ravine. Upon reaching the lake, one branch of the trail runs north a short distance to the park boundary, while the other branch heads south to the small grassy beach. The shoreline trees run right down to the lakeshore, to give the waterfront a "Mississippi River" sort of feel. The portion of the trail that parallels the shore follows the level terrace that lies between the steep slopes of the bluff and the lake. This area appears to be an old, formerly submerged, wave-cut terrace that was exposed when the lake was lowered in 1916–17. Each winter, Lake Washington is lowered to reduce erosion, exposing a succession of sandy pocket beaches along the shore.

The Seminary Trail (0.6 mile) leaves the west side of the seminary building as a service road and weaves gently down a broad ridge to the lakeshore. The steep Grotto Trail (0.3 mile) begins at the southwestern corner of the lawns and drops steeply down the side of another ravine to join the Seminary Trail near the water. South Canyon Trail (0.6 mile) follows the floor of a ravine south of the seminary. The Watertower Trail (0.5 mile) climbs steeply

Woodpecker holes in a western red cedar offer habitat for wildlife.

up the backbone of the ridge to the south of South Canyon near Bastyr University before swinging west to form the South Ridge Trail (1 mile). The Orchard Loop Trail (0.6 mile) offers a gentle sloped path on a small knoll south of the seminary.

The Arrowhead Trail leaves the playfield and runs out to the northeastern corner of the park to emerge at Juanita Drive Northeast. The Volunteer and Juanita Trails are located on this wooded flat at the northeastern corner of the park. The Plateau Trail connects the Arrowhead Trail with the Watertower Trail.

Human History   Marshall Blinn acquired 260 acres in the area in 1879. He logged the land, and skid roads to the south of the seminary were visible for many years. In 1921, Miller Freeman, a publisher, bought the property for a country home, then sold it to live farther south on Groat Point near Meydenbauer Bay. The land was purchased in 1926 by Bishop Edward J. O'Dea, then Bishop of the Archdiocese of Seattle. O'Dea bought the property with his own personal inheritance, and donated it to the diocese for use as a seminary for Catholic priests. Saint Edward Seminary, named for Edward the Confessor, was in operation from 1931 to 1977. Nearby Saint Thomas Seminary (now Bastyr University) was established in 1958 to educate theology students.

Faced with declining enrollment, the Seattle Archdiocese closed Saint Edward Seminary. The land was slated to be sold and developed, but local outcry brought about its acquisition for a state park. In 1977, the Archdiocese sold 316 acres of the land to the state of Washington for a park, retaining 50 acres and Saint Thomas Seminary. Saint Edward State Park was opened to the public in 1978. The seminary building is used for park administrative offices, while the now-public swimming pool is managed by the King County Parks System.

Natural History   This luxuriant mixed forest contains good-sized Douglas-fir, western hemlock, and western red cedar trees, along with red alders, bigleaf maples, cascaras, and Pacific dogwoods, yews, and madrones. The most common trees along the shoreline are black cottonwood, Pacific willow, red alder, and Oregon ash. Notice the red alders leaning along the lakeshore; southwesterly storm winds, combined with soggy ground, provide unstable footing for these trees.

Just offshore the southwest corner of the park is a submerged forest of Douglas-firs. About a thousand years ago, a massive landslide broke from the hillside along a buried layer of clay and carried an entire stand of Douglas-firs right into the lake. The submerged trees are preserved upright in the cold waters of Lake Washington.

The lower part of the North Trail winds among salal and black cottonwood trees.

Many moisture-loving plants attest to the park slopes' abundant water. Sword ferns reign year-round, lady and maidenhair ferns join them in spring, and licorice ferns decorate Douglas-fir trunks. Moist areas in the damp ravines hold shrubby thickets of salmonberry, thimbleberry, red elderberry, California hazelnut, devil's club, and stinging nettle. Near the lake, in damp areas on the flat bench, are common horsetail, Cooley's hedgenettle, skunk cabbage, and Indian plum. Red huckleberry grows on stumps and logs, orange honeysuckle is common along the trails, and shrubs such as salal, Oregon grape, and ocean spray grow on drier areas of the park. Other herbaceous plants in the park include bedstraw, candyflower, large-leaved avens, fringecup, youth-on-age, vanilla leaf, and western trillium. Himalayan blackberry, English ivy, and English holly are among the non-native invaders.

Mountain beavers, coyotes, muskrats, Pacific moles, garter snakes, and bats are among the animals that take refuge in the park. Birds include barn owls, red-tailed hawks, black-capped chickadees, brown creepers, red-shafted flickers, varied thrushes, spotted towhees, ruffed grouse, bushtits, winter wrens, and pileated and hairy woodpeckers. These residents are joined in the spring and summer by western tanagers, rufous hummingbirds, Pacific-slope flycatchers, and violet-green, barn, and cliff swallows.

---

12 ◆ Kirkland
O. O. Denny County Park

Highlights: Forest, large Douglas-firs and western red cedars, stream, Lake Washington beachfront, views of Seattle and the Issaquah Alps
Size: 37.5 acres; 1.6 miles of trails
Ownership: City of Seattle, managed by King County Parks System
Season: Year-round
Terrain: Flat to moderately steep
Facilities: Restrooms, water fountain, phone, picnic tables, and grills at beach
Interpretive Programs: None
Hours: Dawn to dusk
Wheelchair Accessibility: No
Pets: Leash and scoop, prohibited on beach
Horses: No
Bikes: No
Bus: Metro 234, 258 (get off on Juanita Drive Northeast and walk down Holmes Point Drive Northeast)
Driving Directions: From downtown Seattle, take I-90 or Highway 520 east to I-405. Drive north on I-405 to exit 20A, Northeast 116th Street. Turn left (west) at the bottom of the exit ramp onto Northeast 116th Street.

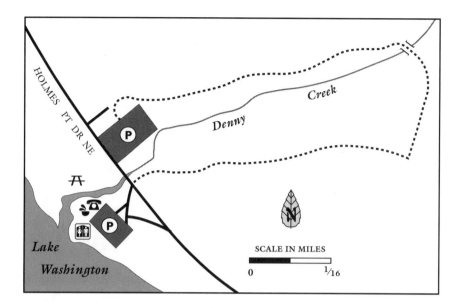

Follow Northeast 116th Street toward the lake, and continue through the intersection at 98th Avenue Northeast. West of this intersection, the road becomes Northeast Juanita Drive. In about 2 miles, turn sharply left on 76th Place Northeast, which changes to Holmes Point Drive Northeast and curves right to parallel the lakeshore. The main parking lot for the park is on the left, with an overflow lot just a bit farther on the right.

Park Overview   This gem of a park lies on the northeastern shore of Lake Washington in a secluded neighborhood. The quiet park, carefully tended by dedicated local residents, consists of a beach, a groomed picnic area, and an upland forest in a stream ravine, with some huge cedar and fir trees that missed the logger's ax of the last century. The small gravelly beach is a good place to put in with a kayak or watch the sun set over the Seattle skyline.

Trail Layout   Across the road from the main parking lot lies a lush, forested ravine, with a dirt/gravel loop trail that leads up one side and down the other of the small canyon. You will find the trailheads by the overflow parking lot: the southern trailhead is just across the street from the main parking area, and the northern one is at the back of a lawn area that adjoins the overflow parking lot.

 Much of the northern trail follows narrow, slippery planks and boardwalks over poorly-drained ground. A side trail (often muddy and overgrown) branches off to the left of the loop trail and winds uphill through big trees to emerge at a backyard. Several overlooks on the southern side of the ravine have no guardrails, so keep an eye on children. Above the eastern clearing,

The base of a broken-off Douglas-fir, once the largest in King County, still dwarfs pilgrims.

the trails peter out—loop back on the gravel road across the creek and walk up the road to re-enter the woods and travel back down the southern branch of the trail on the other side of the ravine.

Human History   Orion O. Denny, the son of Seattle pioneer Arthur Denny, was a businessman and the first white male child born in Seattle, in 1853. He purchased the future park land for a summer home, which he called Kla-hanie. Denny's widow Helen left the property to the city of Seattle after her death in 1922. In 1926 the park was set aside for a time as a camp for children from Seattle, with buildings salvaged from the first Carkeek Park (see Carkeek Park description).

Natural History   The trail leads through a moist forest of bigleaf maples and red alders, with some splendid western red cedars and Douglas-firs. In an area of especially large trees, in one of the muckiest parts of the northern trail, a huge trunk is snapped off about 60 feet up. Until a windstorm in January 1993 claimed it, this was the largest Douglas-fir in King County. According to a plaque which has since been removed, the tree towered 255 feet tall, was 26.5 feet around (8.5 feet in diameter), and was then about 575 years old.

The impressive cedars that grow in the park are little more than a century old. (The park's old-growth cedars were destroyed in a late-nineteenth-century forest fire that scarcely charred the thick bark of the Douglas-firs.) The remarkable size of these young cedars can be attributed to favorable growing conditions—the ravine provides abundant moisture and shelter from winds, encouraging the growth of large conifers. Other trees in the park include western hemlock, cascara, grand fir, and one of the largest black cottonwoods in the Seattle area, measuring 5 feet in diameter and over 16 feet around.

Shrubs in the park include California hazelnut, false Solomon's seal, baldhip rose, Indian plum, salmonberry, Pacific blackberry, and stink currant. Salal and Oregon grape grow in the higher, drier areas, and red huckleberry festoons old stumps. Herbaceous plants such as vanilla leaf, foamflower, candyflower, bleeding heart, Pacific waterleaf, skunk cabbage, bedstraw, fringecup, water parsley, and youth-on-age blanket the mucky streambanks. Mushrooms abound in season. Sword ferns grace the hillsides, accompanied by lady and bracken ferns in summer, while licorice ferns adorn the trunks of bigleaf maples.

Coyotes, squirrels, and an assortment of coniferous and mixed-forest birds reside here. Year-round residents include spotted towhees, brown creepers, pileated woodpeckers, hawks, red-breasted nuthatches, Hutton's vireos, golden-crowned kinglets, winter wrens, and black-capped and chestnut-backed chickadees. Spring and summer visitors include western flycatchers, western tanagers, Swainson's thrushes, and black-throated gray warblers.

Nearby Park
Big Finn Hill Park

Farther north along Juanita Drive Northeast lies Big Finn Hill Park, named for a close-knit neighborhood of Finnish immigrants. This 220-acre tangle of trails is used by mountain bikers and horses, so the dirt/gravel trails can get very muddy. Terrain and vegetation vary. Much of the western part of the park is forested and flat, sloping down through paths mown through blackberries and Scot's broom toward another forest area that borders busy Juanita Drive Northeast. The open forest is made up of bigleaf maple and red alder trees, with some western red cedars, Douglas-firs, western hemlocks, and Pacific madrones. There is a parking lot for cars near Juanita Drive Northeast and 138th Street Northeast.

---

13 ◆ Kirkland
Juanita Bay Park

Highlights: Wetlands
Size: 118 acres, includes 45 acres across the street along Forbes Creek; 3,000 feet of Lake Washington shoreline; over 1 mile of trails
Ownership: Kirkland Parks and Community Services
Season: Year-round
Terrain: Flat to gently sloping
Facilities: Restrooms, water fountain, and picnic tables near parking lot
Hours: Dawn to dusk
Interpretive Programs: Extensive interpretive signs
Wheelchair Accessibility: Entire park accessible through paved paths and boardwalks
Pets: Leash and scoop
Horses: No
Bikes: Allowed on former road
Bus: Metro 234, 255, 258, 275, 931

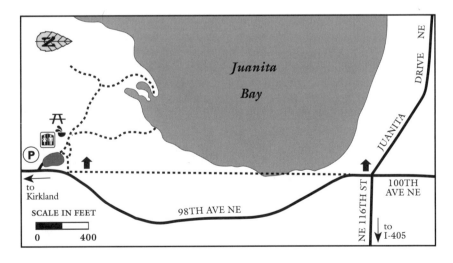

Driving Directions: From downtown Seattle, take I-90 or Highway 520 east to I-405. Drive north on I-405 to exit 20A, Northeast 116th Street. Turn left (west) at the bottom of the exit ramp, and continue on Northeast 116th to 98th Avenue Northeast. Turn left on 98th Avenue Northeast and drive about 0.5 mile along the lakeshore to the parking lot on the right.

Park Overview   This beautiful wildlife sanctuary on Lake Washington's eastern shore is Kirkland's largest park. Boasting 3,000 feet of shoreline, these wetlands host nearly 120 species of birds, and are the remnant of extensive marshes that once bordered the entire lake. Birdsong and frog noise compensate for the traffic sounds from nearby 98th Avenue Northeast. The park is especially beautiful at sunset, with the Seattle skyline visible across the lake to the west.

Trail Layout   Two boardwalks and an abandoned highway bridge along the shoreline offer access into the wetlands. A long, sloping lawn above the marshes with paved asphalt paths has benches and picnic tables placed to overlook the site.

Human History   The Indian name for the south side of Juanita Bay was Paint, since at Nelson Point (the shoreline to the west of the park), pigments were scraped from rocks and baked in a campfire for face paint. The water level of the lake was about 9 feet higher before the construction of the ship canal in 1916–17, and Native Americans paddled to the head of the bay to gather wapatos. These edible bulbs were harvested in about 5 feet of water, and tasted a little like sweet potatoes. Once the lake was lowered, the shoreline wetlands were severely affected. Stranded wetland plants perished, and it took years for zones of vegetation to become reestablished. The wapato in this area never recovered.

The drop in water level brought many changes to Juanita Bay. Once-busy steamship docks at Juanita had to be abandoned and the bay ceased to be a lake port. The area gained 150 acres in land, and a newly uncovered shallow sandy beach at the north end of the bay attracted picnickers and swimmers.

In 1915, the property on which the park sits was leased to two Frenchmen. They planned to use a pond on the property to raise frogs and then sell frog legs commercially to Seattle restaurants. They imported a large species from France, which escaped through the fences and propagated in the lake. Eventually, in 1932, the swampy ground was filled in with thousands of truckloads of cedar bark, sawdust, and dirt to construct a golf course. When the course closed in 1975, citizens voted for funds to save it as a park.

Natural History   This park has some of the best-presented interpretative signs you will ever find. The signs are liberally scattered, detailing the area's history and its wetland ecology and habitats. Spend some time reading and observing, and note how water lilies flourish in open water, how cattails and yellow irises thrive in marshes, and where to look for what animals.

The wetlands contain five major plant communities associated with variations in water depth. The open-water community consists of floating white water lily and duckweed, with submerged European water milfoil.

The marsh is dominated by cattails, interspersed in areas with rushes, reed canary grass, yellow irises, and willows. Water parsley, foxtail, spike rush, bulrush, bur-reed, marsh cinquefoil, knotweed, water plantain, pondweed, bladderwort, and invasive purple loosestrife also grow in this area.

The wet meadow occurs in a wide band along the southernmost part of the wetland. Creeping buttercup, a wetlands-indicator herb, turns this meadow yellow every spring. Other typical plants include horsetail, marsh speedwell, sedges, reed canary grass, soft rush, skunk cabbage, and yellow monkey flower.

The wooded wetland contains the greatest number of plant species. Red alder is dominant, followed by black cottonwood. The thick varied understory includes lady fern, salmonberry, and climbing nightshade. Some Douglas-fir and bigleaf maple trees grow on higher ground in the park.

The shrub wetland occurs north and south of the wooded wetland; its dominant plants are willows.

Animals spotted in the park include raccoons, beavers, muskrats, black-tailed deer, opossums, coyotes, striped skunks, mice, voles, snakes, frogs, painted turtles, and salamanders. Forbes Creek is one of the few remaining spawning streams into Lake Washington, a refuge for coho salmon and cutthroat trout.

Open-water resident birds include American coots, double-crested cormorants, and pied-billed grebes. Winter visitors include ring-necked and ruddy ducks, American wigeons, northern pintails, canvasbacks, lesser scaups, goldeneyes, buffleheads, mergansers, and several species of gulls and grebes. Teals visit the wetlands in the spring.

Resident marsh and shoreline birds include several species of herons, belted kingfishers, Virginia rails, killdeer, spotted sandpipers, common snipe, red-winged blackbirds, and marsh wrens. Sora and common yellowthroats return in spring.

In the thickets and forest, look for resident ring-necked pheasants, woodpeckers, band-tailed pigeons, chickadees, sparrows, Steller's jays, bushtits, Bewick's wrens, kinglets, pine siskins, spotted towhees, purple finches, and dark-eyed juncos. Spring and summer visitors include rufous hummingbirds, willow flycatchers, Bullock's orioles, cedar waxwings, warblers, swallows, black-headed grosbeaks, and Swainson's thrushes. Raptors in the park include hawks, bald eagles, ospreys, and owls.

Boardwalks offer views of beaver dams at the edge of Juanita Bay.

---

14 ◆ Redmond
Farrel-McWhirter Park

Highlights: Forest, stream with spawning salmon, farm
Size: 68 acres; 2 miles of trails
Ownership: Redmond Parks and Recreation Department
Season: Year-round
Terrain: Flat to gently sloping
Facilities: Restrooms in converted silo near farm; swings, picnic shelters, and tables in meadow; barn with farm animals
Hours: 8 A.M. to dusk
Interpretive Programs: Park brochures available at the operations building; groups can arrange pony and wagon rides, farm tours, and nature walks for a fee; orienteering competitions sponsored by Cascade Orienteering Club (See Appendix B for phone numbers)
Wheelchair Accessibility: Paved Charlotte's Trail runs the length of the park, with access to the barn area
Pets: Leash and scoop
Horses: Yes, on certain trails
Bikes: Yes
Bus: Metro 251
Driving Directions: From downtown Seattle, take Highway 520 east to Redmond and get off at the Avondale Road Northeast exit. Go north and in about 1.5 miles, turn right on Novelty Hill Road. Drive 0.25 mile and turn left on Redmond Road. Continue another 0.5 mile to the park entrance on the left. Parking is available here at the south parking lot. To reach the north parking lot, continue on Redmond Road to Northeast 116th Street. Turn left and in just under 0.5 mile, turn left again on 196th Avenue Northeast. Drive about 0.25 mile to the entrance on the right. The north parking lot may be crowded with horse trailers on weekends.

Park Overview This pastoral homestead of meadows and forest now harbors barnyard animals, a stream with salmon runs, and an equestrian arena at the north end of the park. A restored barn with old farm implements holds pigs, rabbits, goats, ponies, and other animals, and is a particular favorite of children. A nature trail winds through second-growth forest and emphasizes the importance of watersheds.

Trail Layout A large central green, with an orchard and farm, is surrounded by second-growth forest. Paved Charlotte's Trail links the southern farm area to the Mackey Creek Watershed Trail (0.5 mile) and the horse facilities at the northern end of the park. An equestrian trail (1.5 miles) borders the park and links to the Puget Power/City of Redmond Multi-Use Trail, which gives

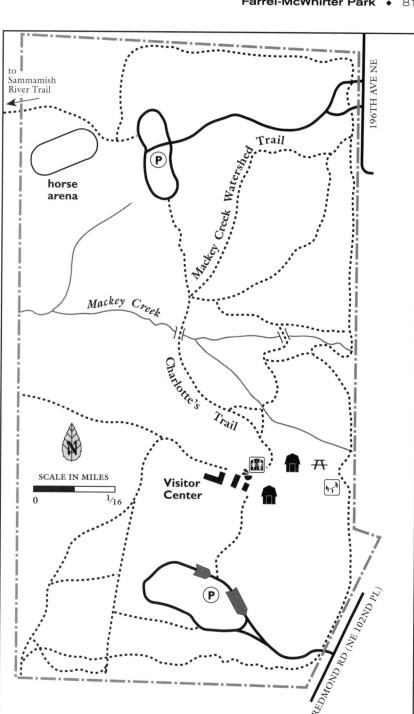

Mushroom hunters study a specimen in Farrel-McWhirter Park.

access to the Sammamish River Trail and the Redmond Watershed Park. If you choose to walk on one of the horse trails, follow proper etiquette and move to the side of the trail when a rider approaches. The dirt/gravel horse trails can be muddy after a rain, so bring appropriate footwear.

Human History The park area was originally homesteaded by Sally and Charles W. Hutcheson, who settled on the property in 1890. The John Peterson Sawmill, one of the largest and most successful in the area, was located on park land at the turn of the century, and milled cedar logs from the

Hutcheson place. Springboard notches are still visible in the park's cedar stumps.

Sally Hutcheson later sold the property to the McWhirters of Seattle in 1936 for $8,000. They established the farm as a summer home, which soon became their permanent residence. Elise Farrel-McWhirter was an avid horse-woman, and trained her horses here. She left 68 acres of her land to the City of Redmond for a park when she died in 1971, and the park was opened to the public in 1978.

Natural History Mackey Creek flows though a mixed forest of Douglas-fir, bigleaf maple, red alder, western hemlock, western red cedar, and black cottonwood trees. The emphasis in this park is on explaining the importance of watersheds, both for salmon habitat and flood control. Coho salmon come up Mackey Creek to spawn in the fall. The best time to see them is from about late September through early October.

Vine maples add color in the fall, and shrubs in the park include native salal, salmonberry, Indian plum, coast red elderberry, red huckleberry, and Pacific blackberry. Flowering plants such as stinging nettle, creeping buttercup and violets are joined by sword, bracken, licorice, and lady ferns. Evergreen blackberry, Himalayan blackberry, and English holly are non-native invasives.

Columbia black-tailed deer, squirrels, raccoons, and coyotes are among the animals in the park. Birds include forest residents such as black-capped chickadees, bushtits, red-breasted nuthatches, golden-crowned kinglets, song sparrows, spotted towhees, Steller's jays, dark-eyed juncos, red-tailed hawks, downy and hairy woodpeckers, and Bewick's and winter wrens. Barn swallows and Swanson's thrushes are spring and summer visitors.

Nearby Park
Redmond Watershed Preserve

The area was acquired by the city of Redmond in the 1920s as a source of water from Seidel Creek. The system worked well for a few years, then encountered serious problems with water quality and was abandoned. The first phase of park development in 1996 established a trail running north-south through the second-growth forest of western red cedars, Douglas-firs and red alders.

To reach the southern end of the park, head east on Novelty Hill Road to where the pipeline crosses the road. A parking lot is under construction, along with restrooms and a phone. Be careful—traffic is frequent and fast on this road. The northern end of the park can be reached by going north on Avondale Road and turning right on Bear Creek Road. Take a right soon on

Seidel Road, which turns into Northeast 133rd Street, and proceed until you see the trail gate on your right. There is currently parking for only a few cars on the shoulder. No pets (except guide dogs). Selected trails are accessible, and bikes and horses are allowed on designated trails. Call to obtain a map (see Appendix B).

---

15 ◆ Redmond
Marymoor Regional Park

Highlights: Progression from open fields through bottomland woods and freshwater marsh to the shallow freshwater shoreline of Lake Sammamish
Size: 524 acres; 2.25-mile loop trail
Ownership: King County Parks System (see Appendix B for phone number)
Season: Year-round
Terrain: Flat
Facilities: Restrooms near off-leash area parking lot and at eastern entrance near playing fields, water fountain
Hours: Dawn to dusk
Interpretive Programs: King County naturalists offer free nature walks; school programs on wetlands; annual wetlands teachers' workshop
Wheelchair Accessibility: Paved asphalt trail leading to boardwalk over marsh (one large step up to boardwalk)
Pets: Leash (except within off-leash area, and then under voice control) and scoop
Bikes: Yes (forbidden on wetland nature trail)
Bus: Metro 251, 253, 254 (0.5-mile walk from bus stop on West Lake Sammamish Parkway).
Driving Directions: From downtown Seattle, take I-5 north to Highway 520 and go east across Lake Washington. Take the West Lake Sammamish Parkway exit, and turn right at the bottom of the exit ramp. In 1 block, take a left at the next light into the park. Drive past the park buildings on the right, and take a right about 1 mile from the park entrance into a gravel parking lot in an open field. The sign for the interpretive nature trail begins at the southeastern corner of the lot.

Park Overview This multi-use park is the second largest in King County. This is not an isolated wilderness area—heavy use and nearby traffic disturb the quiet of the grounds. However, a nature trail tucked into the southeastern end of this spacious park showcases the process of natural succession, where land is slowly reverting back from open meadow to shrub-scrub wetlands.

The marshes of the Sammamish River harbor many species of wildlife.

The park is located at the north end of Lake Sammamish, with a boardwalk through fragile marshes. The Sammamish Slough flows out of Lake Sammamish on the west side of the park, with good opportunities for bird-watching.

Trail Layout   A paved trail leads from an open meadow through bottom-land woods, to a boardwalk over delicate marshes, and then to an overlook of the northwest corner of Lake Sammamish. A round trip on this trail is just under 1 mile. For a longer walk (approximately 2 miles), follow the Sammamish River from the lake overlook through the off-leash area. When you reach the windmill, cut across the lawns to the parking lot. This route is muddy in the rainy season.

Human History   Indian use of this area has been documented back to 11,000 years ago. From 1964 to 1970, archaeologists from the University of Washington identified four pre-Columbian sites, two in Marymoor Park and two just outside the park along the Sammamish River. Excavation of one of the sites yielded a variety of stone tools for hunting and fishing dating from 3,000 to 6,000 years ago. The material and shape of some of the tools suggest a possible link to inhabitants of central Washington. These artifacts are now stored at the Thomas Burke Memorial Washington State Museum on the University of Washington campus.

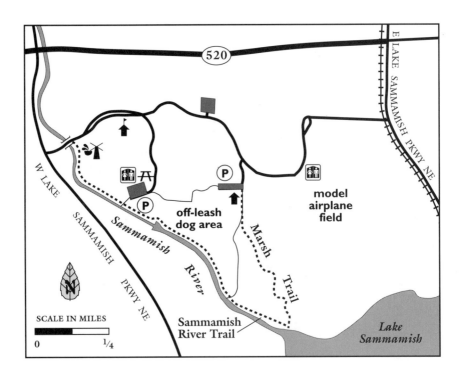

At the time of the first contact with white settlers, between 100 and 200 native people lived in several permanent villages in the valley, both in permanent log houses and temporary cattail-mat houses similar to teepees. They visited the Marymoor area to gather plants and catch and smoke salmon; in some areas, the soil is saturated with fish grease to a depth of several feet.

White settlers came to the Sammamish Valley in the 1860s. The first homesteader on the land where Marymoor Park now sits was John Tosh, an Irish immigrant, who claimed 160 acres in 1876. Tosh and his brother Adam commuted by canoe down Lake Sammamish to work in coal mines near Issaquah. John Tosh's rich bottomland soil grew such an excellent hay crop that the men were eventually able to quit their mining jobs to concentrate on farming.

Loggers began felling trees in the area in the early 1880s, and by the 1930s, most of the timber on the hills surrounding the Sammamish Valley had been harvested. Pilings on the bank's western shore (visible from East Lake Sammamish Parkway) mark the site of the old Campbell Sawmill. Logs were moved along the Sammamish Slough to Lake Washington, where they were rafted together and pulled across the lake.

In 1904, 78 acres along the slough were purchased by James W. Clise, a Seattle banker, from Tosh for use as a bird-hunting preserve. Dubbing his retreat "Willowmoor" for the abundant Pacific willows growing along the Sammamish River, he cleared the land and built a hunting lodge. (Later, the name was changed to Marymoor by the manager of the dairy farm in the 1940s, in honor of a daughter who had died.)

The lodge was expanded, eventually becoming the mansion that now houses the Marymoor Museum. Clise raised prize-winning Morgan horses and Scottish Ayrshire cattle, and his wife was an avid gardener, known for her orchid collection, which she later donated to the Volunteer Park Conservatory in Seattle. She had the grounds planted with numerous imported European and Oriental trees and shrubs, some of which remain today. A free pamphlet found on the outside of the green park building describes trees on the property.

Following the sale of Willowmoor Farm in 1928, the estate had a series of owners and continued as a dairy farm until 1956. The land was then slated for commercial or residential development, but in 1963, the passage of a bond issue enabled King County to purchase the historic farm for a park.

Natural History The Sammamish River has drained into Lake Washington since the valley was carved at the end of the last ice age. The shallow river, lined by willows, cattails, and rushes, was a main avenue of transportation until it became unnavigable with the lowering of Lake Washington in 1916–17. Barges and small steamers carried people, supplies, and crops, and often had to dodge floating logs and logging debris. The mature river was full of meanders—boat crews joked that captains could shake hands across the goosenecks of tight bends. In 1966, the Army Corps of Engineers dredged and straightened the river for flood control. Lombardy poplars line what was once the formal drive leading to the mansion—the continuation of these poplars on the opposite side of the river shows the old location of the Clises' bridge.

The Marsh Trail starts in an open meadow. As the trail progresses, wildflowers and shrubs such as blackberries and salmonberry replace the grasses. The path continues through a deciduous forest of Oregon ash, black cottonwood, and red alder, then the ground becomes progressively wetter and the path graduates to a boardwalk over a marsh area.

This wetlands area provides critical habitat for numerous aquatic creatures, as well as birds and mammals. Marsh plants here include common cattail, bulrushes, sedges, rushes, willows, hardhack, red-osier dogwood, yellow iris, and skunk cabbage. The sometimes rank odor of the marsh comes from hydrogen sulfide and methane gases, byproducts of the decomposition of marsh vegetation. In these cold waters, decomposition is slow and incomplete. As a result, partially decomposed vegetation settles to the bottom and forms layer after layer of peat. As peat builds up along the shore, the overlying water becomes shallower. Eventually, shrubs and trees that tolerate high water levels, such as willow, red-osier dogwood, and hardhack colonize newly emergent areas, as they have here. As the peat and silt accumulate, this marsh and shoreline will extend farther outward into the lake. Given enough time, a pond or lake will completely fill in, forming first a bog, then a meadow, and finally a forest.

The boardwalk ends at the edge of Lake Sammamish. Plants in the open water of the lake include yellow pond-lilies and invasive European water milfoil. A bottomland forest grows in a backwater of the lake, and is a transitional stage between the marsh and the drier, more open forests at the beginning of the trail. Look for skunk cabbage, water parsley, willow, and red-osier dogwood in the wetter areas, and Indian plum, sword fern, red elderberry, evergreen blackberry, red alder, black cottonwood and even young western hemlock in the drier places.

The park is also home to abundant wildlife. Small mammals such as mice, voles, shrews, and moles live in the fields; they attract predators such as Cooper's and red-tailed hawks, eagles, northern harriers, and American kestrels, as well as coyotes and bobcats. Other animals in the park include an occasional beaver or deer, raccoons, muskrats, and many amphibians.

The birds of the open fields include resident killdeer and ring-necked pheasants, with savannah sparrows, American goldfinches, and common yellowthroats visiting in the spring and summer.

Forest birds include resident sparrows and dark-eyed juncos, with hummingbirds and Swainson's thrushes visiting in the spring and summer.

Birds in the marsh include resident American coots, red-winged blackbirds, marsh wrens, northern shovelers, green herons, belted kingfishers, and hooded mergansers. Wintering species include dunlins, and ducks such as northern pintails, green-winged teals, and American wigeons.

16 ◆ Bellevue
Bridle Trails State Park

Highlights: Conifer forest and wetlands
Size: 482 acres; 28 miles of trails
Ownership: Washington State Parks and Recreation Commission
Season: Best summer through early fall
Terrain: Flat to moderate
Facilities: Restrooms, water fountains, grills, and picnic tables, and phone
near horse show facilities by parking lot
Hours: Dawn to dusk
Interpretive Programs: None
Wheelchair Accessibility: Hard-packed ground access to horse show
facilities

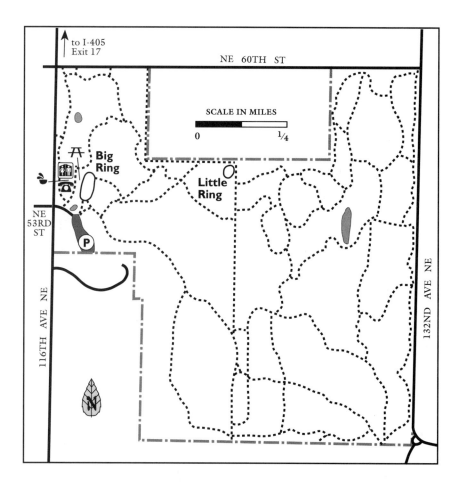

Pets: Leash and scoop
Horses: Yes
Bikes: No
Bus: Metro 251
Directions: From downtown Seattle, drive east on I-90 or Highway 520 to
I-405. Drive north on I-405 to exit 17, Northeast 70th Place. At the stop
sign, turn right on 116th Avenue Northeast and drive approximately 0.8
mile to Northeast 53rd Street. The park entrance is on the left.

Park Overview This large park, crisscrossed by miles of trails, is located on
a plateau and features a second-growth Douglas-fir forest with a smattering of other conifers, along with deciduous trees. Several wetlands areas also
lie in the park, giving this area several varied habitats for animals and plants.
The park is frequented by equestrians and the area is also popular with
orienteering groups.

Trail Layout The arena and bleachers on the west side of the park near the
entrance are used by horse clubs who hold both English and western riding
competitions here virtually every weekend from spring through fall, which
are free to spectators. There is no place to rent horses in the park and the
stables are private—do not visit the stable property. Walkers should also remember that horses have the right-of-way. When approached by a rider, move
to the side of the trail and stand quietly.

Although the park is well-used by horses and riders, the trails are so numerous that at any time of year, you may be in the area for several hours and
not see a rider at all. The action of heavy hooves tends to churn large sections of the dirt/gravel trails into muck, especially during the rainy season,
so footwear suitable for mud is highly recommended.

The maze-like trails in the forest are unmarked and their meandering
routes can be confusing. The only wide-open trail is a straight service road
under a power transmission line running north-south that splits the park. It
is easy to get lost, but not to stay lost. Orient yourself by the noises from the
clatter of a refuse transfer station near the northwest corner of the park, the
rush of traffic from I-405 just to the west, or glimpses of the surrounding
neighborhoods.

Human History The park site was set aside in the 1880s as a school trust
land, and logged to provide revenue for schools. At the time, the land was
heavily timbered, with many bears and cougars. The Newcastle Trail ran
through the park land, providing an important connection between Redmond
and the busy coal mines at Newcastle.

By the early 1930s, equestrians transformed the area's old logging skid
roads into a network of riding trails. The Lake Washington Saddle Club was

The peaceful forest of Bridle Trails State Park is tended by equestrians.

formed in 1945 to act as the park's caretakers. Money raised at horse shows is used to fund park maintenance and improvements.

Natural History   The park is located on a plateau with porous, sandy soil that dries out during the summer. These conditions favor the growth of coniferous woods; deciduous trees and other plants that require reliable moisture during the summer months are largely restricted to poorly drained areas, including several marsh areas in the park. The forest contains many second-growth Douglas-firs, with a smattering of other conifers such as western hemlocks and western red cedars. Bigleaf maple, black cottonwood, red alder, willow, vine maple, Pacific madrone, and bitter cherry are among the deciduous trees that grow here. This coniferous lowland forest was once typical of the entire Puget Sound region. Huge stumps bear witness to past logging in the area, begun over a hundred years ago.

Dense thickets of red alder, vine maple, and devil's club surround a sizable marsh in the center of the east section of the park, and a smaller one in the northwest corner. Other plants in the park include bracken, sword, and licorice ferns, starflower, western trillium, salmonberry, California hazelnut, Indian plum, and some of the largest red huckleberry in the area, reaching up to 12 feet high. Oregon grape and salal grow in drier areas in the park.

The panther amanita, a poisonous mushroom, is common here. This tan mushroom has mottled white spots on its cap. Ingesting panther amanita can induce hallucinations, raging muscle cramps, and deep, comalike sleep.

Park animals include typical area forest inhabitants such as coyotes, squirrels, and deer mice. The birds found in the park are those species found in coniferous and mixed forests. They include chestnut-backed chickadee, brown creeper, red-tailed hawk, great horned owl, and several species of woodpeckers. Flycatchers visit in spring and summer, and varied thrushes winter here.

---

17 ◆ Bellevue
Mercer Slough/Bellefields Nature Park

Highlights: Wetlands, bottomland woods
Size: 320 acres; almost 5 miles of trails
Ownership: Bellevue Parks and Community Services Department
Season: Best spring through fall
Terrain: Flat to moderate
Facilities: Restrooms and water fountain at Winters House and Overlake Blueberry Farm; portable toilet outside Pacific Science Center Mercer Slough Environmental Education Center; phone at Metro Park and Ride.

Mercer Slough encourages bird-watching at an early age.

Hours: Dawn to dusk; Winters House 10 A.M. to 4 P.M., Monday through Saturday, noon to 4 P.M. Sunday

Interpretive Programs: Interpretive signs; free nature brochures; naturalist walks and canoe tours (see Appendix B for phone numbers); historical interpretation at Winters House

Wheelchair Accessibility: Winters House; periphery trail; Overlake Barn to boardwalks and bridge

Pets: Leash and scoop

Horses: No

Fishing: No

Boats: No motorized boats

Bikes: Yes, on paved bike trail

Bus: Metro 226, 235, 240, 340

Driving Directions: From downtown Seattle, take I-90 east to Bellevue Way and head north. Pass the Park and Ride and blueberry farm on your right, and then turn right into the Winters House parking lot. To reach the Bellefields area on the east side of the park, continue north past the Winters House. Bear right at the Y onto 112th Avenue Southeast, then right on Southeast 8th Street, then right on 118th Avenue Southeast. Drive about 0.5 mile to the small parking lot. Put in canoes at Enatai Beach Park just south of the I-90 interchange off Bellevue Way, or at Sweyolocken Park Boat Launch, the first right off Bellevue Way, just north of I-90.

Park Overview The largest remaining wetlands adjacent to Lake Washington, this lush area supports one of the most diverse ecosystems in the Puget Sound region. The Mercer Slough, a 1.5-mile waterway that connects Kelsey Creek to Lake Washington, is located just north of the I-90/I-405 interchange, south of downtown Bellevue. Come see great blue herons hunt in cattails and garter snakes slither off the paths, or catch a glimpse of a furtive coyote. Even if you do not see many animals, you will hear them. Although the rush of nearby freeways is always audible, the rustling thickets hint at the abundant life here in these wetlands.

Trail Layout Some of the lower trails in the Bellefields area of the park are made of sleeves of wood chips that float on top of the bog. Wood-chip paths wind through soggy ground, with short boardwalks and little bridges over the wettest areas. The upland forest has dirt/gravel trails, and a gravel trail runs south of Overlake Farm. Two miles of canoeing paths allow access to the marshes, and a paved bike/jogging path (3 miles) encircles the park periphery. The park is at the western terminus of Bellevue's Lake-to-Lake Trail, a trail system that reaches from Lake Washington to Lake Sammamish.

Human History As late as the eighteenth century, Salish Indians had at least seven winter villages located along the eastern shore of Lake Washington. They

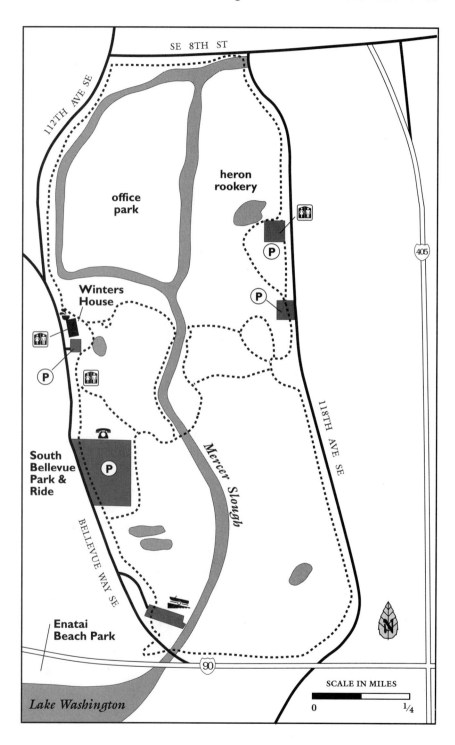

camped near the mouths of streams, erected weirs to catch fish, and gathered roots, berries, and wapato, a form of water chestnut which grew along shoreline reeds. Two or three longhouses were located on the eastern shore of the Mercer Slough, one north of I-90 in the vicinity of 118th Avenue Southeast. During the Indian Wars of 1855–56, warriors from eastern Washington found refuge and stored supplies there.

In 1869, Aaron Mercer farmed 80 acres along the western edge of the slough that bears his name, reaching from the lake on the south, to Southeast 24th Street on the north, and inland to 112th Avenue Southeast. Before the completion of the ship canal, the waters of Mercer Slough were 4 to 5 feet higher, and the swamp along the lakeshore extended as far north as present-day Main Street in Bellevue. The Mercers erected a log cabin about 0.5 mile from Lake Washington on the west shoreline of the slough.

When the water level of Lake Washington was lowered in 1916–17 with the opening of the Lake Washington ship canal, Mercer Slough became completely unnavigable. Former marshes dried up and died, bog building ended, and the ground evolved to other types of wetlands. New marshes became established at lower elevations. In the upland forest on the eastern side of the slough, the lower boundary of the stand of western red cedars and bigleaf maples at the base of hill marks the former shoreline.

After the lake was lowered, canals were dug to further drain the rich bottomland, and blueberries were grown in the bogs along the western border of Mercer Slough. (The blueberry farm here now leases its land from the city of Bellevue.) The fallen ruins of a greenhouse, and an array of daffodils, irises, rhododendrons, and azaleas are remnants of a bulb farm once run by the Winters family.

Natural History   The Winters House, along Bellevue Way on the northwestern part of the park (north of the blueberry farm), was built in 1929 and now serves as the Interpretive Center for the park. The Mercer Slough Environmental Education Center, a partnership with the Pacific Science Center, offers environmental education programs for children and adults.

Many species of birds, mammals, and amphibians, and hundreds of species of plants can be found here. Six wildlife-enhancement ponds were built in the park to create more habitat, making this one of the most diverse ecosystems in King County. The ponds create open water and a wetland edge, where animals adapted to more than one habitat can meet various needs. These combination habitats often support the highest diversity of species. Interpretive signs in the park identify the different kinds of wetlands according to their elevation above the waters of the slough.

The park features one of the region's most varied deciduous woodlands. The wet ground in the area supplies the moisture that these trees require

A western red cedar along the Bellefields Nature Park loop trail marks the location of the former shoreline of Lake Washington.

during the dry summer months, and discourages competition from conifers. The highest parts of the upland forest hold bigleaf maple, western red cedar, and Douglas-fir trees. Other deciduous trees growing in the forest and along the edges of the slough include red alder, black cottonwood, Oregon ash, Pacific crabapple, bitter cherry, vine maple, cascara, paper and swamp birches, and thirty-five species of willows.

Native shrubs include Pacific ninebark, red-osier dogwood, Indian plum, hardhack, California hazelnut, Labrador tea, straggly gooseberry, black twinberry, Nootka rose, snowberry, swamp gooseberry, and Pacific blackberry. Salal and Oregon grape grow on the hillsides, along with lady and sword ferns. Flowering plants include stinging nettle, fireweed, creeping buttercup, large-leaved avens, deadly nightshade, skunk cabbage, water parsley, water lilies, cattails, and rushes. Invasive non-native blackberry, canary reed grass, and loosestrife create dense monocultures that crowd out native plants in some areas of the park.

Animal life exists within every level of the park, from open water to upland forest. Look for coyotes, red foxes, porcupines, beavers, mink, raccoons, weasels, deer, muskrats, river otters, and squirrels. Dragonflies, painted turtles, Pacific treefrogs, toads, and salamanders reside in the marshes. Freshwater crayfish and mussels are found here, as well as western tiger swallowtail, veined white, red admiral and silvery blue butterflies.

A busy thoroughfare for birds, the slough is used by some species for nesting, others for wintering, and as a rest area by migratory birds. Over 100 species have been sighted (obtain a list at the visitor center). Great blue herons roost high in the tops of fir, cedar and cottonwood trees in the northeastern corner of the park, and cliff swallows build mud nests under the I-90 bridge. Raptors include bald eagles, ospreys, and several species of hawks and owls.

Look for resident ruffed grouse, California quail, and ring-necked pheasants in the fields. In the forests and thickets, you may spot resident woodpeckers, kinglets, warblers, red-breasted nuthatches, band-tailed pigeons, sparrows, Steller's jays, American goldfinches, cedar waxwings, wrens, spotted towhees, and pine siskens. These are joined in the spring and summer by western tanagers, rufous hummingbirds, red-eyed vireos, thrushes, flycatchers, swallows, water pipits, Bullock's orioles, black-headed grosbeaks, and other species of warblers and sparrows.

Marsh birds include Virginia rails, soras, common yellowthroats, killdeer, common snipes, marsh wrens, red-winged blackbirds, and several species of herons.

The open waters of the slough host resident double-crested cormorants, belted kingfishers, pied-billed grebes, American coots, and ducks such as gadwalls, northern shovelers, mergansers, and wood ducks. Fall and winter bring wintering ducks including northern pintails, canvasbacks, buffleheads, goldeneyes, scaups, ruddy and ring-necked ducks, and American and Eurasian wigeons. Teals visit in the spring and summer.

---

18 ◆ Bellevue
Bellevue Botanical Gardens at Wilburton Hill Park

Highlights: Garden displays, forest, wetlands
Size: 103 acres with 36 acres of gardens; several miles of trails
Ownership: Bellevue Parks and Community Services Department
Season: Best spring through fall
Terrain: Flat to moderately rolling
Facilities: Restrooms, water fountain, gift shop at visitor center; picnic tables on lawn
Hours: Dawn to dusk; visitor center open daily 10 A.M. to 4 P.M. (see Appendix B for phone number)
Fee: None
Interpretive Programs: Monthly bird walks through East Lake Washington Audubon Society; plant workshops at visitor center
Wheelchair Accessibility: Paved walkway and fine gravel paths around visitor center gardens
Pets: Prohibited in gardens; allowed in east side of park

The garden's award-winning Perennial Border attracts admirers.

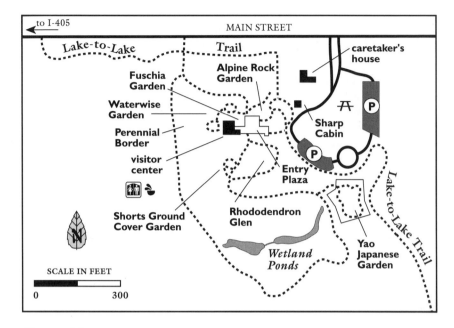

Horses: No

Bikes: Not in gardens; allowed in east side of park

Bus: Metro 340

Driving Directions: From downtown Seattle, take I-90 east to I-405 and head north. Take exit 13 to Northeast 8th Street and head east. Turn right on 120th Avenue Northeast, and then take a left onto Main Street. The park entrance is on your right in approximately 0.5 mile.

Park Overview   In this lovely hillside park, you would never know you were so close to downtown Bellevue, were it not for the wind-like whoosh of I-405, unseen to the west. The star attraction of this area is the Bellevue Botanical Gardens at the western edge of the park. In 1996, *Garden Design* magazine voted the gardens as one of the top 50 public gardens in the United States. Here you can stroll among spectacular perennial beds, a Japanese garden, wooded wetlands, a glen of rhododendrons, a fuchsia garden, an alpine rock garden, and a demonstration garden that features plants suited to our dry summer climate. A visitor center offers information, a gift shop, and workshops on various garden topics.

Trail Layout   The land is flat to moderately sloping, with gravel paths. Within the Perennial Border are delightful little paths made of hazelnut shells that entice you to explore within. The park is a major link in the Lake-to-Lake Trail, which runs through Bellevue parks and neighborhoods from Lake Washington to Lake Sammamish. Follow the marked trail east through the forest on the eastern side of Wilburton Park to reach Kelsey Creek Park, about 0.25 mile away.

Human History There were Indian longhouses at one time in the area near the park, probably to the west near the Mercer Slough. The Sharp Cabin, located near the parking lot at the edge of the garden area, was relocated to its present site. It is the second story of a historic local cabin—an accompanying plaque explains its history.

A Civil War veteran and loner named Clark M. Sturtevant took advantage of the federal law that granted former servicemen 160 acres as a reward for having served in the war. In 1873, he paddled up Mercer Slough to settle, breaking through seven beaver dams along the way. (Before Lake Washington was lowered in 1916–17, Mercer Slough had a higher water level and was navigable farther up.) Sturtevant's land was located at the edge of the Slough, just to the west of Wilburton Park, near the site of Bellevue's City Hall.

In the 1880s, other settlers moved to the area, cleared the trees, and farmed. Around the turn of the century, loggers moved into the area and the Wilburton area became a logging boomtown, with several large logging camps that employed up to 700 men. Wilburton got its name from Manley Wilbur, one of the partners in the Wilbur and England logging camp. A cooperative sawmill was started just below the head of Mercer Slough (where the Bellevue City Hall is now located). The mill went bankrupt, and was taken over in 1904 by the Hewitt Lumber company, headed by Wilbur and Henry Hewitt, Jr. A company town was platted, taking its name from the mill, which ran night and day. A train delivered the logs to the head of the slough, where they floated down to the mill. The lumber was then shipped out of the mill by steamboat. With the construction of the ship canal in 1916–17, the water level of Mercer Slough fell, making the slough unnavigable. The sawmill business was forced to close in 1918, since steamboats could no longer reach the mill to load lumber. The mill sued King County for $125,000 in damages for being deprived of means of transportation for its product, and eventually won in 1920.

In 1947, the property on which the botanical gardens sit was purchased by Calhoun and Harriet Shorts, who had a custom home built on the grounds. In 1984, the Shorts donated the house (now the visitor center) and 7 acres to the City of Bellevue, which set aside the property and 29 additional acres for the park in 1989. The gardens were opened to the public in 1992, developed as a joint effort between the City of Bellevue and the Bellevue Botanical Garden Society.

Natural History The second-growth upland forest located in the park includes bigleaf maples, red alders, and Douglas-firs, with native shrubs such as salal and Oregon grape. A short loop trail encircles 19 acres of forested wetlands to the south of the gardens.

The park's mission is to develop, maintain, and display plant collections in a park setting for the purposes of horticultural demonstration, education, and recreation. A waterwise demonstration garden displays plants that require little water during our dry summer months. Educational opportunities for homeowners include pamphlets and workshops on low-water landscaping, shade gardens, and soil preparation.

The botanical gardens feature several different types of displays. A colorful dahlia bed is planted near the Sharp Cabin, and the marvelous Perennial Border occupies 17,000 square feet on the slope bordering the back lawn of the visitor center. The Shorts Ground Cover Garden offers a look at varieties of low plants you can grow in gardens, while the Rhododendron Glen in the forest is a prime highlight in the spring.

The Fuchsia Garden, located in front of the visitor center, is a test garden to determine favorable light and temperature conditions for growing fuchsias. Most of the fuchsias featured in the garden are the originally wild, species *fuchsias* that grow as erect shrubs, and from which hybrid fuchsias have been developed. (The familiar hanging fuchsia was developed in the 1930s after a century of hybridizing.) A species map is available at the visitor center.

The Alpine Rock Garden features 250 tons of boulders and hundreds of plants. The Yao Japanese Garden features contemporary and traditional Asian garden concepts using plants native to Asia and the Pacific Northwest.

The second-growth woods harbor the usual assemblage of local forest animals. The park's varied habitats of forest, wetlands, meadows, flower beds, and lawns attract numerous birds. Residents include red-winged blackbirds, northern flickers, Steller's jays, red-breasted nuthatches, pine siskins, song sparrows, spotted towhees, and Bewick's wrens. Buffleheads visit in the winter.

---

19 ◆ Bellevue
Kelsey Creek Farm and Community Park

Highlights: Forest, stream, farm animals
Size: 149 acres; 2.5 miles of trails
Ownership: Bellevue Parks and Community Services Department
Season: Best spring through fall
Terrain: Flat to moderately steep
Facilities: Restrooms, water fountain, picnic tables, and play areas are located between the parking lot and the farm buildings; park can be rented for special events (see Appendix B for phone number)
Hours: Dawn to dusk; animal barns open daily 9 A.M. to 4 P.M.
Interpretive Programs: Naturalist walks; unique children's recreational programs, such as pony care classes, farm tours, and classes
Wheelchair Accessibility: Access to farm buildings on paved road

Pets: Leash and scoop; prohibited in farm area
Horses: No
Bikes: No
Bus: Metro 273, 274
Driving Directions: Take I-90 east across Lake Washington, then head north on I-405. Take exit 12 to Southeast 8th Street. At the exit ramp stoplight, turn right (east). Drive under a tall railroad trestle and through two stoplights, crossing the Lake Hills Connector road (Southeast 8th becomes Southeast 7th Place). At the stop sign at 128th Avenue Southeast, turn left (north) and then turn right (east) on Southeast 4th Place. Follow the road into the park.

Park Overview   The pastures and woods of this park are tucked away in the midst of a quiet Bellevue neighborhood, and give the feeling of being farther out in the country. The main attractions are two historic barns built in the early 1920s, farm animals, and a moist hillside forest with trails.

Trail Layout   A small bridge crosses Kelsey Creek and leads to a dirt trail (1.5 miles) that climbs a forested hillside in the eastern section of the park. Trails are often mucky in this very moist forest, even in summer, but bridges and

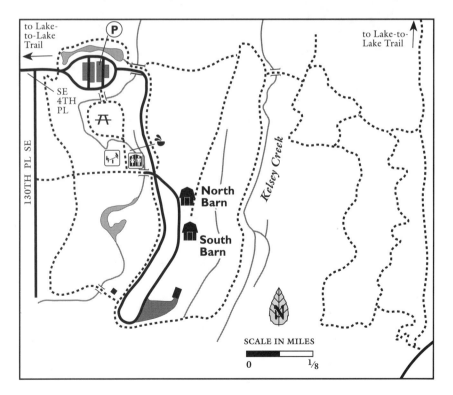

The moist forest surrounding Kelsey Creek supports treacherous stinging nettles and graceful vine maples.

boardwalks cross over the wettest places. A gravel service road (1 mile), popular with joggers and cyclists, loops around the farm. The park is a major link in the Lake-to-Lake Trail, which runs through Bellevue parks and neighborhoods from Lake Washington to Lake Sammamish.

Human History   The Daniel W. Fraser cabin, erected in 1888, was moved to Kelsey Creek Park in 1976 and is one of Bellevue's few remaining pioneer structures. The park is named for Henry E. Kelsey, a bachelor from New York, who arrived in 1884 to teach at the first school established for the children of Bellevue and Mercer Island. In 1888, Kelsey bought 160 acres from the Northern Pacific Railroad, with the center of his tract located at Northeast 8th and 140th Avenue Northeast, northeast of the park. Kelsey Creek, which crossed his land, was named for him. He married, then later moved to Hawaii, where he became well known as an educator.

In 1921, the W. W. Duey family rented some of the land that had been logged for the Wilburton mill, and started a dairy farm. When the Dueys moved to Bellevue, the only access to their house was via the bed of an abandoned logging railroad. They loaded their belongings in a truck and drove to their new home on the old railroad ties. Duey cleared the land, erected two barns, and started a dairy, the Twin Valley Farm, named for the two valleys on either side of the barn area. The dairy operated until 1942. In 1968 and 1990, the city of Bellevue purchased the park land.

Natural History A written account of the area in 1895 noted that Douglas-fir trees were 200 to 300 feet high, with some up to 12 feet in diameter. Since then, those tall Douglas-firs and other conifers have been logged, and a mainly deciduous forest of bigleaf maples, red alders, and vine maples now dominates. Some western red cedars, Douglas-firs, and Sitka spruce are still scattered on the hillside. Along Kelsey Creek, black cottonwoods, red alders, and willows grow in the wet ground.

The hillside is very moist, with many rivulets trickling down the hill, even in summer. These moist conditions are evident in the lush thickets of shrubs on the moist hillside, which include salmonberry, Pacific blackberry, Indian plum, California hazelnut, thimbleberry, straggly gooseberry, and red-osier dogwood. Red huckleberry shrubs spring from the tops of the old western red cedar stumps. Luxuriant gardens of lady ferns and sword ferns cover the ground, and licorice ferns fringe the bigleaf maple trunks. Herbaceous plants include stinging nettle, Cooley's hedgenettle, skunk cabbage, water parsley, fringecup, youth-on-age, bedstraw, enchanter's nightshade, and candyflower.

Farm animals include chickens and ducks, rabbits, pigs, goats, sheep, ponies, and cows, with baby animals in the spring. The park's "Adopt a Critter" program encourages farm animal "adoptions" to support the farm and give children a sense of connection to the animals (without the responsibility).

Kelsey Creek, (once called Duey Creek) which runs through the park, rises from Larson Lake, drains most of Bellevue and part of Kirkland, and empties into the Mercer Slough. Visit in late September through October, and you might see migrating chinook, sockeye, or coho salmon, descendants of once magnificent salmon runs. During the Depression, hard-up farmers survived the winter on salt-salmon and potatoes, and, at the end of spawning season, speared the salmon carcasses with pitchforks, to use as fertilizer.

Other animals in the park include typical local forest species, such as raccoons and foxes. The moist areas also harbor Pacific treefrogs, which are especially audible during spring nights. The forest trails are home to numerous light-brown snails. These snails don't seem to have a common name, but they are known to zoologists as *Allogona townsendia*.

Birds include resident black-capped chickadees, great blue herons, northern flickers, winter wrens, spotted towhees, Steller's jays, golden-crowned kinglets, song sparrows, downy woodpeckers, red-tailed hawks, great horned owls, red-breasted nuthatches, and brown creepers. Vireos and warblers visit in spring and summer as well as barn swallows, which frequent the barn area. Wigeons winter in the park.

20 ◆ Bellevue
Lake Hills Greenbelt

Highlights: Wetlands, lakes, farming history, community gardens
Size: 150 acres; 5 miles of trails
Ownership: Bellevue Parks and Community Services Department
Season: Year-round
Terrain: Flat
Facilities: Restrooms, free brochures at Lake Hills Greenbelt Ranger Station,
    15416 Southeast 16th Street; restrooms, water, and nonmotorized boat
    put-in at Phantom Lake; fishing from docks at Phantom and Larsen Lakes
Hours: Dawn to dusk; ranger station noon to 4 P.M. Saturday
Interpretive Programs: Guided naturalist walks; school programs
Wheelchair Accessibility: Yes
Pets: Leash and scoop
Horses: No
Bikes: Yes
Bus: Metro 273
Driving Directions: From downtown Seattle, take I-90 east to exit 11B,
    148th Avenue Southeast. Drive past the Mormon temple and Robinswood
    Park to Southeast 16th Street. To reach the northern part of the park, keep
    straight here: the trailhead will be on your right in approximately 0.75 mile.
    Limited parking is available at Larsen Lake Blueberry Farm. To visit the
    ranger station, turn right on Southeast 16th Street, and drive 0.5 mile to
    the community gardens parking lot on the left. To reach the southern park-
    ing lot near Phantom Lake, continue on Southeast 16th Street to 156th
    Avenue Southeast, and turn right. The parking area will be on your left.

Park Overview   This area is reverting to natural vegetation after a long history of cultivation, and the wide variety of environments creates a myriad of
wildlife habitats and a much-needed animal corridor. The park's lakes, wetlands, meadows, shrubs, and deciduous and coniferous woods support over
a thousand species of plants, and hundreds of species of birds and mammals.

Trail Layout   The trail links Larsen Lake in the north to Phantom Lake in the
south, snaking through wetlands, meadows and forests. This single path reduces habitat impact, and its curves provide a sinuous line, called "the curved
edge of nature." The nonlinear trail resembles natural paths and gives animals
quicker access to cover. The flat, packed gravel trail makes for an easy walk.
    In the bog area of the park, the trail was carefully designed to avoid

*The observation platform at Larsen Lake is a good place to view raptors perched in
nearby trees.*

disturbing the natural flow of water through the peat. Heavy-duty black plastic was laid on the ground and covered with 18 inches of wood chips. The plastic was flattened over the top of the chips and the flaps were sewn together. This flattened tube was then covered with gravel and compacted, so it literally floats on top of the bog.

An asphalt path (2.5 miles) encircles Phantom Lake. The park is a major link in the Lake-to-Lake Trail, which runs through Bellevue parks and neighborhoods from Lake Washington to Lake Sammamish.

Human History   Parts of the trail follow the route of an old Indian trail that led from Phantom Lake to Kirkland, with a winter encampment at Larsen Lake, as well as a branch to another encampment near Mercer Slough. A trading route ran from Phantom Lake, east to near Fall City, and south over Naches Pass to the Yakima area.

In 1883, a settler named Henry Thode settled on 160 acres near Phantom Lake. The lake was then somewhat connected to Larsen Lake during the winter rainy season. Drainage was northward, from Phantom Lake north to Larsen Lake, the headwaters of Kelsey Creek. However, in order to drain the land for crops, Thode single-handedly dug a new outlet for the Phantom Lake, causing it to drain east toward Lake Sammamish. Early some mornings, a pillar of fog with the appearance of a human profile came up the new channel. When it got over the lake it faded, and this phenomenon inspired the name Phantom Lake. Some of the Thode property was logged in 1905, and the family owned the land until 1951.

Ove Peter Larsen, a Dane, gained title in 1889 to 160 acres at the lake named for him. He worked in the Newcastle coal mines and came home on weekends, probably walking or riding a horse along the Redmond–Newcastle trail.

Japanese immigrants may have arrived in the area as early as 1894. They were brought in to clear the land for farming, and later some arranged to lease the land. By 1913 they were well-established farmers, and eventually grew 95 percent of the strawberries produced between the lakes, as well as other produce. In 1942, the Japanese-Americans in this area were evacuated to internment camps in Oregon. Less than half of the ousted families returned to the area at the conclusion of World War II.

Because this area has such a rich history, one purpose of the park is to preserve Bellevue's agricultural heritage. The seasonal farm stand at 156th Avenue Southeast and Southeast 16th Street sells produce grown on the leased park fields to the east, and the commercial blueberry farm near Larsen Lake is also leased.

Natural History   West of the farm stand are demonstration gardens managed and maintained through a cooperative partnership with the King County Master Gardeners and the Washington State University Cooperative

Extension Service. Nearby community gardens offer land-poor gardeners a chance to till the soil.

Staff at the adjacent Lake Hills Greenbelt Ranger Station, in partnership with the Department of Wildlife, educate the public, developers, and businesses on the use of native plants to establish habitats in backyards and on corporate grounds. The grounds of the ranger station include wildlife enhancement gardens, designed to make backyards more attractive to hummingbirds, butterflies, and amphibians. The program also shows how to select native plants to create a grassland, wetland meadow, or forest-edge environment.

The forested areas contain deciduous and coniferous species. Deciduous trees include red alder, willow, bitter cherry, and cascara. Douglas-fir, western red cedar, western hemlock, and grand fir are among the native coniferous trees; non-native species include blue and Norway spruce, and shore and lodgepole pine.

Plants in wetland areas include red-osier dogwood, hardhack, cattail, and

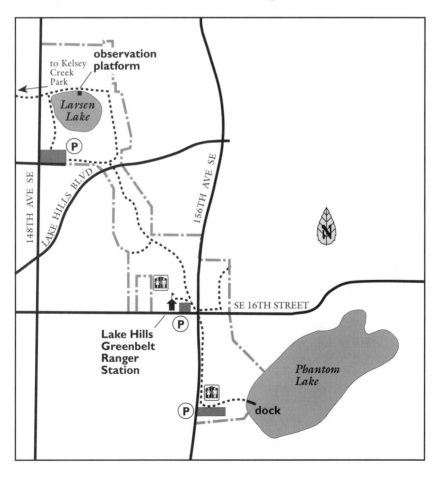

creeping buttercup. The many invasive plants show the recent disturbance of the area, with reed canary grass, evergreen and Himalayan blackberry, Scot's broom, English ivy, and English holly constantly targeted for removal by park staff.

The sinewy nature of the park acts as a wildlife corridor for animals, and the park maintains many microhabitats to increase species diversity. These habitats attract coyotes, muskrats, and many species of birds.

In the lakes, look for resident pied-billed grebes, gadwalls, and hooded mergansers. The observation platform on Larsen Lake offers a good vantage point for watching wintering species such as wigeons and ring-necked ducks. Along the marshy shores, resident great blue herons, red-winged blackbirds, killdeer, and spotted sandpipers are joined in the spring by common yellowthroats.

---

21 ◆ Bellevue
Lakemont Trail System

Highlights: Forest; stream ravine; views of Mount Rainier and the Cascades, Lake Sammamish, and Lake Washington
Size: Over 100 acres; approximately 7 miles of trails
Ownership: Bellevue Parks and Community Services Department
Season: Year-round
Terrain: Moderate to steep
Facilities: Restrooms, water fountain, and phone at Lakemont Community Park; playground at Lakemont Highlands Park
Hours: Dawn to dusk
Interpretive Programs: Naturalist-led walks (see Appendix B for phone number)
Wheelchair Accessibility: Asphalt path in field below restrooms at Lakemont Park
Pets: Leash and scoop
Horses: Permitted unless otherwise noted
Bikes: Permitted unless otherwise noted
Bus: Metro 210
Driving Directions: From downtown Seattle, take I-90 east to exit 11A, 150th Avenue Southeast. Bear right on the exit ramp, turn right at the stop sign, and continue approximately 0.5 mile south, up a hill. Turn left at Southeast Newport Way, drive approximately 1 mile, then turn right on 164th Avenue Southeast. Drive for 2 miles, and then turn left on Lakemont Boulevard. Take the first right, onto Village Park Drive Southeast, and the Lakemont Community Park entrance will be on your left. To reach the trailhead for the Lakemont Highlands Park, bear right onto Lakemont

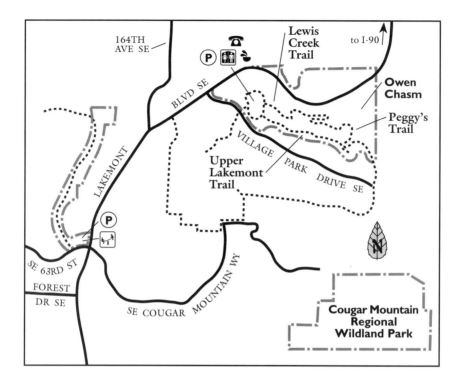

Boulevard off 164th Avenue Southeast, take a right at Southeast 63rd Street, and the park is on the corner.

Park Overview   The Lakemont Trail System is located on the north side of Cougar Mountain above, below, and within several luxurious housing developments. This fragmented park results from efforts to preserve open space, wildlife corridors, and access to the Lewis Creek gorge within the developed area. Some parts of the trail system offer spectacular views of the Cascades, Lake Sammamish, and Lake Washington. The area is quiet, with some noise from local traffic and the distant whoosh of I-405 and I-90.

Trail Layout   The well-groomed trails are composed of dirt, bark, or gravel. They are well-drained on the slopes, but some sections of the moist gorge are mucky after a rain. From Lakemont Community Park, the Lewis Creek Trail leads down into the gorge and joins up with Peggy's Trail to lead into Owen Chasm with its beautiful cascades and waterfalls. (Peggy's Trail was established by local residents Ralph and Peggy Owen so she could commute to work on foot.)

   The Upper Lakemont Trail climbs very steeply out of the gorge, and then heads south and west up through narrow greenbelts within the neighborhoods. At times, the trail follows sidewalks within the development. The trail eventually borders a low meadow area, which is the headwaters of Lewis Creek, then loops back through a large street culvert to the parking lot.

The Lakemont Highlands Trail (1 mile) starts from the playground behind the basketball court and leads up a ridge through a narrow greenbelt area between houses. It emerges onto a flat field with panoramic views of the Cascades, Lake Sammamish, Lake Washington, and Mount Rainier. The Cougar Mountain trail system can be accessed farther south along Lakemont Boulevard. In the future, a trail will join the two parks.

Human History   Early settlers cleared some of the area for farming. Since the area lacked the forest resources to justify a railroad spur from Lake Sammamish, timber in the most accessible areas was removed with oxen teams. The Somerset area was probably logged by the 1920s, which made the deforestation between Lake Washington and Lake Sammamish complete.

The history of the long battle between development and preservationists in the area is detailed in the Issaquah Alps Trails Club publication, *Hiking and Strolling Trails of Cougar Mountain Regional Wildlands Park*. Plans to construct a road from I-90 to Coal Creek Parkway by way of Lakemont Boulevard were fought by local residents in the 1970s. The boulevard is expected to be completed in late 1998.

Because of this pressure from local neighborhood groups, the developers were required to set aside open areas for parkland and wildlife corridors. Homeowners work with the Bellevue Parks and Community Services Department in a Neighborhoods for Habitat program to develop a buffer of native plants between their property boundaries and the trail.

Natural History   Lewis Creek, which flows into Lake Sammamish, has sliced a deep damp ravine into the north side of Cougar Mountain. The area marks where the Vashon Ice Sheet came up against the bedrock that composes the Issaquah Alps, and ground into the cliff on the north side of Cougar Mountain known locally as the Precipice. The cascades and waterfall in Owens Chasm spill over bedrock ledges of brown sandstone, while salt-and-pepper granite boulders left by the glaciers dot the slopes and lie in the streambed.

Since the park lies on the north side of Cougar Mountain, it is protected from southwestern winter storms. Also, its northern exposure exposes it to less sunlight than surrounding areas, so temperatures are cooler, moisture evaporates more slowly, and the humidity within the forest remains at higher levels year-round. As a result, ferns are plentiful here. Wood, sword, and lady ferns decorate the slopes. Licorice ferns grow on the trunks of bigleaf maples, and maidenhair ferns thrive in the moist air near the stream and its waterfalls. Mushrooms sprout when the cooler fall weather arrives.

The mixed forest is dominated by large bigleaf maples and red alders,

The peaceful trails of the Lakemont Gorge belie their nearness to I-90.

Small animals find shelter beneath the plants of the forest floor.

with western hemlocks, western red cedars, and Douglas-firs. A few remnants of old-growth Douglas-firs are scattered on steep slopes, and cedar stumps show the size of the old-growth trees. Black cottonwoods flourish near the streams, and cascara and vine maples dot the forest understory.

The hillsides hold many moisture-loving plants, such as salmonberry, devil's club, coast red elderberry, thimbleberry, stink currant, California hazelnut, youth-on-age, creeping buttercup, and Himalayan blackberry. Red huckleberry bushes spring from old cedar stumps, and salal and Oregon grape grow on the drier upper slopes of the park.

Look for signs of coyote and deer. Ring-necked pheasants and California quail seek cover in the fields. Forest birds include resident downy woodpeckers, white-crowned sparrows, and cedar waxwings. Golden-crowned
sparrows visit in winter. Birds of prey in the park include red-tailed hawks,
owls, bald eagles, and osprey.

---

22 ◆ Issaquah
Cougar Mountain Regional Wildland Park

Highlights: Forest, stream, coal-mining history
Size: 4,000 acres; 50 miles of trails
Ownership: King County Park System
Season: Best spring through fall
Terrain: Flat to moderately steep
Facilities: Portable toilets at Red Town trailhead and at Radar Park; picnic
tables at Radar Park
Hours: Dawn to dusk
Interpretive Programs: Guided walks by King County naturalists and mem-
bers of the Issaquah Alps Trails Club; Return to Newcastle Days Festival
(first Saturday in June)
Wheelchair Accessibility: None except road to Radar Park
Pets: Leash and scoop
Horses: Yes, on 12 miles of trails
Bikes: No
Bus: Metro 210
Driving Directions: From downtown Seattle, take I-90 east to exit 11A,
150th Avenue Southeast. Bear right on the exit ramp, turn right at the
stop sign, and continue approximately 0.5 mile south, up a hill. Turn left
at Southeast Newport Way, drive about 1 mile, then turn right on 164th
Avenue Southeast. Drive for 2 miles until the road turns into Lakemont
Boulevard. To get to the Radar Park entrance, continue for 2 miles on
Lakemont Boulevard and turn left on Cougar Mountain Way. In about 1
mile, the road becomes Southeast 60th Street. Just beyond, turn right on
Cougar Mountain Drive and continue 0.75 mile to a gate and drive uphill
to Radar Park (if gate is closed, park here and proceed on foot). To get to
the Red Town trailhead, continue past Cougar Mountain Way, and the park
entrance is on your left, at a hairpin turn.

Park Overview Lush vegetation drapes the ruins of the Eastside's early coal-
mining site in this largest of King County parks. This huge area covers a variety of habitats, from wetlands to streams to meadows and forests, and was
saved from development by strong citizen support. The region, underlain by
miles of hollowed-out areas, is riddled with mine openings. Do honor the

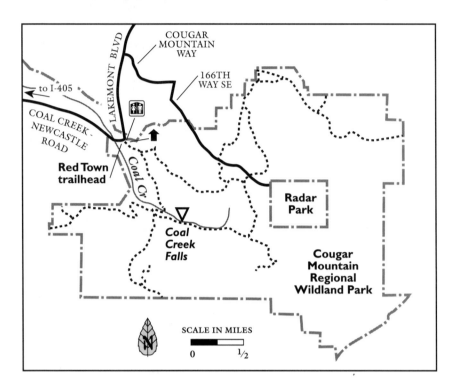

safety signs—some of the openings emit carbon monoxide, and small animals have been overcome near openings that have since been capped. Tiny fragments of coal can still be spotted in the hillsides or along the streams.

Trail Layout   The dirt/gravel trails can be muddy in spots in this moist forest. Walkers should also remember that horses have the right-of-way. When approached by a rider, move to the side of the trail and stand quietly.

Radar Park is a flat open area, offering a panoramic view of the Cascade Mountains north to Mount Baker and the Sammamish Valley. Free trail maps can be found at the Radar Park and Red Town trailheads—the trouble is choosing among the dozens of trails.

Human History   The Duwamish Indians lived in the area and artifacts, such as grinding stones and scrapers, have been found along the park's creek bottoms. The area's Duwamish Trail is believed to date back over 8,000 years. Coal was mined in this area for a century after its discovery in 1863, and Seattle evolved from a small village to a major city largely because of the mining activity here during the late 1800s. For a while, King County was known as the Pennsylvania of the West. The long-abandoned townsite

Trail markers on Cougar Mountain hint at 50 miles of choices.

A.A. RIDGE TRAIL
← COUGAR PASS
CLAYPIT PEAK
LOST BEAGLE TRAIL
KLONDIKE SWAMP
NIKE PEAK →

of Coal Creek was located near the Red Town trailhead, and the old Newcastle townsite was located just to the west.

Faint signs of the old structures are visible only if you know where to look—better yet, go on a guided walk. Along the Steam Hoist Trail, you can see the cemented Ford Slope Mine shaft, as well as the foundation of the building that housed the hoist used to pull the cars up from the mine. A plant-covered mound marks the site of the old washhouse, where miners could shower after work. Along the Bagley Seam Trail, a long, sunken hollow marks where a seam of coal was strip-mined on the surface, and slag heaps lie underneath thick vegetation.

A burned snag offers fertile ground for shrubs.

The Newcastle and Coal Creek townsites had 600 houses between them. Since they were company-owned, the old buildings, which were built on posts and blocks, rather than on foundations, were removed in the 1930s and 1940s. The neighborhood of Red Town took its name from its houses, all painted the same shade of red. A school was built in 1914 on an old smoldering waste dump, and some students used the hot dump area to warm up containers of soup for lunch. Few signs now remain of the towns of Coal Creek, except the old road (now a trail). Look for boards nailed to trees that mark the former location of telephone lines.

A meadow along the Red Town Trail marks the location of the former ballfield. Each mine in the Newcastle and Issaquah areas had at least one baseball team. Area teams played against those from other mines as far north as Nanaimo, B.C., and as far east as Roslyn. This ballpark dates only from 1921; an earlier one was located about 0.75 mile from Red Town.

The mines, never very profitable and frequently plagued by fires and labor strikes, went out of business after the development of cheap hydroelectric power. During World War II, the military installed anti-aircraft guns on Cougar Mountain to protect Seattle and its industries. During the Cold War, the gun bases were upgraded to Nike missile and radar sites. Strong citizen support for open space saved the area for a park, and in 1984, King County purchased 1,000 acres of the property for six million dollars to form the center of the park.

Natural History   One of the Issaquah Alps, Cougar Mountain is a remnant of an ancient chain of mountains that ran from Cape Flattery on the coast to Yakima, before the Olympic or Cascade Mountains even existed. The coalbeds in the area formed from plants that grew when the climate was warmer and moister. Swamps covered the area with plants such as magnolias, figs, palms, and giant tree ferns. When many layers of the remains of this flora were buried deep underground by geologic forces, high pressures and temperatures turned them into layers of coal. Eleven layers of coal exist in this area, and seven of them were mined.

Unlike the desolate piles of mining tailings found on the arid slopes of the Rocky Mountains, the slag heaps in this area are thickly covered with vegetation. Most of the old-growth trees were cut for support beams in the mines, or for buildings, although some large cedars remain. The second-growth forest is dominated by red alder and bigleaf maple trees, with Sitka spruce, western red cedars, Douglas-firs, and western hemlocks.

Other shrubs and herbaceous plants include swamp gooseberry, coast red elderberry, salmonberry, Oregon grape, snowberry, red-flowering currant, western bleeding heart, youth-on-age, and stinging nettle. Sword, bracken, licorice, and lady ferns also grow in this moist forest.

Many giant charred snags remain, riddled with woodpecker holes, reminders of the past forest. Old stumps and logs support vegetation such as red huckleberry and salal, and mushrooms return with the fall rains. The meadow where mining teams once played baseball has been restored and planted with native plants such as yarrow and lupine.

The park attracts a variety of wildlife. Coyotes, cougars, bobcats, and black bears reside here, as do black-tailed deer, mountain beavers, porcupines, weasels, raccoons, flying squirrels, rabbits, and frogs.

Forest and thicket birds include resident pileated woodpeckers, band-tailed pigeons, brown creepers, Hutton's vireos, cedar waxwings, varied thrushes, chickadees, red-breasted nuthatches, golden-crowned kinglets, sparrows, and spotted towhees. These species are joined in spring and summer by hermit and Swainson's thrushes, red-eyed vireos, and several species of warblers and sparrows.

Ruffed grouse and California quail seek cover in the fields, while bald eagles and several species of hawks and owls hunt in the meadows of Radar Park. At the marshy headwaters of Coal Creek, look for resident American dippers, great blue herons, wood ducks, hooded mergansers, Virginia rails, red-winged blackbirds, and marsh wrens.

---

23 ◆ Newcastle
Coal Creek Canyon Park

Highlights: Forest, stream, mining history
Size: 303.5 acres; 4.3 miles of trails
Ownership: King County Park System
Season: Year-round
Terrain: Flat to moderately steep
Facilities: Portable toilet at Red Town trailhead
Hours: Dawn to dusk
Interpretive Programs: Interpretive walks offered during Return to Newcastle Days Festival (first Saturday in June); Issaquah Alps Trails Club leads walks throughout the year
Wheelchair Accessibility: None
Pets: Leash and scoop
Horses: Allowed below falls
Bikes: No
Bus: Metro DART (dial-a-ride) service (see Appendix B for phone number)
Driving Directions: From downtown Seattle, take I-90 east to I-405 south. As you bear onto I-405, stay in the right-hand lane and get off at the next exit, exit 10, onto Coal Creek Parkway. Turn left at the bottom of the hill at the parking light, and drive 1.5 miles. After you cross Forest Drive Southeast, the western park trailhead for the west side of the park is at the bottom of the hill on your left. To continue to the eastern (Cougar

Mountain/Red Town) trailhead, continue on Coal Creek Parkway and pass a shopping center. Take a left at the light, onto Southeast 72nd Street, then turn left at the top of the hill onto Newcastle–Coal Creek Road. Drive 1.9 miles, and as the road curves sharply left after crossing over a stream, the Red Town trailhead is on your right. Walk across the street to pick up the Coal Creek Trail.

Park Overview The lush peacefulness of this moist stream valley belies its identity as an industrial center during the last century. The fern-covered, hummocky slopes are covered mine tailings, while the stream was once boarded over so a narrow-gauge railroad could run on top. The creek holds center stage in this now quiet ravine, and a beautiful waterfall flows close to the eastern trailhead.

Trail Layout The trails are composed of dirt and coal-mine tailings of shale and sandstone. They are mucky in wet spots in this moist ravine, especially along the western end of the park. Boardwalks and steps near the central and eastern areas of the park help cross over the stream and muddy spots. A small kiosk near the eastern end of the park displays historical photos of the area during its coal-mining days.

The main Coal Creek Trail (3 miles) begins on Coal Creek Parkway, crosses the creek over a primitive log footbridge, and climbs the ravine to follow parts of the old railroad bed to the eastern entrance, across from the Red Town trailhead at Cougar Mountain Regional Wildland Park. North Creek Falls is 0.3 mile from the eastern trailhead; the Cinder Mine area is 1 mile from the Red Town trailhead. The Primrose Trail leads off the Coal Creek Trail down the hill to Sandstone Falls, the farm pond, and Scalzo Creek and mine. This trail may be difficult to follow during the flood season.

In the center of the park, the Coal Creek Trail follows a gravel road in the center of the park. Keep an eye out for the well-marked trail entrances back into the forest. Much of the trail system runs along the tops of piles of tailings. Stay back from the edges of the unstable bluffs.

Human History A few concrete foundations, holes in the ground, slag heaps, and old railroad grades mark the location of former boomtowns. When most of Bellevue was covered by deep forests, the two mining towns of Coal Creek and Newcastle were Washington's second largest community (Seattle was the largest). Until 1886, Newcastle had the only post office and voting precinct on the Eastside.

Known mine openings have been sealed—a 1980s survey identified 166 such holes and land subsidences in the area, and a large sealed opening is obvious near the eastern entrance of the park.

Coal Creek was much used during the coal-mining heyday. In 1878, a narrow-gauge railroad, built to carry coal, extended from Seattle to where the Newcastle–Coal Creek Road crosses the stream. The upper part of the creek was boarded into a covered channel, with the railroad tracks running on top of the structure. (Look for the remains of the 12-inch timbers in the creek.) Coal Creek was dammed with bales of hay and brush after an 1894 mine explosion, and its course was diverted into one of the mine shafts to quench the fire that continued burning underground for decades.

Extensive bunkers and a coal-washing plant sat right at the eastern park boundary, while just to the east was a town center with a hotel, stores,

Winter winds dislodge trees rooted in the unstable mine debris along Coal Creek Canyon.

community halls, and hundreds of homes scattered over the surrounding slopes. A concrete foundation in a meadow near the eastern trailhead is part of the boiler room for the old hotel.

Approximately 0.5 mile from the eastern park entrance are the remains of the old railroad turntable. Trains came up the valley, reached the station, then were disconnected and backed down via a bypass track to the turntable, where the engine was turned, then backed up to connect with loaded cars. The turntable was so finely balanced that children later used it as a merry-go-round.

Rock from the mine was sorted and washed, and the tailings dumped into Coal Creek Canyon. These dumps contained low-grade coal, which would often ignite by spontaneous combustion and burn, producing a haze of smoke, fire, and noxious gases. The ovenlike temperatures in the waste piles turned the mixture of sandstones and shales bright red. One main dump area located along the Coal Creek Trail was called the Cinder Mine and smoldered for 55 years.

After the mines closed in the 1930s, independent miners leased rights and continued to mine until the early 1960s. They mined seams close to the surface that had been left by earlier mines, resulting in numerous collapses. A bog caused by water drainage from the Scalzo mine on the north side of Coal Creek has been identified for removal, due to the presence of quicksand.

Natural History   The coal in this area is found in the Renton Formation, and dates from the late Eocene to early Oligocene period, approximately 35 million years ago. The climate was warmer and moister then, and the region was a large swampy floodplain covered with magnolias, figs, and giant tree ferns. As plants died, they were covered and buried among stream sediments and ash layers from occasional volcanic eruptions. Under the high pressure and temperature of deep burial, the organic matter turned to coal and the silt and ash were converted into sandstone and shale. Later land movements tilted and further buried the coal strata, which extend in a 18-mile arc from this area to east of Issaquah. At Newcastle, the coal belt was 890 feet wide at the surface, and was mined down along the steeply dipping seams. The subbituminous coal was not of high quality, but it was close to market and suitable for steam boilers.

During the last century, the streambed along Coal Creek Parkway at the west entrance of the park was a swamp, and was 25 to 30 feet lower. The area was eventually filled in with mine tailings and overlain with dirt from the I-90 freeway construction on Mercer Island. Coal and cinder fragments can be seen in the stream, and higher up the drainage, small coal seams outcrop in the streambanks.

The lushly vegetated mounds of tailings in the park reflect the restorative powers of nature. The original conifer forest, logged for mine shafts and building timbers for the townsites, is replaced by a mostly deciduous forest of large bigleaf maple, red alder, and black cottonwood trees that also

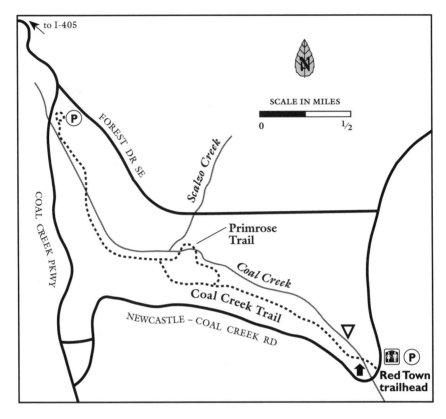

contains some western red cedars, Douglas-firs, and western hemlocks. Other shrubs and herbaceous plants in the moist ravine include Oregon grape, salmonberry, snowberry, creeping buttercup, youth-on-age, and Himalayan and evergreen blackberry. Ferns and mosses show the abundant moisture in the ravine.

The hillsides are covered by beautiful sword ferns which appear to flow down the hillsides. Trees sometimes do lean and fall down the slopes, their shallow roots undermined by the downhill creep of the tailings piles that support them.

The park harbors forest animals typical of the Eastside, including coyotes, black-tailed deer, and an occasional black bear or cougar coming down the wildlife corridor from the Cascade Mountains via Cougar Mountain Park. Many forest birds seen in Cougar Mountain Regional Wildland Park are probable in this adjoining park. These include resident pileated woodpeckers, band-tailed pigeons, varied thrushes, brown creepers, Hutton's vireos, cedar waxwings, chickadees, red-breasted nuthatches, golden-crowned kinglets, sparrows, and spotted towhees. These species are joined in spring and summer by red-eyed vireos, hermit and Swainson's thrushes, and several species of warblers and sparrows.

24 ♦ Mercer Island
Pioneer Park

Highlights: Forest
Size: 120 acres; several miles of trails
Ownership: Mercer Island Parks and Recreation Department
Season: Year-round
Terrain: Flat to moderately sloping
Facilities: None; restrooms, water fountain and phone at shopping center
    adjacent to park and 0.5 mile north at Island Crest Park
Hours: Dawn to dusk
Interpretive Programs: None
Wheelchair Accessibility: None
Pets: On leash or voice control
Horses: Trails in the northwest section
Bikes: No
Bus: Metro 202
Driving Directions: From downtown Seattle, take I-90 east to Mercer Is-
land. Get off at exit 7, and follow Island Crest Way a little over 3 miles
south to Southeast 68th Street. Park at this corner, along Island Crest Way,
or turn right onto Southeast 68th Street, then left into the shopping cen-
ter parking lot. You can also park at Island Crest Park, 0.5 mile back along
Island Crest Way.

Park Overview   This forested oasis provides an important natural haven in
the midst of Mercer Island's suburbs and playing fields. Located toward the
southern end of Mercer Island, it is the largest park on the island, and hints
at how Mercer Island appeared when it was occupied only by summer homes,
before its bridges made it an accessible suburb.

Trail Layout   The park consists of three adjacent quarter-mile sections. The
generally flat, northwest section is used by equestrians. The southeast section slopes gently to the east. The northeast section, level near Island Crest
Way, slopes down to a moist ravine in the northeastern part. The main gravel
trails are good for jogging. The park is quiet except for local traffic and the
distant, wind-like whoosh of I-405 across Lake Washington to the east.

Human History   The local Indians thought Mercer Island haunted due to
several myths that shrouded the island. They used it for hunting and berry
picking during the day, but avoided staying the night. One myth said that
once there had been a small island in the center of the lake between Madison
Park and Kirkland, inhabited by about thirty Indians. One night, the island
disappeared, taking everyone down with it. There are several standing sunken

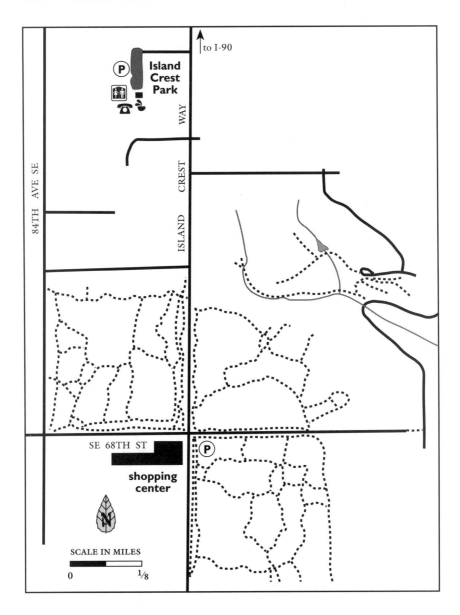

forests in Lake Washington where landslides carried an area of shoreline deep out into the lake. Perhaps such an occurrence gave rise to this myth. One such sunken forest stands off the southern tip of Mercer Island.

When the federal survey of the region was made in 1860, surveyors found the island populated only by game and birds, and the land known only to hunters, trappers, and berry pickers. In 1876, Vitus Schmidt, a wagon-maker from Germany, came with John Wenzler, a cobbler from Chicago, and filed a 160-acre homestead claim on the east-central part of Mercer Island. When Schmidt's cabin was crushed by a falling tree, he left his claim and went back to Chicago, but returned 13 years later. In 1889, C. C. Calkins bought acreage on the north side of the island and built a resort he dubbed East Seattle. The resort failed in 1902, and the hotel burned in 1908, but soon afterwards, Seattleites began to build summer homes on the island.

The park land was privately owned until 1931, when Mrs. Maud Walker-Ames willed the property to the University of Washington. Mercer Island became incorporated in 1960, and when the land then known as "the University properties" became available, a bond issue was passed to acquire it in 1964. Over the last several decades, advocates have tried three times to have portions of the park developed into a municipal golf course. The land was recently placed into an open-space conservancy trust, in an effort to discourage further pursuit of the idea.

Natural History Pioneer Park, like the rest of Mercer Island, had been logged of most of its virgin timber before the turn of the century, although some logging also may have occurred in the 1920s. The skid roads left by the loggers on the island rapidly became covered with devil's club, red huckleberry, and blackberry, and the second-growth forests were so full of deer, grouse, and other game that hunters became a nuisance.

The dominant conifers in the park are Douglas-firs, but as the forest continues to mature, western red cedars and western hemlocks will again become the main coniferous trees. The old cedar stumps are relics of the earlier old-growth forest, as are a few large conifers growing in the bottom of the ravine. Other tree species include bigleaf maple, red alder, Pacific madrone, and Pacific dogwood.

The type of vegetation in the park differs between the two higher sections and the northeast ravine. The soil on the two upper sections is less fertile, more sandy, and less prone to hold water. These conditions favor the growth of conifers and shrubs like salal, Oregon grape, red huckleberry, ocean spray, and sword, bracken, and wood ferns. The trees and shrubs that grow here must be able to withstand several months of little or no rainfall. Because salal, Oregon grape and conifers all remain active during the winter and have thick, leathery, or waxy leaves designed to retard water loss, they can survive in this environment.

In the ravine, however, the soil is relatively rich and holds enough moisture during dry summer months to support deciduous trees. The understory is varied and lush, with abundant maidenhair, lady, and licorice ferns, salmonberry, red elderberry, twinflower, devil's club, skunk cabbage, youth-on-age, horsetails, rushes and sedges.

The upper edge of the ravine is a good place to search for birds of the forest canopy such as band-tailed pigeon, golden-crowned kinglet, Swainson's thrush, and Western tanager. In the spring, migratory grosbeaks, warblers,

Salal occupies the higher, drier portions of Pioneer Park.

vireos, and hummingbirds are attracted by the stream water and abundant plant life. An extensive bird list of the park's seventy-four species of birds, as well as its plants, is found in an excellent booklet on the natural history of the park, available for a small fee through the Mercer Island Parks and Recreation Department.

Nearby Park
Island Crest Park

This 40-acre park shelters a delightful little pocket of moist deciduous and coniferous forest with dirt trails and a long suspension bridge over a mucky stream area. From Pioneer Park, go approximately 0.5 mile north on Island Crest Way; the park is on the left. Park in the larger parking lot and head west from the center of the lot or from the restrooms down into a damp forested hollow.

South King County

25 • Burien
Ed Munro / Seahurst Park

Highlights: Forest with some large trees, stream, saltwater beach with views
of Puget Sound, Vashon Island, and the Olympic Mountains
Size: 185 acres; approximately 1 mile of saltwater shoreline; several miles of
beach and forest trails
Ownership: City of Burien Parks and Recreation Division
Season: Year-round
Terrain: Level to moderately steep forest trails; level beach path
Facilities: Restrooms, water fountain, picnic shelter and tables at beach
Hours: Dawn to dusk
Interpretive Programs: Possible—call for information (see Appendix B)
Wheelchair Accessibility: Hard-packed level gravel trail above beach
Pets: Leash and scoop
Horses: No
Bikes: Yes, on level gravel walkways
Bus: Metro 135, 136 (get off at Ambaum Boulevard Southwest and South-
west 144th Street, and walk about 1 mile to the beach)
Driving Directions: From downtown Seattle, take I-5 south to Burien. Get
off at exit 154 (the Sea-Tac airport exit), and go west on Highway 518,
which turns into Southwest 148th Street west of Highway 509. At
Ambaum Boulevard Southwest take a right, then in a few blocks, turn left
on Southwest 144th Street, which is marked by a park sign. In three blocks,
at another park sign, turn right on 13th Avenue Southwest, which changes
to Southwest 140th Street as it winds down to the park. There is an upper
parking lot on the left after you enter the park, and a lower beach parking
lot at the end of the road.

Park Overview   This deep forested ravine plunges west to almost a mile of
cobbled beach bordering Puget Sound. Some large Douglas-firs and western
red cedars, overlooked by earlier loggers, grow in the forest. A wide, level,
packed gravel path parallels the sand and cobble beach and offers a vantage
point for bird-watching and for viewing Puget Sound, the Olympic Mountains, ferries crossing to Vashon and Bainbridge Islands, and cargo ships on
their way to and from Tacoma. The park can be crowded in the summer, especially on weekends, but is quiet the rest of the year.

Trail Layout   The forest trails can be accessed from the middle of the upper parking lot on the south side, or by crossing the footbridge at the southern end of the lower parking lot, then veering left up the hill. The dirt trails are steep or narrow in some spots and can be muddy after a rain. Fallen western red cedars and Douglas-firs can block some of the trails on this moist hillside. Steps have been cut in some fallen logs; however, in other spots, you may have to climb over a log and look for where the trail picks up again. A small stream must be forded on logs and rocks, so parties with small children or others unsteady on their feet may want to turn back and retrace their steps. A wide, level, packed gravel path south of the lower parking lot parallels the beach and offers an easy walk.

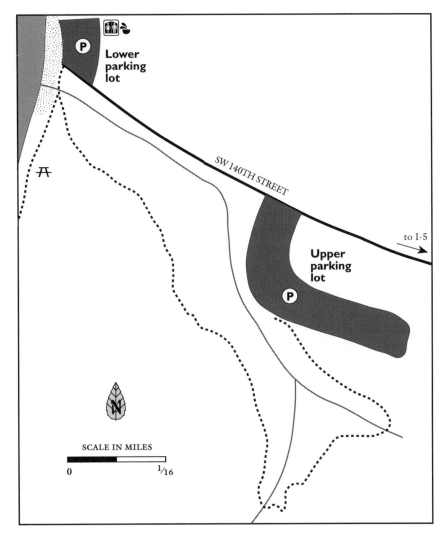

Licorice ferns festoon the trunk of a Douglas-fir.

Human History This lush ravine owes its preservation to the steep slopes that made it unattractive to developers. Native Americans used its shores for summer fishing and clam digging, then wintered farther inland. In the 1930s, Mr. Fox, a construction and lumber mill baron, built an estate on the site. During Prohibition, Fox built a sea wall that had gates to allow rum runners from Canada to smuggle alcohol into the area at night during high tide. The liquor was hidden in caves dug into the hills above the beach.

Low tide exposes the intertidal zone at this Puget Sound park, encouraging exploration.

King County purchased the land for a park in the late 1960s, and officially opened Ed Munro/Seahurst Park in 1975. Former King County Commissioner Ed Munro helped establish the park. There was controversy over whether to develop the park more aggressively, but ultimately, the area was preserved with a focus toward ecology.

Natural History   Large conifers, along with old conifer stumps, are relics of the first-growth forest that dominated this area before white settlers arrived. After the conifers were logged, deciduous trees became established. Today, the lush forest consists of second-growth woods of bigleaf maple and red alder, with some good-sized Douglas-firs, western red cedars, and western hemlocks. Eventually, conifers will shade out the deciduous trees and again dominate this area.

The moisture in this west-facing ravine is evident from its abundant mosses and ferns. The sword and wood ferns are evergreen, the lady and maidenhair ferns die back in winter, and the licorice ferns thrive in winter but die back in the warm days of summer. Other moisture-loving plants include stink currant, coast red elderberry, salmonberry, bedstraw, sweet cicely, candyflower, youth-on-age, and western trillium. Red huckleberry plants thrive here on stumps, and red currant, salal, and Oregon grape occupy higher, drier areas of the forest. Invasive English holly and Himalayan blackberry also grow in the park.

Note the various pools and drops of the stream within the forest. Fallen logs and branches help determine the shape, stability, and aquatic habitats of small forest streams. Pools that form behind large woody debris create critical habitats for fish and other aquatic life. The deposition of sediments in these pools slows down the removal of nutrient-rich debris from the forest, allowing decomposing organisms time to work on the materials before they are washed downstream and lost to the forest community. The stream profile of alternating pools and drops stabilizes the streambed and reduces erosion.

Animals in the park include the usual forest assemblage in this region, as well as the ensatina salamander. At low tide, look for (but do not disturb) intertidal animals such as purple and green shore crabs, sea cucumbers, clams, barnacles, and mussels. A barge was sunk off the beach in 1971 to create a haven for sea stars, octopuses, rockfish, sea perch and other marine life. Seals may also be seen in the area.

Forest birds sighted here include resident winter wrens, cedar waxwings, spotted towhees, song sparrows, and varied thrushes. The abundant snags and proximity to water for fishing also offers habitat for bald eagles and belted kingfishers. The waters off the cobble beach harbor wintering ducks such as Barrow's and common goldeneye, and bufflehead, along with common loons, grebes, scoters, and gulls. Nearshore eelgrass beds attract migrating brants in the spring.

---

26 ♦ Kent
Soos Creek County Park

Highlights: Progression from open fields to bottomland woods through freshwater marsh

Size: 436.9 acres; 4.4-mile trail

Ownership: King County Parks System

Season: Year-round

Terrain: Flat to gently rolling

Facilities: Restrooms, water fountains, picnic shelters, and playgrounds at Gary Grant and Lake Meridian Parks; portable toilet and picnic tables at the park maintenance yard at 148th Avenue Southeast and Southeast 249th Street

Hours: Dawn to dusk

Interpretive Programs: King County naturalists offer free nature walks, and school programs on wetlands are offered for a fee (see Appendix B for phone number); self-guided trail pamphlet available at trailhead

Wheelchair Accessibility: Paved asphalt trail

Pets: Leash and scoop

Horses: Yes, mostly on a parallel dirt trail

Bikes: Yes

Bus: Metro 163, 169 (call for directions; see Appendix B for phone number)

Driving Directions: From downtown Seattle, take I-5 south to I-405. From I-405, take Highway 167 south, and exit at South 212th Street in Kent. At the exit ramp, turn left onto 212th and go up a long hill. The street changes to Southeast 208th Street. After you cross 132nd Avenue Southeast, the Gary Grant Park trailhead is on the left.

Park Overview   The park follows Soos Creek from Gary Grant Park in the north to Lake Meridian in the south, traveling through varied wetlands of cattail marshes, wet meadows, willow thickets, and forested swamps. The stream valley passes between upland forests, and an occasional house or barn is seen in the distance. On clear days, Mount Rainier looms to the south.

Trail Layout   This wide curving trail is used by walkers, cyclists, joggers, and inline skaters, with horses trotting alongside on a separate dirt trail—a more rural version of Seattle's Burke-Gilman Trail. The trail cuts across several neighborhood roads, so use caution when crossing these intersecting streets, especially when on a bike. The paved, gently graded trail offers a great hike on a rainy day, so long as one is equipped with umbrella and boots.

Human History   Soos Creek takes its name from the Skopamish Indian village that was located at its mouth on the Green River. From the mid-to-late 1800s, most of the land in the Soos Creek area was owned by the Northern Pacific Railroad. At the end of the nineteenth century, large logging companies, including Weyerhaeuser, purchased and logged the timber, then sold the land to settlers, mostly Finnish, Norwegian, and Swedish farmers. Rumor has it that with no roads leading up to the hill, one Finn carried his

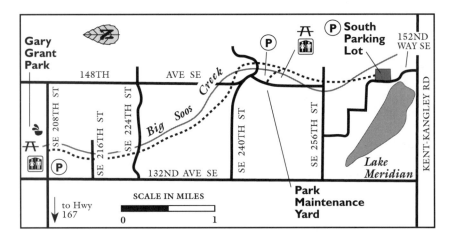

The multi-use Soos Creek Trail passes through over four miles of wetlands.

cast-iron stove in on his back. After clearing the land with horse and oxen, the early settlers mainly raised fruit and vegetables, and some established dairies. Old fruit trees can still be seen along the trail.

The Forward Thrust bond issue of the 1960s saved the Soos Creek area from development. Gary Grant Park at the north end of the park was named in honor of a former King County Council member who was instrumental in the creation of the park during the mid-1980s.

Natural History   Soos Creek is an active salmon-spawning stream that starts on the Fairwood plateau and drains into the Green River. The trail passes through several wetland environments, with a corresponding change in plant life, including pond, marsh, wet meadow, shrub-scrub wetland, and forested wetland.

Trees in the upland forest above the trail include good-sized Douglas-firs, western red cedars, Sitka spruces, western hemlocks, bigleaf maples and red alders. Sword, licorice, and lady ferns grow in the forest, and bracken ferns grow in clearings. Forest shrubs include salmonberry, thimbleberry, snowberry, coast red elderberry, Pacific ninebark, and Oregon grape. Flowering plants include stinging nettle, skunk cabbage, and deadly nightshade. Wetland plants are found in their zones: forested wetlands hold skunk cabbage, while shrub-scrub wetlands feature hardhack, willow, red-osier dogwood, Nootka rose, fireweed, and Scot's broom. Wet meadows hold reed canary grass, creeping buttercup, and horsetail. Cattail and common rush grow in marshes, and duckweed and European water milfoil appear in open water.

Animals in the park include coyotes, little brown bats, mice, shrews, garter snakes, red-legged frogs, and many birds, including bald eagles, several resident species of hawks, and owls. Killdeer lay their eggs in the horse pasture at the northern end of the park, and resident ring-necked pheasants, ruffed grouse, and California quail find shelter in the fields.

Marsh residents include great blue heron, Virginia rail, belted kingfisher, and wood duck.

Forest birds include many resident woodpecker species, including northern flicker, red-breasted sapsucker, and pileated, downy, and hairy woodpecker. Trees also harbor resident cedar waxwings, wrens, sparrows, pine siskins, bushtits, and chickadees. Spring and summer add red-eyed vireos, willow flycatchers, orange-crowned warblers, brown-headed cowbirds, and violet-green, tree, and barn swallows.

---

27 ♦ Kent
Lake Fenwick Park

Highlights: Lake, forest
Size: 127 acres; 20-acre lake; several miles of trails
Ownership: Kent Parks and Recreation Department
Season: Year-round
Terrain: Flat to moderately steep
Facilities: Portable toilets and picnic tables at central and southern parking lots; picnic tables on island; public fishing
Hours: Dawn to dusk
Interpretive Programs: None
Wheelchair Accessibility: Boardwalk over lake
Pets: Leash and scoop
Horses: No
Bikes: No
Bus: Metro 166 (see Appendix B for phone number)
Driving Directions: From downtown Seattle, take I-5 south to exit 149. At the bottom of the exit ramp, take a left on Kent-Des Moines Road (State

Route 516), and travel east down a long hill into the Kent Valley. Near the bottom of the hill, take the first right at Reith Road, then a left in 0.2 mile onto Fenwick Road. Bear left onto Lake Fenwick Road at the intersection with South 254th Street. The park entrance is on your left in about 1 mile. There are three parking areas—the largest one, at the first entrance on your left, is near the hillside trailhead, with two others farther south along Lake Fenwick Road.

Park Overview   This small lovely lake is located in a beautiful little glen tucked between Puget Sound and the Kent Valley. This quiet, peaceful park is lush and languid in summer, save for local traffic, or a passing flight from Sea-Tac airport to the west. Fishermen come here to fish for trout and bass off the attractive boardwalk or among private pocket beaches on the forested island. The marshes offer great bird-watching, especially during the winter months. A broad trail climbs high above the east side of the lake to cross a ridge and descend down a huge staircase within the forest to the base of the Kent Valley.

Trail Layout   A boardwalk/pier area connects tiny Lake Island to the mainland, and offers forested alcoves for watching marsh birds or fishing on the western shore. The Park Lake trail on the western side of the park winds uphill to a local neighborhood.

   The wide dirt/gravel trail that leads up the ridge east of the lake is easier than it looks from the bottom. The trail offers great views of the lake on the way up, with a few well-placed benches along the way. Travel north a short distance along the ridge, then descend via a huge metal grating staircase down the other side of the ridge to the Kent Valley floor. The towering stairway provides a fine viewpoint for observing birds in the forest canopy. At the base of the stairs, a fairly well-drained bark trail leads north to a long wooden

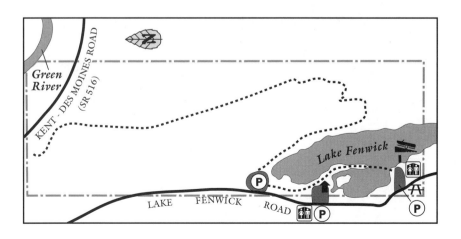

boardwalk that skirts apartments and a pond to emerge at Highway 516 across from the Green River. A plan is in the works to link Lake Fenwick Park to the Green River Trail via Highway 516. Train and traffic noise is more obvious on the eastern side of the park than it is by the lake.

Human History Native Americans in the Kent Valley lived in loosely organized family groups and wintered together at permanent village sites along the rivers. Tribes along the White and Green River drainages had ties to the Duwamish and were the ancestors of the tribes that now live on the Muckleshoot Reservation. In 1855, frustrated by encroachment on land that contained sacred grounds or traditional fishing and plant-gathering sites, Indians attacked several pioneer families in Auburn. Many settlers in the valley fled to the village of Seattle to winter in its blockhouse, which was attacked in January 1856, and defended by a U.S. warship dispatched to the area. Many of the White River homesteaders sold their claims and never returned.

In 1859, Thomas Moody Alvord bought 320 acres between Lake Fenwick (originally called Long Lake) and the White River (the present bed of the Green River). The White River became a busy thoroughfare and Alvord established a river landing and a warehouse. There were few roads in the heavily forested area—a trip to Seattle made as late as 1875 by horseback or wagon took two to three days in good weather. All supplies for the White River settlement were delivered by steamboat, and Alvords Landing was the designated upriver terminus for river boats. Farmers from miles around brought their produce to Alvord for shipment to Seattle. In the 1860s and 1870s, Alvord was also a successful farmer in his own right. In 1896, however, the failure of the local hops industry forced him into bankruptcy and he sold his land at public auction.

The Lake Fenwick Country Club was located south of the present park land during the 1920s and 1930s. This private club consisted of nine small cabins, each one built by a member. The area of the northernmost parking lot was an old lakeside resort. The city of Kent bought 47 acres of the land about 1970, with funds from a bond issue matched by state and federal funds. More acreage was later added to the park land.

Natural History The Kent valley, on the east side of the park, now holds the course of the Green River. However, once the White River flowed here, and before that, the valley was part of Puget Sound. Around 5,000 years ago, an eruption on Mount Rainier sent a mass of mud and rock, known as the Osceola Mudflow, into the southern part of the Sound at the present site of Auburn. Afterwards, the White River cut a new channel from its glacial source

The peaceful waters of Lake Fenwick offer a haven for waterfowl and fishing aficionados.

on the mountain down through the surface of the mudflow. Over the course of time, a delta built up in the bay, and the White River Valley emerged from the sea. By the beginning of the nineteenth century, the White River was a mature river system, and the dominant drainage in the valley. Semi-annual flooding blanketed the valley floor with a layer of rich alluvium, creating fertile bottomlands.

North of Auburn, the Green River then emptied into the White River as one of its tributaries. The White River merged with the Black River (then the outlet for Lake Washington) at Tukwila, and together they formed the deep Duwamish River, which flowed into Elliott Bay across a vast delta. In 1906, the year of the Great Flood, the raging White River shifted its flow to drain south into the Puyallup River. A concrete dam built at Auburn permanently diverted its waters south to restrict valley flooding, and the Green River took over the White River's drainage.

In the late 1970s, residential development on the hills to the west of Lake Fenwick caused increased soil run-off into the little valley. The small stream that drained into the lake at its northwest corner became laden with silt, which then entered the lake. Excessive runoff from the stream was diverted to a natural pond near the lake's northwest corner, which traps silt and pollutants before they reach the lake. Native vegetation was planted along the shoreline and timber bulkheads built to discourage erosion. To improve the low oxygen content of the bottom water, an aerator (the blue raft in the lake) mixes air from the atmosphere via an onshore compressor (the building in the middle parking lot) into the lake water. This process adds oxygen to improve fish habitat, and helps control phosphorus, a nutrient that promotes excessive algae growth in lakes.

The combination of forest and lake habitats supports a variety of plant species. The forests surrounding the lake consist of mixed woods of red alders, bigleaf and vine maples, medium-sized Douglas-firs and western red cedars, western hemlocks, black cottonwoods, cascaras, willows, and small coast redwoods. Sword ferns on the slopes stay green year-round, joined by deer ferns in the spring. Licorice ferns cover the trunks of bigleaf maples.

Salal and Oregon grape grow in the drier soils of the park, and native shrubs in moister areas include snowberry, and red and blue elderberry. Herbaceous plants include creeping buttercup, youth-on-age, cattail, yellow pond lily, yellow iris, and water parsley. Himalayan blackberry, English ivy, and English holly are among the invasive non-native plants in the park.

Nineteenth-century pioneer accounts of the area mention lynx and beaver in the swamps, as well as weasel, coyote, black-tailed deer, and bear. The White River then contained chinook, coho, chum, pink, and sockeye salmon runs. The park now harbors black-tailed deer, raccoons, coyotes, muskrats, and river otters. The Washington State Department of Game stocks the lake with trout, and bass have also been caught.

The park offers varied habitats for many species of birds. Forest birds include resident band-tailed pigeons and song sparrows, with tree swallows and Bullock's orioles visiting in the spring and summer. Great blue herons and marsh wrens frequent the marsh. Waterfowl include resident pied-billed grebes, mallards, American coots, and wood ducks. Wintering buffleheads and ring-necked ducks find shelter on the lake.

---

28 ♦ Des Moines
Saltwater State Park

Highlights: Forest, saltwater beach, stream

Size: 88 acres; 1,445 feet of sandy and rocky saltwater shoreline; 2 miles of trails

Ownership: Washington State Parks and Recreation Commission

Season: Year-round

Terrain: Flat to moderately steep

Facilities: Restrooms, water fountain, phone, playground at parking lot; picnic shelters and tables, and grills along shorefront and forest; sandy swimming beach (no lifeguard); summer camping from April to Labor Day; concession stand open during camping season; artificial offshore diving reef

Hours: Dawn to dusk

Interpretive Programs: Campfire program on Saturday nights from Memorial Day to Labor Day

Wheelchair Accessibility: Paved trail along shoreline; road into camping area; footbridges over creek

Pets: Leash and scoop

Horses: No

Bikes: Yes

Bus: Metro 130

Driving Directions: From downtown Seattle, take I-5 south to exit 149. At the bottom of the exit ramp, turn right and head west on Highway 516, the Kent–Des Moines Road. Cross Pacific Highway South (Highway 99), and take a left at Marine View Drive (Highway 509). Head south, and in about 1 mile, where Marine View Drive bears left, turn right on South 251st Street, then left on 8th Place South. The park entrance is ahead in 2 blocks. Large brown park signs along the way will assist your search.

Park Overview Located on the East Passage on Puget Sound, this forested ravine offers views of Vashon and Maury Islands, and gorgeous sunsets over the Olympic Mountains. A sandy saltwater beach and an on-site campground make this the most heavily used state park on Puget Sound. Most of the park activity centers on the beach, so hikers can still find some solitude on the trails that climb up to the upland forests. For a quieter walk, come in midweek or between Labor Day and Memorial Day.

Trail Layout Dirt/gravel trails climb to wooded ridges around the ravine, descending to pass through picnic and camping areas. On top of the hills, the trails are mostly level and fairly well-drained, though mucky in spots and on the lower slopes after a rain. The group camping area offers spectacular views of the Sound from the bluff. When not crowded with campers, the park is fairly quiet, except for local traffic passing overhead on Highway 509. However, if you like watching planes, head for the eastern end of the park on the forested ridge to watch flights on low approach to Sea-Tac airport, just to the north.

Human History Indians from the Kent Valley who lived along the White and Green Rivers (ancestors of tribes now on the Muckleshoot Reservation) traveled to the beach area in summer to harvest clams. Shell middens have been found on the beaches near the mouth of McSorleys Creek. On the bluffs above the beach, lookouts scanned for approaching raiders from the north, since Tlingits from southern Alaska and Haidas and Tsimshians from northern British Columbia often came to Puget Sound to capture slaves. The Haidas came in long black canoes, carved from a single cedar log, that measured more than 80 feet in length and carried 40-60 passengers. An example exists at the Burke Museum on the University of Washington campus.

Early white settlers knew the area as McSorleys Gulch. James McSorley, a farmer from Ireland, homesteaded the park land from around 1875 to 1890. Logging operations were active in the area from 1890 to 1925. Around 1908, K. Otto Anderson and his partner began a logging operation and built a logging chute on the bluff north of the park to dump timber into the Sound.

Timber supplied local mills and provided cordwood for steamers on the Sound. Beginning in the 1850s, Puget Sound was a busy highway for sailing ships, and later steamships. By the end of the nineteenth century, small steamships (called the Mosquito Fleet) sailed the Sound, carrying Seattleites to the resort areas along its banks.

In 1925, the *Seattle Star* newspaper launched a fundraising campaign to purchase the gulch for a public park to be enjoyed by everyone living between Seattle and Tacoma. With the help of the *Tacoma Times* newspaper, and the Seattle/Tacoma Associated Young Men's Business Club, the park land was acquired in seven parcels, the first in 1929 and the last in 1974. The park was dedicated in 1933, in a colorful ceremony where a hatchet was buried at the foot of the flagpole, signifying the end of rivalries between Seattle and Tacoma. From 1935 to 1936, the Civilian Conservation Corps constructed several buildings, picnic tables and stonework in the park, and improved roads

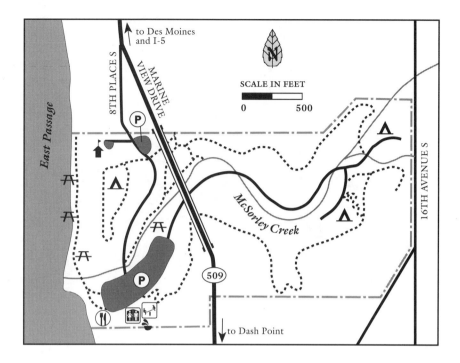

and roughed-in trails. In the early 1950s, the creek bed was moved to the north to enlarge the parking lot and to extend the beach.

Natural History Smith Creek, named after Peter Smith, a landowner in the 1920s, was renamed McSorleys Creek in 1988. Suburban development above the park has contributed to a decline in water quality, due to septic tank leakage and erosion from storm water runoff. A project begun in 1992 seeks to restore the former runs of salmon, and cutthroat and steelhead trout in McSorleys Creek.

Little marine life is found on the sandy beach. However, a barge and tires were sunk 150 yards offshore near the southern edge of the park to form an underwater reef. The structure attracts marine life such as fish, plumose anemone, nudibranch, starfish, and an occasional octopus. The beach is also a handy place to put in with a kayak.

The forest consists mostly of bigleaf maples and red alders, with some Douglas-firs, western hemlocks, western red cedars, and Pacific madrones. Vine maples in the understory add fall color. Many tree trunks are covered with English ivy, and non-native European mountain ash, holly, and Himalayan blackberry also exist in the park.

This is a moist forest, as evidenced by shrubs such as salmonberry, Indian plum, red elderberry, and false Solomon's seal. Other moisture-loving plants include common horsetail, creeping buttercup, large-leaved avens,

A close look at the forest floor reveals mosses and mushrooms.

youth-on-age, trillium, fringecup, waterleaf, enchanter's nightshade, and western starflower. Sword ferns grow year-round, and licorice ferns cover bigleaf-maple tree trunks. Wood, lady, and maidenhair ferns can be found in the park during the growing season. Oregon grape and salal grow on drier hillsides.

Before the white settlers, deer, cougars, bears, and perhaps elk lived in the area. Now, the forest shelters rabbits, chipmunks, squirrels, weasels, raccoons, and skunks. Saltwater birds include resident ducks, gulls, pigeon guillemots, and belted kingfishers, with wintering common loons, surf scoters, horned grebes, Bonaparte's gulls, and Barrow's goldeneye. Brants make a spring stopover on their way to Alaska to feed on nearshore eelgrass beds, and bald eagles find hunting grounds. Forest birds include resident spotted towhees, finches, Steller's jays, Bewick's wrens and song sparrows. Several species of swallows and warblers nest here in the spring.

---

29 ◆ Federal Way
West Hylebos State Park

Highlights: Diverse wetland communities, old-growth Sitka spruce
Size: 150 acres, 1.5 miles of trails
Ownership: Washington State Parks and Recreation Commission
Season: Year-round

Terrain: Flat
Facilities: Portable toilet at parking lot
Hours: Dawn to dusk
Interpretive Programs: Interpretive signs along boardwalk and trail; Friends of Hylebos Association newsletter available at trailhead
Wheelchair Accessibility: Level boardwalks must be reached by short gravel trail
Pets: No
Horses: No
Bikes: No
Bus: Metro 174, 194, 195, 196, 197
Driving Directions: From downtown Seattle, take I-5 south to exit 147B (Highway 161 South, Puyallup). At the bottom of the exit ramp, turn right (west) on South 348th Street. After crossing Pacific Highway South (Highway 99), continue west for another 0.5 mile, and watch for 4th Avenue South, an obscure single-lane road on the left. Turn in here, and in 2 blocks turn left into the parking area and trailhead.

Park Overview   This marvelous enclave preserves wetlands at the headwaters of Hylebos Creek. Despite its location in booming Federal Way, these wetlands comprise probably the wildest, most diverse, least disturbed headwater swamp in King County. The primordial jungle of giant Sitka spruces, western red cedars, and Douglas-firs towers over impenetrable thickets of deciduous trees and shrubs, providing a haven for dozens of species of plants.

Trail Layout   A remarkable boardwalk loops through the forest and bog to keep visitors just above the soggy ground. In fact, the area would be inaccessible without it. Safety mesh on the wooden planks offers a nice degree of security. Interpretive signs show photographs of the plants in bloom, identify plant and animal activities, and describe glacial geology. A side trail leads to Mar Lake. There are a few scattered benches and picnic tables, and the park is quiet, except for the distant noise of the nearby freeways and shopping centers.

Human History   Portions of the area were logged sometime in the late nineteenth century. This wetlands preserve exists through the foresight, generosity, and hard work of Ilene and Francis Marckx. They recognized the value of the unique wetlands and launched the park process in 1981 by donating 24.5 acres of land to the state. Other small parcels have been acquired from local residents with the aid of community groups. The development of the nature trail has been an ongoing labor of love for the Friends of the Hylebos, a group that tends the area, publishes a newsletter, and leads special events. An interpretive center has been in the works for some time, but cutbacks in state funds have continually delayed its development.

Natural History The park features magnificent Sitka spruces, western red cedars, and western hemlocks, some over 500 years old. The Sitka spruce, fairly common in the West Hylebos Wetlands, is rare in the rest of the Puget Sound region, since its strong but light wood was prized for early airplane construction. Douglas-firs are uncommon here, due to the wet conditions. Thickets of red alder and cascara, with Oregon crabapple, bitter cherry, Pacific dogwood, Oregon ash, and bigleaf and vine maple, are among the deciduous trees in the park. The shallow roots of the trees in these wetlands make them vulnerable to wind, and storms in 1990 and 1993 brought down numerous trees and damaged large sections of boardwalk, which have been repaired.

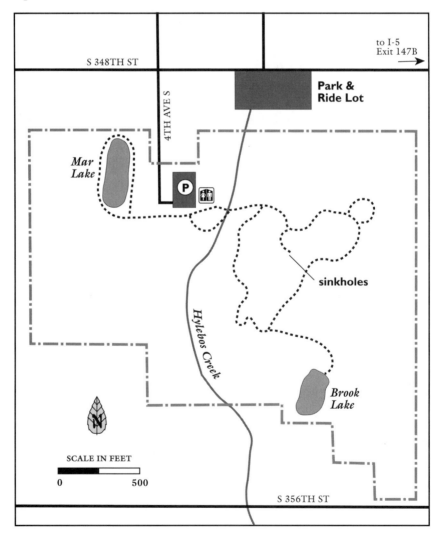

A wooden walkway leads into the forested wetland of West Hylebos State Park.

The shrub layer includes red-osier dogwood, coast red elderberry, salmonberry, black twinberry, straggly gooseberry, Labrador tea, swamp laurel, swamp birch, hardhack, red huckleberry, Indian plum, stink currant, Nootka rose, wild azalea, and native and imported blackberries. Flowering plants include stinging nettle, Cooley's hedgenettle, swamp violet, bog orchid, skunk cabbage, false lily-of-the-valley, bleeding heart, Pacific water-leaf, water parsley, creeping buttercup, youth-on-age, duckweed, trillium, and common horsetail.

Numerous types of ferns, including wood ferns growing on deadwood, and lady, bracken, deer, and licorice ferns support the lush feel of the place, as do the twenty-five types of moss, eighteen types of lichens, six species of liverwort, and many types of fungi and mushrooms that grow here.

An arboretum planted by the Marckxes contains three specimens of almost every conifer found in Washington State. Included are coast redwood, giant sequoia, dawn redwood, and gingko, which no longer grow in the area but were common in the lush semitropical forest that covered North America during the Tertiary Period some 30 million years ago.

Forest birds and waterfowl use the park area—114 species at last count. Several small lakes host resident great blue herons, double-crested cormorants, mallards and wood ducks, and wintering ring-necked ducks, goldeneyes, and buffleheads. Forest birds include resident downy woodpeckers, Steller's jays, spotted towhees, chickadees, bushtits, Bewick's wrens, and pine siskins. Ruby-crowned kinglets visit from fall through spring. Animals include little brown bats, Pacific treefrogs, Douglas and flying squirrels, garter snakes, and coyotes, while mountain beavers live further downstream.

A series of low, elongated glacial ridges, or drumlins, account for the area's wavy topography. As the last ice sheet withdrew around 14,000 years ago, meltwater collected in the depressions between the drumlins. Gradually, these depressions collected sediments, and pioneer wetland plants such as sedges and rushes invaded the area. Shrubs and trees followed, as ponds evolved into marshes, marshes into bogs, bogs into forested swamps, and swamps into bottomland woods and thickets. Today, the West Hylebos Wetlands contains samples of all of these types of wetlands, most of which are underlain by thick deposits of peat. In cool northern wetlands such as this one, the decomposition of dead plants proceeds slowly, and is often incomplete. Plant materials, often mixed with silt deposited by streams, pile up layer by layer, forming peat and gradually creating new land by filling in lake margins and bottomlands.

Several 17-foot-deep sinkholes in the park remain a mystery. They might be the remnants of a shallow lake that once covered the area, or might be a sign of deep underground springs. Even after a prolonged dry period, the water level in these holes never falls more than 14 inches below the surface. Also unknown is the reason why some portions of the forest floor lack understory plants, while adjacent areas are overgrown with shrubs, ferns, wildflowers, and mosses.

---

30 ◆ Federal Way
Rhododendron Species Botanical Garden and Pacific Rim Bonsai Collection

Highlights: Collections of rhododendrons (RSBG) and bonsai (PRBC)
Size: (RSBG) 22 acres; approximately 2 miles of trail; (PRBC) 1 acre
Ownership: (RSBG) The Rhododendron Species Foundation; (PRBC) The Weyerhauser Company
Season: (RSBG) Best spring and fall; (PRBC) Year-round
Terrain: (RSBG) Flat to gently rolling; (PRBC) Level
Facilities: Both collections share a gift shop, restrooms, and water fountain; two additional water fountains in RSBG; no picnicking on grounds
Hours: (RSBG and PRBC) March through May, 10 A.M. to 4 P.M. (closed Thursdays); June through February, 11 P.M. to 4 P.M. (closed Thursdays and Fridays)
Fee: (RSBG) Admission fee March through October; discounts for students, seniors, and groups; children under 12 and school groups free; memberships available; no fee for PRBC
Interpretive Programs: (RSBG and PRBC) Group tours by appointment

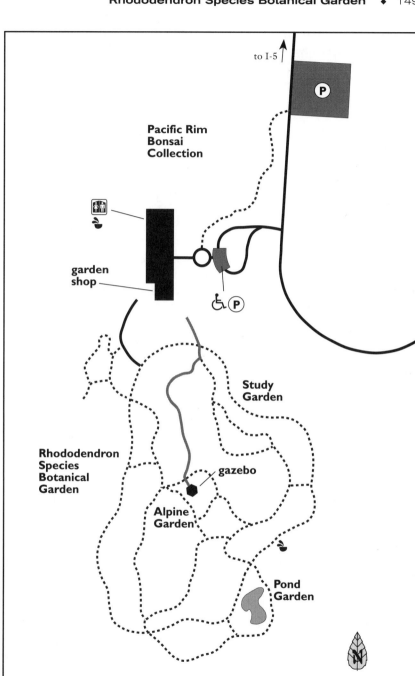

(See Appendix B for phone numbers); (PRBC) Free tours each Sunday at
noon; bonsai video runs continually in outside shelter, free bonsai booklet
Wheelchair Accessibility: (RSBG and PRBC) Handicapped parking area at
entrance; level, fine gravel paths
Pets: No
Horses: No
Bikes: No
Bus: Metro 181
Driving Directions: From Seattle, take I-5 south to exit 142A (Highway 18
East). Stay in the far right-hand lane and take the first exit to Weyerhaeuser
Way South. At the stop sign, turn left on Weyerhaeuser Way South; drive
for approximately 0.5 mile and take the first left. Follow the signs to Gar-
den Parking and turn right into the parking lot.

Park Overview   The forested grounds of the Weyerhaeuser headquarters
harbor two separate public gardens that feature the plants of the Rhododendron Species Botanical Garden and the Pacific Rim Bonsai Collection. Croaking frogs and the songs of birds slightly dampen the whoosh of traffic from
nearby I-5. Forgot your umbrella? You can borrow one at the gift shop.

More than 2,100 different varieties of wild rhododendrons are displayed
in the Rhododendron Species Botanical Garden, comprising one of the largest collections in the world. A succession of blooms can be seen throughout
the spring; colors vary according to the time of season. Peak bloom time is
mid-March through mid-May, when blooming rhododendrons are joined by
spring bulbs, perennials, and flowering trees and shrubs. In general, red
blooms are most spectacular from February through March, lavenders appear in April, and white and pink flowers open in May. A small number of
plants bloom in June and July. Call the visitor center for a report. Selected
rhododendrons, azaleas (a type of rhododendron), perennials, ferns, and
bonsai plants are for sale throughout the year in the plant sales pavilion next
to the gift shop.

The Pacific Rim Bonsai Collection is owned and operated by the
Weyerhaeuser Company, and is one of the finest public bonsai displays in North
America. The collection was opened in 1989 to honor the art and cultures of
the Pacific Rim nations where the company has maintained business relation-
ships for over 30 years.

Trail Layout   The gravel trails of the Rhododendron Species Botanical Garden are well drained, and often blanketed with fir needles. Benches, conve-
niently placed in cozy alcoves, invite visitors to stop and enjoy the
surroundings. The centrally located gazebo offers covered seating and is a
popular spot for garden weddings.

A graceful gazebo appears through the trees north of the Pond Garden.

The Pacific Rim Bonsai Collection is located in an impressive ivy-covered maze with raked gravel paths and frequent benches.

Human History The Rhododendron Species garden literally began in someone's backyard—actually several backyards in and around Eugene, Oregon. The Rhododendron Species Foundation, a nonprofit organization, was established in 1964 by an Oregon group of species *Rhododendron* enthusiasts.

In 1974, the Weyerhaeuser Company was approached about providing a home for the foundation's plants. George Weyerhaeuser thought it a great idea, and in 1974, the Company donated the use of a portion of its grounds. The company funded the clearing of the land and the construction of office space, greenhouse, access roads, and an irrigation system. The initial agreement was later recast as a lease on the land, with ownership of the facilities retained by the foundation. The gardens were first opened to the public on a limited basis in 1980.

Natural History The Rhododendron Species Botanical Garden is located in a mixed second-growth forest of Douglas-firs, western red cedars, western hemlocks, bigleaf maples, vine maples, Pacific dogwoods and Pacific madrones. Native shrubs include Oregon grape, salal, and huckleberry. Many stumps and nurse logs have been left to nourish plants. A collection of Japanese maples have been planted throughout the area, and display striking golden-orange foliage in the fall.

There are more than 800 species in the genus *Rhododendron,* including the Pacific rhododendron *(Rhododendron macrophyllum),* Washington's state flower. In this special place, you'll find giant rhododendrons the size of small trees, and tiny alpine shrubs with leaves the size of a child's fingernail. The rhododendrons featured here are all species that grow in the wild; the hybrid rhododendrons popular in local gardens are derived from these plants. Many of the plants look similar to the hybrid variety, and even unfamiliar-looking species display the distinctive rhododendron leaves. Most of the species are labeled by name, height, color, month of bloom, fragrance, habitat, altitude, and country of origin. Collections of ferns, heathers, magnolias, and carnivorous plants are also featured in the garden.

A favorite attraction is the Alpine Garden, where tiny rhododendrons that look more like groundcovers grow among 200 tons of granite boulders brought from the Cascade Mountains. This area simulates a natural mountain landscape, and features alpine plants from North and South America, Asia, Europe, and New Zealand.

The Pacific Rim Bonsai Collection features an astonishing outdoor maze with individual "rooms" that each feature tables with several bonsai plants, some hundreds of years old. Some trees have accompanying companion plants to indicate a sense of place or season, or as an artistic complement to the tree.

Individual signs describe the age of the specimen and how many years it has been "in training."

This incredible collection includes dwarfed yews, junipers, maples, larches, azaleas, Japanese black pines, bald cypresses, Engelmann spruces, olives, and a coast redwood. The trees' striking, graceful lines seek to convey large old trees in miniature. The fall foliage season is especially stunning. A foot-tall maple holds fall foliage of tiny orange and gold leaves; a larch lies surrounded by its fallen golden needles, and a crabapple supports dozens of cherry-size crabapples dripping from its branches. There is also a greenhouse that protects tropical bonsai plants.

Garden birds include resident black-capped and chestnut-backed chickadees, brown creepers, golden-crowned kinglets, and white-crowned sparrows. Rufous hummingbirds visit in spring and summer.

Nearby Park
Blue Heron Marsh

This wetlands area is a nesting area from late spring to early summer for great blue herons. The large nests can be seen in the tops of tall red alder trees, from near the parking lot (former trails in the marsh have been abandoned, since the herons were being disturbed). Call the Rainier Audubon Society (see Appendix B for phone number) for information on the site.

To reach Blue Heron Marsh from the Rhododendron Species Botanical Garden, come out the South 320th Street entrance and turn right. Go down the hill through Peasley Canyon, and turn right onto West Valley Freeway, then immediately turn right again into the small gravel parking lot at Blue Heron Marsh.

Vashon and Bainbridge Islands

31 • Vashon Island
Burton Acres

Highlights: Forest, saltwater shoreline on Quartermaster Harbor
Size: 68 acres; approximately 1 mile of trails
Ownership: Vashon Park District
Season: Best spring through fall
Terrain: Flat to gently sloping
Facilities: Restroom (open April to September), picnic tables and boat launch at parking lot; kayak rentals from June 1 to September 15 through Vashon Island Kayak Company (see Appendix B for phone numbers)
Hours: Dawn to dusk
Interpretive Programs: None
Wheelchair Accessibility: None
Pets: Leash and scoop
Horses: Yes
Bikes: Yes
Bus: Metro 118 (via Fauntleroy ferry), to Burton, several-mile walk to park
Driving Directions: From downtown Seattle, take the car ferry to Vashon Island. Once off the ferry, drive south on Vashon Highway Southwest to the town of Burton. Turn left (east) on Southwest Burton Drive, then take a right on 97th Avenue Southwest, which turns into Southwest Bayview Drive and encircles the Burton peninsula. Drive around to the northern side of the peninsula, and turn right into the park entrance and boat ramp area. The trailheads are across the road from the parking lot.

Park Overview   This is an endearing little forest, and the names of park areas on the Scout map at the trailhead support this feeling, with labels like Enchanted Forest, Willow Wild, Elfin Dell, and Ivy Land. The boat ramp at Jensens Point offers easy access to Quartermaster Harbor, a protected bay perfect for kayaking—during the summer you can rent kayaks here. Nearby Camp Burton runs a retreat center for nonprofit organizations.

Trail Layout   The Vashon-Maury Island Chamber of Commerce publishes a map of the island, which includes park, restaurant, store, and bed-and-breakfast information. Pick up a free copy at their office in downtown Vashon or at several island realties. Free maps showing all the parks on the island are available at the park district office in Ober Park.

The trails in the park start directly across from the boat ramp parking lot, or, if you walk up the road a half block, you will see a walker sign that leads to the trailhead where a park map and plant information are tacked to a plastic-covered kiosk. The flat to gently sloping dirt trails are muddy in the rainy season, and are also used by horses. (When approached by a horse, stand quietly by the side of the trail to let it pass.) A primitive amphitheater within the forest offers low log seats for a rest. The park is very quiet, with occasional local traffic noise from the peninsula road.

Human History This sleepy little peninsula has a long and varied history. The Suquamish Indians claimed all territory between Gig Harbor and the northern end of Bainbridge Island. A local branch, known as the Shomamish

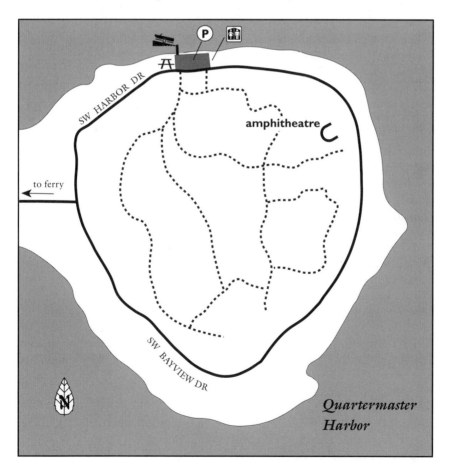

tribe, had longhouses on the shores of Quartermaster Harbor until the arrival of the white settlers. A Indian longhouse also stood on the south side of the Burton isthmus in 1850. Early natives lived on game, fish, clams, wild berries and roots. In the 1920s and 1930s, many agate and jasper arrowheads were found on the beaches of Quartermaster Harbor, and arrowheads and tools have been found near Judd Creek, which flows into the harbor just north of the peninsula. To the south of the park, Indian Point, south of Magnolia Beach, was used by the Indians to harvest and dry clams.

The first white settler on the Burton peninsula was Lars John Hansen, a Norwegian immigrant, who acquired a 138-acre homestead claim for ten dollars in 1869. Hansen lived on the north side of the peninsula at the mouth of Judd Creek, near the present-day town of Burton. He made his living through logging and farming. His wife was a native woman, Katie, whose mother Lumne-i, or Lemai as she was called, lived with the Hansens. Lemai had received $800 in gold pieces from the U.S. government for the sale of some land, and she kept the stash buried somewhere near the mouth of Judd Creek. One day, she was taken ill suddenly and died, without telling anyone where the gold was hidden. People used to see Hansen looking for the buried gold afterwards, but none was ever found.

The Burton area was home to many logging camps, with additional camps scattered around Quartermaster Harbor. Judd Creek had Burton's first sawmill, which supplied wood for homesteaders and the wood-burning engines of the many steamers that cruised the Sound. Before Puget Sound communities were linked by roads, Quartermaster Harbor occupied a crucial site between Seattle and Tacoma.

In the late 1800s, local farmers found that strawberries did well in the climate and poor soil of the island, and berry farming became a source of revenue. Shipping records from 1895 from two berry farmers on the Burton peninsula indicate crops of strawberries, raspberries, currants, gooseberries, and cherries.

Lucy Gerand, the last Indian princess of Vashon Island, and her husband Tom lived on a houseboat where the park boat ramp is located at Jensens Point. She died in the 1940s at the age of 100 and was buried in the Vashon cemetery.

In 1995, the Vashon Park District took on the management of twelve King County Parks on the island, including Burton Acres. Islanders supported a park levy to acquire the parks to have more local control, and community stewardship groups help develop a master plan for each park and determine the uses appropriate for each park environment.

Natural History A photograph taken around 1920 shows a view of the logged Burton peninsula covered with young trees about 20 to 30 years old, with some occasional tall conifers.

Lush vegetation carpets the ground beneath the peninsula's second-growth forest.

The current mixed coniferous and deciduous forest has large second-growth western red cedars, western hemlocks, Douglas-firs, bigleaf maples, red alders, hazelnuts, and Pacific yews. In these moist woods, large cedar nurse stumps are festooned with ferns, red huckleberry, vanilla leaf, and club moss. Some areas of the forest are more open, with shrubby wet meadows. Bracken ferns and native Pacific blackberry bushes grow in the open clearings, licorice ferns decorate bigleaf maples, and lady and sword ferns blanket the forest floor. Willow trees and salmonberry, thimbleberry, coast red elderberry, snowberry, wild rose, and stinging nettles form thickets in the moist areas of the park. Pacific madrone trees and Oregon grape, salal, red currant, ocean spray, and evergreen huckleberry shrubs are found on higher, drier ground. English ivy and holly represent invasive species.

Burton Acres harbors numerous species of forest birds, including resident spotted towhee, Bewick's wren, bushtit, black-capped chickadee, brown creeper, red-breasted sapsucker, northern flicker, American goldfinch, and red-breasted nuthatch. These species are joined in spring and summer by black-headed grosbeak, hermit thrush, and several species of sparrows, vireos, and warblers.

Resident pigeon guillemots and belted kingfishers breed in burrows in sand bluffs around Quartermaster Harbor, and Barrow's goldeneyes and black scoters winter in the harbor. Robinson Point on Maury Island to the east is known for good winter bird-watching: parasitic jaegers, loons, grebes, scoters, double-crested cormorants, and Eurasian wigeons are among the birds seen here. Mileta Creek Wildlife Refuge on Maury Island has one of the largest great blue heron rookeries in King county, and the birds are often seen on the shores of Quartermaster Harbor.

---

32 ◆ Bainbridge Island
The Grand Forest

Highlights: Forest, wetlands
Size: 240 acres; several miles of trails
Ownership: Bainbridge Island Parks and Recreation District
Season: Best spring through fall
Terrain: Flat to moderately sloping
Facilities: None
Hours: Dawn to dusk
Interpretive Programs: Available for groups (see Appendix B for phone number)
Wheelchair Accessibility: None
Pets: Leash and scoop
Horses: Yes
Bikes: Yes
Bus: Kitsap Transit (see Appendix B for phone number)
Driving Directions: Drive north from Winslow on State Highway 305 for almost 1 mile and turn left (west) on High School Road. Follow High School Road for about 2 miles until it comes to a T with Fletcher Bay Road. Turn right (north) on Fletcher Bay Road (which becomes Miller Road) and continue for 1.3 miles to the intersection with Tolo Road. Drive past the intersection and park on the right shoulder. There is also limited parking at the bend in Mandus Olson Road. Cyclists are encouraged and bike racks are planned.

Park Overview This peaceful forest of evergreen and deciduous trees lies in the middle of Bainbridge Island. The park also harbors a wetlands habitat. The combination of habitats supports a wide variety of plants and birds in this quiet refuge.

Trail Layout The three segments of the park are separated by private land. To cross from one segment to another, walk down Mandus Olson, Koura,

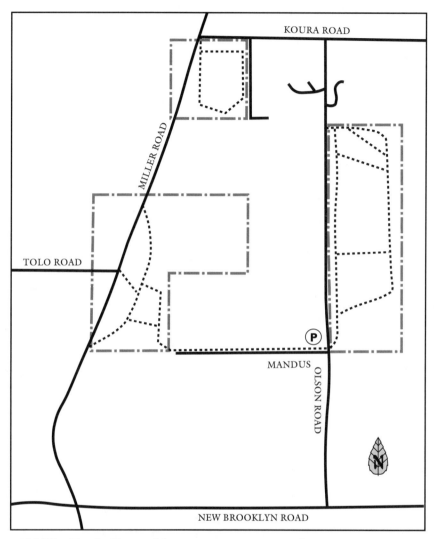

and Miller Roads. Be careful not to trespass across private property.

The flat, wide, dirt/gravel trails are shared with horses and their riders. (When approached by a horse, stand quietly by the side of the trail to let it pass.) In keeping with the equestrian use of the park, and to avoid the impact of heavy machinery, a bridge in the marsh area was put into place with a handsome team of Percheron horses.

Human History   Indians probably came to the Grand Forest land to hunt and gather berries, but typically lived along the shores of the island. When Washington became a state, a portion of each township was set aside to support the construction of public schools. These lands, owned and operated by

the state's Department of Natural Resources (DNR), were usually leased to timber companies, and the sale of the harvested timber generated state income for public schools. Since the Grand Forest area was always DNR-owned, no settlers ever homesteaded on park land. On the southeastern side of the island, just south of Winslow, the Port Blakely mill was in full swing in the late 1800s. Said to have been the largest lumber mill in the world at the time, it was a center for sawmills and shipbuilding.

The interior of the island began to have its timber harvested in the 1880s. Immigrant farmers (first Norwegians, and later Japanese), cleared the remaining stumps and developed the land for agriculture. Demand for produce from the community at Port Blakely fostered the island's agricultural development, and the island became known for its strawberries, vegetables, and flowers.

In 1989, a number of school trust lands, including The Grand Forest area, were reclassified as "transitional" lands and made available for purchase. Local residents, concerned about the possibility of a large-scale housing development that would destroy the forest, tried to have the designation changed, but their efforts failed. However, with the help of the Bainbridge Island Land Trust, the Park and Recreation District, state funding, and local volunteers, a 1991 bond issue overwhelmingly passed to save the land. The Grand Forest received its name in a contest sponsored by the Park District among local elementary school children.

Natural History   Issei Creek runs through the park, its name reflecting respect for the first-generation Japanese immigrants who settled on Bainbridge Island. Although coho salmon runs have been restored in the stream, they do not extend upstream as far as the park.

The forest is a mixed woods of deciduous and coniferous trees, consisting of red alders, bigleaf maples, western red cedars, western hemlocks, and Douglas-firs. Red-osier dogwood, cascara, filbert, Sitka spruce, seedling cherry, mountain ash, Indian plum, Pacific madrone, black cottonwood, and willow trees also grow here.

Salal and Oregon grape grow in drier sections of the park, and foxglove, fireweed, and Scot's broom thrive in clearings. Sword, lady, licorice, deer, wood, and bracken ferns are present in the park.

Shrubs include wild rose, snowberry, red huckleberry, blackcap, thimbleberry, salmonberry, dewberry, coast red elderberry, and evergreen and Himalayan blackberry. Flowering plants include trillium, stinging nettle, vanilla leaf, pearly everlasting, wild ginger, red willow-herb, bedstraw, large-leaved avens, yellow parentucellia, false Solomon's seal, and foamflower.

Wetland plants include open water plants such as duckweed, and marsh plants like marsh speedwell, cattails, sedges, and common rush. Wet meadow

The rustic bridge in the western section of The Grand Forest was constructed using French draft horses.

areas contain creeping buttercup, reed canary grass, bulrushes, sedges, rushes, horsetails, and yellow monkeyflower; and shrub-scrub wetlands have stands of hardhack. Forested wetlands hold skunk cabbage, and cranberry grows in bog areas.

Animals in the park include black-tailed deer, coyotes, Douglas squirrels, mice, mink, opossums, rabbits, raccoons, red foxes, shrews, spotted skunks, Townsend's chipmunks, voles, and river otters. Frogs, tree toads, garter snakes, and salamanders comprise the amphibian population.

The combination of forest and marsh habitats, combined with the proximity to the waters of Puget Sound, brings many different types of birds to The Grand Forest. Resident forest birds include band-tailed pigeon, dark-eyed junco, black-capped chickadee, American goldfinch, bushtit, cedar waxwing, wren, golden-crowned kinglet, purple finch, Hutton's vireo, yellow-rumped warbler, pine siskin, red-breasted nuthatch, spotted towhee, varied thrush, song and white-crowned sparrows, and several species of woodpeckers. In the spring and summer, add Swainson's thrushes, warbling vireos, Bullock's orioles, rufous hummingbirds, western tanagers, and several species of warblers, flycatchers, swallows, and grosbeaks. Fall and winter bring ruby-crowned kinglets, and fox and golden-crowned sparrows.

Ruffed grouse, ring-necked pheasant, and California quail find shelter in fields, while predators like red-tailed hawks, great horned owls and bald eagles hunt in the park. In the marsh area, look for resident belted kingfishers, hooded mergansers, wood ducks, Virginia rails, common snipes, marsh wrens, red-winged blackbirds, and green and great blue herons. Buffleheads winter in the park, while spring and summer bring common yellowthroats.

---

33 ◆ Bainbridge Island
Bloedel Reserve

Highlights: Carefully landscaped gardens, meadows and ponds within a natural forest setting; spectacular view of Puget Sound and the Cascade Mountains.

Size: 165 acres; several miles of trails

Ownership: The Arbor Fund

Season: Year-round

Terrain: Flat to moderately sloping

Facilities: Restrooms and water fountain at visitor center and gatehouse

Hours: Admittance by reservation only (call to reserve) and limited to 200 visitors daily; open 10 A.M. to 4 P.M., Wednesday through Sunday (closed federal holidays)

Fees: Admission fee, senior discount (65 and over), children under 5 free; annual memberships available

Wheelchair Accessibility: Paved service roads offer good accessibility to many areas; two free wheelchairs available (call to reserve)

Interpretive Programs: Free maps; excellent booklets on the birds and trees of the reserve available for a small charge

Pets: No (guide dogs allowed)

Horses: No

Bikes: No

Bus: Kitsap Transit (see Appendix B for phone number)

Driving Directions: From downtown Seattle, take the Bainbridge Island ferry to the town of Winslow. Drive straight out of town from the Winslow ferry dock, heading north on Highway 305. Just before the Agate Pass Bridge, take a right on Northeast Agatewood Road. The reserve is at the end of the road before it bears to the left and turns into Agate Point Road.

Park Overview   On this marvelous estate, it is easy to pretend that you are a guest of the owners, with free rein to wander about its lovely gardens, forests, wetlands and ponds. This former private home on the northeast shore of Bainbridge Island, now a nonprofit reserve, encourages such fantasies. Allow at least two hours to visit the grounds.

Summer offers the lushness of the forest and blooming wildflowers. Autumn brings one of the most spectacular color displays in the region, with oranges, reds and golds, from the foliage of both native and non-native trees. In winter, the park is beautiful with a dusting of snow on the evergreen trees and shrubs; musicians often play at the visitor center during the holiday season. In spring, cherry blossoms, rhododendrons, and jonquils fill the air with fragrance.

The visitor center, a former residence, is flanked by stately imported trees.

Note: There is no food service or picnicking allowed. This rule is strictly enforced.

Trail Layout   Manicured paths and casual trails lead you in a loosely choreographed sequence of landscapes. You can either study the plants or simply enjoy whatever portion of the grounds you feel like visiting. The reserve's bridges and boardwalks are stunning in their grace and simplicity. The grounds are quiet, with occasional distant traffic noise from the highway that is well masked by birdsong.

Human History   Suquamish Indians once lived in the area where the reserve is now located. In 1827, a Hudson Bay Company man recorded a stop at a Suquamish village, looking for Chief Seattle. The site was described as a beautiful sandy beach with groves of huge cedar trees lining the edges of a dry marsh and estuary. From the location description, the village was probably a temporary summer camp located at the mouth of the stream running through the reserve property.

In 1855, the Point Elliott Treaty set up the nearby Port Madison Indian Reservation, with land on Bainbridge Island outside the reservation deeded to the U.S. government. In 1862, a large tract of land (now the southeastern part of the reserve) was purchased by George Meigs, and the revenue from this sale was probably used to set up the new Territorial University (that later became the University of Washington). Meigs harvested the timber, which was processed at his mill at Port Madison and shipped to Seattle, where it was used to erect the first university building.

After her husband's death in 1903, Angela Collins bought much of what is now the reserve land in 1906 for a summer and weekend retreat. During the early part of the twentieth century, she described Port Madison Bay as being filled with the black canoes of Haida Indians visiting from the north. In 1931, Mrs. Collins's eighteenth-century French country style house was completed (an especially impressive undertaking, since all the surrounding houses were small log and frame summer cabins).

After Mrs. Collins's death, the land was bought in 1950 by Prentice and Virginia Bloedel, who renamed the Collinswood estate Agate Point Farm. Bloedel and his wife both came from prominent timber families. Bloedel entered the family business, but he also had an innate sense of connection to the land and felt a responsibility to conserve and protect it for future generations. Although he incorporated ideas from famous landscape designers, his aim was to reinforce the natural qualities of the reserve.

In 1970, concerned that the reserve might not survive as a private entity, the Bloedels deeded the property to the University of Washington, and placed restriction on its maintenance and use. In 1974, they established the Arbor Fund, a nonprofit foundation, and an endowment was created to assure maintenance of the Bloedel Reserve. In 1985, the mansion was converted into

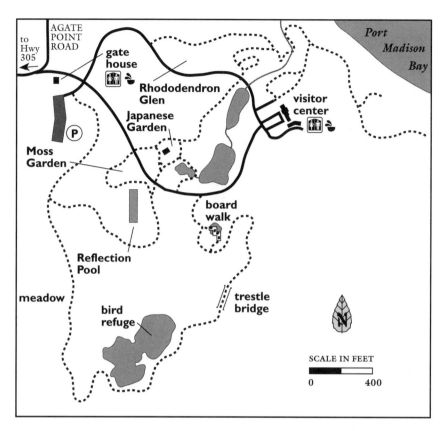

the visitor center. Recognizing the property's limited use to the University, the Arbor Fund bought the Bloedel Reserve back from the university in 1986, dedicating it for the public's enjoyment.

Natural History   About 100 acres of the reserve consist of a second-growth forest of good-sized western red cedars, western hemlocks, Douglas-firs, grand firs, red alders, Oregon white oaks, Pacific yews, cascaras, Pacific dogwoods, madrones, and vine and bigleaf maples. Native shrubs and herbaceous plants include Oregon grape, salal, trillium, salmonberry, rhododendron, skunk cabbage, and ferns. Dead snags show the work of pileated woodpeckers, and old logged stumps demonstrate the size of the old trees.

The rest of the land has been subtly sculpted into gardens, meadows, ponds, and wildlife habitat. The combination of native forest and landscaping is effective; the wilderness of the forest is respected here. The Reserve is a labor of love, the Bloedels' big—very big—backyard. Plants were chosen for their color, texture, and size under the artistic supervision of landscape designers schooled in European and Asian landscape traditions, so plants from all over the world blend with native species.

The plantings in the bird refuge, a man-made pond with islands, were designed to provide food and cover for birds, and include vine maples, native rhododendrons, cattail, red alders, willows, horsetail, native sedges, ferns, blood currants, western azaleas, red-osier dogwoods, Indian plums, hardhack spirea, and moosewood viburnum. Nearby is a beautiful trestle bridge and a boardwalk that crosses through a wooded wetland of conifers, red alders, and skunk cabbage.

Weeping willow, Japanese maple, English elm, Chinese magnolia, Chinese dogwood, empress tree, Katsura tree, Portuguese laurel, parrot tree, Camperdown elm, beech, cypress, American chestnut, and flowering cherries are among the non-native trees near the visitor center. The Rhododendron Glen holds both species and hybrid varieties (best viewed in April and May), including some of Mrs. Collins' original plants. Other plants in this moist glen include Japanese maples, white-flowering hydrangeas, ferns, trillium, lungworts, azaleas, native wild ginger, primula, and the largest display of hardy cyclamen in the Pacific Northwest.

The Japanese Garden was designed in 1956 by Fujitaro Kubota, a local Seattle landscaper. A stone and raked-sand garden lies on one side of the guesthouse, which combines elements of both a Japanese temple and a Northwest Coast Indian longhouse. The house is built of western red cedar and Douglas-fir, with a deck of Alaska yellow cedar. Plantings include pine, dogwood, Japanese maple, blue Atlas Cedar, Katsura, and cherry trees.

Nearby, in the Moss Garden, native huckleberries rise from nurse stumps, ferns abound, and tall alder stumps offer material for woodpeckers. Vine maple, red alder and large-leaved Hercule's walking stick trees provide additional summer shade for the moss that carpets the ground. The startling Reflection Pool was inspired by Finnish and English canal ponds, and is fed by a natural spring. Irish yew hedges surrounded the long, rectangular pool with nearby paper birches, camellias, trillium, anemones, oxalis, violets, and bluebells.

The varied habitats and abundance of plants attract dozens of species of birds. Pinioned trumpeter and tundra swans grace the ponds. Native waterfowl include American wigeons, buffleheads, and wood ducks. Red-winged blackbirds, great blue herons, and belted kingfishers are among the birds in the marsh. Raptors in the reserve include bald eagles, ospreys, and sharp-shinned hawks.

Forest and thicket birds include band-tailed pigeons, rufous hummingbirds, northern flickers, flycatchers, bushtits, swallows, brown creepers, red-breasted nuthatches, cedar waxwings, American goldfinches, pine siskins, spotted towhees, warblers, Swainson's and varied thrushes, golden- and ruby-crowned kinglets, Bewick's and winter wrens, black-capped and chestnut-backed chickadees, purple and house finches, pileated and hairy woodpeckers, and several varieties of sparrows.

Part III
Plants and Animals

This book is not a field guide to animals and plants, so only general information is provided. Readers are encouraged to obtain a good field guide with detailed drawings or photographs (see Appendix A).

Plants

The following section lists the general characteristics, habitat, and uses by indigenous peoples for the more common plants found in local parks.

Trees

Alder, Red *(Alnus rubra)*

Native deciduous tree. The most abundant tree in the area, the red alder grows where fire, logging, or other disturbances have opened up the forest. It prefers moist woods and damp bottomlands along streams and lakes. The roots of the red alder contain symbiotic bacteria that convert nitrogen from the atmosphere into a form useful to plants; so not only can alders grow in poor soil, they improve it for later trees. Red alders are susceptible to heart rot, a fungus disease, and they begin to die after about sixty years.

Red alders are identified by their toothed oval leaves; smooth, light gray bark mottled with lichens; and the showy yellow catkins, or male flowers, that hang down from branches in early spring. The buds and seeds are eaten by birds, while the twigs and leaves are food for beaver, deer, and rabbits. Various Northwest Indian tribes used alder wood for utensils, furniture, masks, and to smoke fish. The bark was used as a dye, a cure for rheumatic fever and tuberculosis, and as an antibiotic for wounds.

Ash, Oregon *(Fraxinus latifolia)*

Native deciduous tree. This tall slender tree grows on riverbanks and lakeshores and in moist bottomlands. Despite its wet habitat, it is resistant to wind, due to a massive spreading root system. The tree's compound leaves consist of five to seven leaflets which turn golden in fall, and its mature bark is closely furrowed and appears cross-hatched. The winged fruits resemble canoe paddles, and are eaten by birds and mammals. Various Northwest Indian tribes used the tree for canoe paddles and digging sticks, and the bark was boiled and drunk for worms.

Cascara *(Rhamnus purshiana)*

Native deciduous tree. This small tree has dark green, finely toothed oval leaves that have a washboard surface and turn yellow in the fall. It grows in fairly dry to wet, often shady sites in mixed forests, and its blue-black berries are eaten by ruffed grouse, raccoons and other animals. The smooth, gray bitter bark of cascara trees is the active ingredient in most commercial laxatives, and has been harvested for over a hundred years. Various Northwest tribes ate the berries, and boiled the dried bark and drank it as a laxative and to relieve heart strain and dysentery. The liquid was also used topically for washing sores and swellings, and as a green dye.

Sprays of flattened leaves give the western red cedar a graceful appearance.

Cedar, Western Red *(Thuja plicata)*

Native coniferous tree. It is found in stream ravines, on bottomlands, and on moist hillsides. Western red cedar is less shade-tolerant than the region's other climax species, western hemlock, but lives much longer (up to 1,000 years) and can grow in soils that are too wet for hemlock. This tree is identified by its peeling reddish bark, wide base, and sprays of flat, overlapping, scale-like leaves.

Cedar was the most important tree in the economy of the Northwest Coast tribes. Cedar wood was used for house posts and siding, roofing planks,

169

canoes, totem poles, boxes, cradles, and other household items. Its fibrous bark was shredded and woven into napkins, towels, blankets, fishing nets, sails, and clothing. Unwoven strips were plaited to make bowls, plates, and mats, and its roots used to weave baskets. Various parts of the tree were also used for medicinal purposes, including remedies for colds, tuberculosis, toothache, kidney trouble, fever, and sores.

Cherry, Bitter *(Prunus emarginata)*

Native deciduous tree. This small, slender tree grows in moist forests, near streams, and in disturbed areas. Its smooth, dark reddish or grayish brown bark is marked by rougher, darker horizontal rings; these pores, called lenticels, permit the passage of air into the trunk. The highly astringent bright red berries are eaten by birds, especially cedar waxwings. Various Northwest tribes used the bark for basketry, and for wrapping the joints of harpoons and arrows. The bark was chewed to facilitate childbirth, or boiled and drunk as a laxative.

Cottonwood, Black *(Populus trichocarpa)*

Native deciduous tree. The tallest and most massive deciduous tree in the Northwest, the cottonwood grows in rich, wet bottomland soils near lakes and streams. Its distinctive heart-shaped leaves turn bright yellow in fall. In the spring, males produce dangling catkins, while females form seed pods which release millions of tiny seeds borne on cottony tufts. Great blue herons, bald eagles and ospreys nest in the tops of cottonwoods; woodpeckers, great horned owls, wood ducks, flying squirrels, raccoons and songbirds nest in their trunks; and beavers use them for food and building materials. Various Northwest tribes used the wood for posts and sweat lodges, the bark for temporary house coverings, and the leaves as an antiseptic for cuts. They used gum from the buds as a remedy for baldness, sore throats, whooping cough, and tuberculosis, as glue for arrowheads, and as a paint ingredient.

Crabapple, Pacific *(Pyrus fusca)*

Native deciduous tree. This small tree, also called the Oregon or western crabapple, prefers the mucky soil of bottomlands, moist forests, thickets, swamps, and streambanks. Its lovely whitish-pink blossoms are followed by tiny, oblong, dark yellow crabapples, which are eaten by ruffed grouse, pheasants, purple finches, deer, elk, and bears. The egg-shaped leaves turn yellow to red in the fall, and the bark contains dangerous cyanide-producing compounds. Various Northwest tribes ate the fruit, and used the strong wood for the prongs of seal spears, and for wedges to split western red cedar. The bark was peeled, soaked in water, and drunk for intestinal disorders, gonorrhea, and lung troubles, or used as a wash for cuts or eyes.

Dogwood, Pacific *(Cornus nutallii)*

Native deciduous tree. This common understory tree can survive in the moist shade of mixed forests, since it can carry out photosynthesis with very little sunlight. Large white "flowers" appear in spring. These are actually bracts (modified leaves) that surround a central cluster of small green flowers to attract insects. Certain butterfly larvae feed on dogwood leaves, and the clusters of orange-red berries are eaten by band-tailed pigeons, flickers, and pileated woodpeckers. The leaves turn orange, red, and purple in the fall. Various Northwest tribes boiled the bark for a brown dye, and used it medicinally as a laxative, a blood purifier, a lung strengthener, and a tonic. In the nineteenth century, they substituted it for quinine to treat malaria. Wood was used for harpoon shafts and gaming pieces.

Douglas-fir *(Pseudotsuga menziesii)*

Native coniferous tree. This misnamed member of the pine family has long puzzled plant classifiers. It is often the first conifer to invade burned or

Douglas-firs display distinctive cones.

The small cones of a western hemlock are less than an inch long.

logged areas, since it requires fire and bare mineral soil to germinate. Intolerant of shade, it grows quickly to keep ahead of the other trees, and can survive a wide range of climatic conditions. Most large Douglas-firs have survived numerous fires, thanks to their thick, corky bark. The needles radiate from all sides of the twigs, and the distinctive cones have three-pronged bracts that protrude from between the woody scales, resembling the back half of a hiding mouse.

The Douglas-fir supports other forms of forest life. Mosses, ferns and lichens grow in moist crevices in its trunk, and bees are attracted by its flowers. Other insects feed on the bark, wood, and leaves, and provide food for birds. Squirrels, chipmunks and mice eat the seeds. Various Northwest tribes used the wood for firewood, and as shafts for spears and harpoons. Fir pitch was put on sores; the buds were chewed to relieve sore throat or mouth sores, and the pitch, bark, or needles were boiled into a tea as a cold remedy.

Hemlock, Western *(Tsuga heterophylla)*

Native coniferous tree. This tree can grow even in deep shade, so its seedlings are usually the most common ones in shady forests. Needing moisture, seedlings commonly sprout from moist stumps and logs. Over time, western hemlocks will replace the other dominant trees in a forest, and live 300 to 400 years. The needles are short, flat, stubby, and loosely arranged in two ranks on opposite sides of a twig, with two white lines on their undersides. The cones have papery scales and are less than an inch long. Various Northwest tribes used the bark as a dye or paint for tanning hides, as storage containers, and to line cooking pits. The pitch was used as facepaint and to prevent chapping or sunburn, or put on the hair to remove vermin. The bark was boiled and the liquid consumed as a laxative and as a treatment for hemorrhages, syphilis, tuberculosis, and sore throat. The liquid was also used topically as a wash for sores or eyes.

Holly, English *(Ilex aquifolium)*

Non-native tree. Birds dispersed the seeds of this Eurasian plant after eating the red berries from imported ornamentals, and now it grows widely in parks throughout the area. The berries should not be eaten.

Madrone, Pacific *(Arbutus menziesii)*

Native evergreen broadleaf tree. This distinctive broadleaf tree, also known as a madrona, has thick, shiny evergreen leaves, reddish peeling bark, and clusters of red berries enjoyed by birds like cedar waxwings. Madrones prefer dry,

A close-up reveals the distinctive bark of the Pacific madrone.

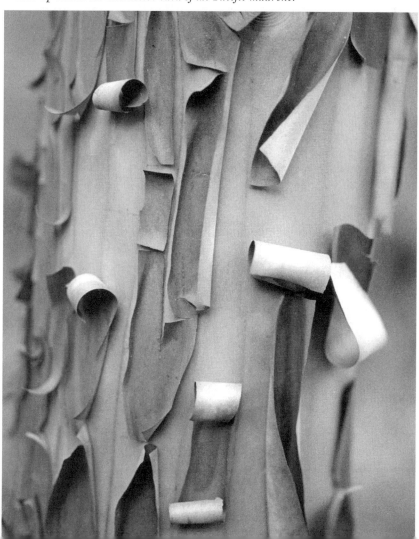

well-drained soils or otherwise poor soils where competition with conifers is reduced. They often have a canker fungus, which girdles year-old stems and kills them, as indicated by black or purplish areas on the bark. Various Northwest tribes ate the berries, boiled the leaves, barks or roots as a remedy for a cold, sore throat, or ulcerated stomach, and made spoons from the bulbous roots.

Maple, Bigleaf *(Acer macrophyllum)*

Native deciduous tree. These maples grow easily in rich bottomland soils and disturbed sites such as logged areas. Their huge leaves are an adaptation to shade—a few large leaves are able to intersect as much light as smaller leaves of comparable surface area, with less energy required to produce them. The smooth trunks are usually padded with moss and festooned with growths of licorice ferns. Burls are large growths whose origin is a mystery but don't appear to harm the tree, and result in a beautiful, swirly wood grain that makes specimens prized for carving. Eastern gray squirrels eat the seeds. Various Northwest tribes used bigleaf maple wood for carvings, dishes, cooking utensils, paddles, and other implements, and to smoke salmon. The bark was woven into rope, and boiled and drunk as a tuberculosis remedy, and the leaves used to cover food during cleaning, cooking, and storage.

Maple, Vine *(Acer circinatum)*

Native deciduous tree. This small tree is one of the few plants that grows well either in deep shade or full sun. Its elegantly contorted branches and flattened sprays of leaves angle to receive maximum sunlight. In October, the leaves turn a variety of colors: usually, those growing beneath the forest canopy turn pale yellow, while those in the open turn fiery shades of red and orange. Various Northwest tribes wove its shoots into open baskets for carrying clams and fish, and also used the wood for firewood, for building fish traps, tongs, and baby swings, and for securing planks on roofs.

Willow *(Salix sp.)*

Native deciduous tree. There are thirty different kinds of willows growing in Washington—while they are easy to distinguish from other trees, individual species can be difficult to identify. Three common species are Pacific, Piper's, and Scouler's willows. Willows require damp, poorly drained soils, near streambanks and lakeshores, where they help to stabilize the banks. Various Northwest tribes used willow bark in basketry and string-making, and made willow-bark tonics to treat headache, fever, sore throat, and other ailments. Acetylsalicylic acid, or aspirin, is a derivative of salicin, the active ingredient in willow leaves and bark.

Yew, Pacific *(Taxus brevifolia)*

Native coniferous tree. Also known as western yew, this tree grows in moist, shady forests. Its flat shiny needles resemble those of western hemlock. It has scaly reddish bark, and instead of a seed cone it produces a single seed surrounded by a bright red, fleshy cup that is poisonous to humans but attractive to birds. Various Northwest tribes prized the tough durable wood,

A Pacific yew displays its distinctive shiny needles.

and used it for bows, arrows, paddles, harpoon shafts, clubs, and many types of household utensils. They smoked dried yew needles. The leaves were used medicinally: they were boiled and consumed to relieve internal injuries, or were chewed and spat on wounds. A potent anti-cancer drug, taxol, has been identified in the bark and other parts of this slow-growing yew.

Shrubs

Blackberry, Evergreen *(Rubus laciniatus)*

Non-native evergreen shrub. This aggressive member of the rose family, introduced from Europe, occurs in dense thickets in open fields and woods, and along streambanks. This plant keeps its leaves through winter, hence, its name.

Blackberry, Himalayan *(Rubus discolor)*

Non-native evergreen/deciduous shrub. This member of the rose family came to the region from India via England and is the most common introduced blackberry in the area. It grows in open fields and woods, and along streambanks, crowding out native species but providing shelter and food for wildlife. This plant often keeps its leaves in winter.

Blackberry, Pacific *(Rubus ursinus)*

Native deciduous shrub. Also known as trailing blackberry or dewberry. This member of the rose family produces smaller fruit than the introduced species, and was used to develop other berries such as loganberries and boysenberries. It grows in open forests, and is often a pioneer species in logged or burned areas. Various Northwest tribes used fresh or dried berries for food. Tea was made from dried leaves, and leaves and roots were used to treat diarrhea, dysentery, cholera, excessive menstruation, fevers, hemorrhoids, and mouth sores.

Broom, Scot's *(Cytisus scoparius)*

Non-native deciduous shrub. This invasive plant bears yellow flowers and grows in meadows, open forests, and disturbed areas. The seeds are spread explosively from their pods, and are also carried away by ants. A member of the legume or pea family, its roots host bacteria that help enrich the soil. This plant contains several toxic alkaloids that can depress the heart and nervous system; children may be poisoned by eating the pods and pea-like seeds.

Currant, Red-flowering *(Ribes sanguineum)*

Native deciduous shrub. The lovely pink flowers are favored by hummingbirds, and its sparse, round, blue-black berries are considered unpalatable. The plant is found in dry open woods and disturbed sites, such as logged areas. The berries were eaten fresh by some Northwest tribes, but were not highly regarded.

Currant, Stink *(Ribes bracteosum)*

Native deciduous shrub. This tall rangy shrub has very large, maple-leaf-shaped leaves, inconspicuous greenish-white flowers, and rough blue-black berries that are generally unpalatable, though birds enjoy them. Named for the skunky odor of its leaves, this plant is common in moist-to-wet shady places in woods, and on streambanks, floodplains and shorelines. Various Northwest tribes ate the bland berries with grease or oil when fresh to avoid constipation or stomach cramps. The stems were used as tubes to inflate seal paunches used as oil containers; the leaves were used to line and cover hemlock bark containers; and a medicine was made of the bark.

Devil's Club *(Oplopanax horridum)*

Native deciduous shrub. This spiny plant has large, maple-leaf-shaped leaves. Its bright red, shiny berries in showy pyramidal clusters are relished by bears. An indicator of water at or just below the surface, it grows in moist woods and on streambanks. Contact with its spines may cause allergic reactions. This important medicinal plant is related to ginseng. Various Northwest tribes used its roots and inner bark to treat ailments including arthritis, ulcers, tuberculosis, and diabetes; to ward off evil influences; and to make fishing lures. The berries were rubbed in the scalp to combat lice and dandruff and to make hair shiny.

Dogwood, Red-osier or Creek *(Cornus stolonifera)*

Native deciduous shrub. This common shrub often forms nearly impenetrable thickets within shrub-scrub wetlands. It has flat-topped clusters of small greenish-white flowers and small, round, bluish-white fruits that make a good food for songbirds, especially cedar waxwings. The leaves turn a brilliant orange and red in the fall, and this shrub is an extremely important winter food for deer and elk. Various Northwest tribes used the stems for basket rims, salmon spreaders, and barbecue racks; the bark and twigs were used in a variety of medicinal preparations.

Elderberry, Coast Red *(Sambucus racemosa)*

Native deciduous shrub. This tall shrub produces plumes of creamy white flowers in early spring, and its dense clusters of scarlet berries are eaten by band-tailed pigeons, ruffed grouse, and cedar waxwings. One of the most common shrubs in forested wetlands, it indicates moisture, and is also found along streambanks, in swampy thickets, and in moist clearings. The stems, bark, leaves, and roots are toxic due to the presence of cyanide-producing glycosides. Since the leaves contain tannin, they are said to provide relief for contact with stinging nettle or poison oak. The plant's berries were an important food for various Northwest tribes; since raw berries can cause nausea, they were steamed or dried, then usually eaten in winter. The fresh leaves were pounded to treat abscesses and boils, or put on sore joints to reduce swelling.

Gooseberry, Black or Swamp *(Ribes lacustre)*

Native deciduous shrub. The stems of this gooseberry are covered by a mixture of small and large spines. Because of these prickles, the plant was thought by Indians to have special protective powers for warding off evil influences. Contact with the prickles may cause allergic reactions in some people. The plant grows in moist forests and thickets, and on streambanks. Its dark purple berries are hairy and edible. Various Northwest tribes peeled off the bark and boiled it into a tea that was drunk during childbirth. The liquid was also used as a wash for sore eyes, or to soothe general body aches.

Gooseberry, Wild or Straggly *(Ribes divaricatum)*

Native deciduous shrub. This tall shrub has maple-leaf-shaped leaves on arched stems, with spines at the stem joints that cause allergic reactions in some people. Its smooth, dark purple berries are edible and relished by birds, while deer enjoy the foliage. It grows in moist open forests and streambanks, but also in drier open forests and clearings. The berries were eaten fresh by various Northwest tribes or baked in cakes; the bark was soaked for an eye wash; and the thorns used for tattooing.

Grape, Low Oregon *(Berberis nervosa)*

Native evergreen shrub. This plant flourishes in second-growth Douglas-fir forests, so it is very common in the Puget Sound area. Each leaf is made up of nine to twenty-one holly-shaped leaflets arranged in pairs along the stem, with a single leaflet at the tip. These shiny leathery leaflets are designed to retard water loss, enabling the plant to grow in dry forest sites. Oregon grape has beautiful yellow flowers and large clusters of edible blue berries, eaten by birds, squirrels, chipmunks, and other small animals. Various Northwest tribes ate the tart berries raw or cooked, sometimes mixed with those of salal or other fruit. The shredded bark of the stems and roots was used to make a bright yellow dye for baskets. The bark and berries were used medicinally to treat ailments including sores, coughs, liver disease, and eye problems.

Oregon grape shrubs display clumps of berries popular among wildlife.

Grape, Tall Oregon *(Berberis aquifolium)*

Native evergreen shrub. This shrub is similar to low Oregon grape, but leaflets are shinier and fewer, with only five to eleven leaflets per stem. *Aquifolium* is usually taller than *nervosa* (as its common name suggests), and is found in dry, sunny spots, such as in clearings and along roadsides.

Hardhack *(Spiraea douglasii)*

Native deciduous shrub. This tall member of the rose family can form almost impenetrable thickets, through which early settlers found it "hard to hack." In late summer, its showy pink plumes of flowers turn to brown seed clusters present year-round. This shrub is found in standing water in wet meadows, bogs and shrub-scrub wetlands. A favorite nesting site of yellowthroats and Virginia rails, Northwest tribes used hardhack stems for roasting salmon and clams. Tea made from the seeds was a treatment for diarrhea. Salicylic acid (aspirin) was first isolated from a *Spiraea*.

Hazelnut, California *(Corylus cornuta* variety *californica)*

Native deciduous shrub. This member of the birch family is common in local forests, shady openings, thickets or clearings, where it prefers moist but well-drained soils. In late winter, before the soft, serrated oval leaves appear, look for distinctive clusters of male flowers that hang in yellow-green catkins. Female flowers develop into pairs of nuts sheathed in light-green bracts (modified leaves) which extend to form a fringed tube. The small nuts, related to commercial filberts, are savored by eastern gray squirrels, Douglas squirrels, chipmunks, mice, Steller's jays, and crows. Various Northwest tribes ate the nuts fresh or stored, and used them in trade (Lewis and Clark bargained for them). The long, flexible twigs were also twisted into rope.

Honeysuckle, Orange *(Lonicera ciliosa)*

Native deciduous shrub. This vine climbs over other shrubs and up into trees, and prefers sunny places in brushy areas and at the edges of woods. The orange tubular flowers are pollinated during the day by hummingbirds, and the red-to-orange berries are eaten by many species of birds, but are inedible to humans. Various Northwest tribes boiled the leaves as a tea for tuberculosis or as a strengthening tonic, or put chewed leaves on bruises.

Huckleberry, Evergreen *(Vaccinium ovatum)*

Native evergreen shrub. This member of the heath family features small, shiny, year-round dark green leaves, with light pink, bell-shaped flowers and deep purplish-black berries. This plant is less common around Seattle than red huckleberry, as it prefers somewhat drier conditions than typically exist in the forests in and around Seattle. It grows at the edges of drier coniferous forests, and near saltwater shorelines. The berries were prized by coastal Indians from northern California to British Columbia and were eaten fresh, often with oil, or dried into cakes.

Huckleberry, Red *(Vaccinium parvifolium)*

Native deciduous shrub. One of the Puget Sound region's most common forest shrubs, this lacy, bright-green plant often grows atop logs and

The California hazelnut shrub is a member of the birch family.

stumps in moist coniferous forests. Its distinctive, square green twigs contain chlorophyll, and enable the plant to capture additional sunlight for use in photosynthesis. Its bright red berries are popular with birds (whose seed-filled droppings distribute seeds on top of stumps), squirrels, chipmunks, and bears. Deer browse its foliage. Various Northwest tribes prized the berries, gathering them from the shrubs with combs. They either dried the berries singly, like raisins, mashed and dried them into cakes for winter use, mixed them with other berries such as salal, or stored them soaked in grease and oil. The watery juice was drunk as a beverage to stimulate the appetite or as a mouthwash, the leaves used for tea, and the bark boiled for a cold remedy.

Indian plum *(Oemleria cerasiformis)*
Native deciduous shrub. Also known as osoberry, this common shrub is found in open, moist coniferous forests, thickets, streambanks, and roadsides. In late February and early March, distinctive clusters of hanging white flowers appear, usually before the leaves. Their rank odor attracts flies and other insects that pollinate the blossoms. The clusters of orange berries ripen to purple, plum-like fruits and are a favorite among birds and small rodents. Various Northwest tribes ate the berries fresh, mainly as a traveling snack or starvation food. The twigs were chewed and applied to sores, and a tea made from the bark was used as a purgative and tonic.

Labrador Tea *(Ledum groendlandicum)*
Native evergreen shrub. This low spindly member of the heath family indicates wet, usually very acidic and nutrient-poor soil, and is common in conifer swamps and bogs. Whorls of droopy, rolled leathery leaves with dense rusty hairs underneath are distinctive, along with white clusters of flowers. Various Northwest tribes made a tea from the leaves which served as a beverage, a laxative, or a treatment for colds, sore throats, and rheumatism. Because the plant contains the toxic compound ledol, it is not recommended that you steep your own tea.

Laurel, Swamp *(Kalmia occidentalis)*
Native evergreen shrub. This shrub has small, glossy, dark green leaves and saucer-shaped pink blossoms. At the slightest touch by an insect probing for nectar, the stamens pop out and dust the insect with pollen. Swamp laurel grows only in acidic bogs and wet meadows. The leaves and flowers contain a substance poisonous to sheep and cattle. When ingested, swamp laurel lowers blood pressure, and causes breathing problems, dizziness, cramps, vomiting, and diarrhea. The Tlingit Indians washed in a liquid of boiled swamp laurel to treat skin ailments.

Ninebark, Pacific *(Physocarpus capitatus)*
Native deciduous shrub. This tall member of the rose family has maple-leaf-shaped leaves, rounded white flower clusters, and edible maroon berries. The name comes from the papery bark which peels on older branches—the main branch was believed to have at least nine layers of bark. Ninebark prefers wet, somewhat open places like streamside thickets, the edges of moist woods, coastal marshes, meadows, lakeshores and streambanks (wooded wetland communities). Various Northwest tribes used the young peeled shoots as an emetic, as a laxative, and for gonorrhea.

Ocean Spray *(Holodiscus discolor)*
Native deciduous shrub. This common plant, also known as creambush, has droopy plumes of hundreds of creamy white flowers that die and persist on the bush as brown sprays. The plant is common in well-drained, dry to moist, open forests, thickets, and clearings. It often grows with salal and is browsed by deer and elk. Called ironwood, or arrow-wood, its hard, strong wood was valued by various Northwest tribes who used it to make

a variety of tools, including canoe paddles, roasting tongs, bows, arrow shafts, digging sticks, and spear and harpoon shafts. They also steeped the fruiting clusters in boiling water to make a tea for diarrhea, measles, and chickenpox, applied the leaves to sore feet and lips, and made an eyewash from the inner bark.

Rhododendron, Pacific *(Rhododendron macrophyllum)*

Native evergreen shrub. This member of the heath family is the state flower of Washington, with large, showy clusters of pink flowers. It grows in moist to fairly dry, open, coniferous or mixed forests. This native rhododendron is found on the coast, on Whidbey Island, at higher elevations on the west side of the Cascades, and in certain areas around Hood Canal and Puget Sound. All parts of the plant are poisonous: chemicals in its leaves, when dissolved in water, will kill the seeds of other plants. This is why few plants grow underneath rhododendrons. Various Northwest tribes boiled the buds into a tea for colds and sore throats, chewed and swallowed the buds for ulcerated stomachs, and chewed and spit bud juice on cuts, which were then bandaged in shredded cedar bark.

Rose, Baldhip *(Rosa gymnocarpa)*

Native deciduous shrub. This rose has small, single flowers and its stems are covered with small, straight, delicate thorns. The crown of sepals falls away early from the small orange-to-red, pear-shaped fruits (rosehips), hence the plant's name. This rose is found in a variety of habitats, from open to wooded, and in dry to moist conditions. Branches of all species of wild rose were used by various Northwest tribes in steaming pits, cooking baskets, and storage pits.

Rose, Little Wild *(Rosa pisocarpa)*

Native deciduous shrub. This rose is found in wet swampy places, and has several clustered pale pink flowers (unlike the single flowers of other wild roses), small, purple, pear-shaped hips, and pairs of thorns just below where the leaves join the stem. Some Northwest tribes ate the hips fresh or brewed the roots into a tea to soothe sore throats. Mothers drank a tea made from the bark just after giving birth.

Rose, Nootka *(Rosa nutkana)*

Native deciduous shrub. This is the tallest (up to 10 feet high) and most common rose in the area, with large, showy pink flowers and large round scarlet hips. It grows in a variety of open habitats, and is found in meadows, thickets, and clearings, and along lakeshores and streambanks. This shrub provides good cover and nesting areas for birds and small mammals. Various Northwest tribes ate the outer rind of fresh or dried hips sparingly as food or as a breath freshener. Tea made from the twigs, bark, and leaves was consumed as a beverage, or used as an eyewash for cataracts or to enhance eyesight. The leaves and bark were dried, toasted, and then smoked. The tender young shoots were sometimes eaten, chewed leaves were applied to bee stings, and the ripe hips were fed to babies with diarrhea.

The glossy, leathery leaves of the salal shrub slow down water loss.

Salal *(Gaultheria shallon)*

Native broadleaf evergreen shrub. This member of the heath family has thick, glossy, leathery leaves coated with cutin (also found on conifers), which reduces moisture loss. This understory shrub is very common in local parks, and is usually found in the drier parts of open coniferous or mixed forests. It has long clusters of pinkish-white, bell-shaped flowers, and its dark purple berries are eaten by many birds and mammals.

Various Northwest tribes ate the berries fresh, mashed and dried into cakes, or mixed with other berries and foods. The young leaves were chewed as a hunger suppressant and to relieve heartburn and colic, chewed and spit on burns or sores, or boiled in a tea to cure a cough, tuberculosis, or diarrhea. The leafy branches were also used to line cooking pits.

Salmonberry *(Rubus spectabilis)*

Native deciduous shrub. A type of raspberry, this tall common shrub indicates moisture. It grows in moist to wet areas in open forests, on streambanks, and in clearings and disturbed areas. The dark pink flowers attract hummingbirds and butterflies, and the yellow, orange, or light red berries are food for raccoons, chipmunks and squirrels, and many kinds of birds.

Most Northwest tribes ate the young sprouts, often with salmon (the name may have come from this practice or the color of the berries). The watery berries are among the earliest to ripen, and were eaten fresh. The bark and leaves have astringent qualities, and were eaten to aid digestion, chewed and spit on burns, or placed on an aching tooth or festering wound.

Serviceberry, Western *(Amelanchier alnifolia)*
Native deciduous shrub. This large shrub grows in moist, well-drained soil in meadows, thickets, dry to moist open forests, roadsides, and streambanks (shrub-scrub and wooded wetland communities). In April and May, it features showy, fragrant white blossoms, which ripen into blue-black fruit by August. Its leaves and flowers are eaten by deer, elk, rabbits, rodents, and ring-necked pheasants. Ruffed grouse and black bears eat the berries. Many Northwest tribes ate the berries both fresh and dried (as did Lewis and Clark), and the tough wood was used as the spreader in halibut lines.

Snowberry, Common *(Symphoricarpos albus)*
Native deciduous shrub. This common shrub is easily recognized during fall and winter by its conspicuous waxy white berries. Its tiny, bell-shaped, pinkish-white flowers bloom from spring to late summer, and its berries are poisonous to humans, but provide food for birds and rodents in winter. This honeysuckle relative grows in both dry and moist habitats, including open coniferous and mixed forests, thickets, and roadsides.

Some Northwest tribes ate the berries to induce vomiting as an antidote for poisoning. They also used the berries as shampoo, applied chewed leaves on cuts, used the bark as a cure for venereal disease and tuberculosis, and made a tea from the leaves as a cold remedy.

Thimbleberry *(Rubus parviflorus)*
Native deciduous shrub. This member of the raspberry family requires both moisture and sun, so it thrives in damp, open, places in forests, clearings and roadsides. Its soft, maple-leaf-shaped leaves, large white crinkled flowers, red hemispherical berries and lack of thorns are distinctive. Birds and bears eat the berries. Many Northwest tribes consumed both the berries and the young shoots. The bark was boiled and used as soap. The leaves were used to wrap food for storage, boiled as a tea for anemia, and burned or dried as a poultice for swellings and burns.

Twinberry, Black *(Lonicera involucrata)*
Native deciduous shrub. This shrub is easily recognized when its pairs of yellow tubular flowers or twinned shiny black berries are present. It grows in moist forests and clearings, in swamps and thickets, and on streambanks. Various Northwest tribes considered the bitter berries inedible, and one tribe believed that eating them would made one unable to speak. The bark and twigs were used to treat digestive tract ailments and as a contraceptive; the berries were used to dye graying hair; and the leaves were chewed to induce vomiting after poisoning.

Flowering Plants
Avens, Large-leaved *(Geum macrophyllum)*
Native herbaceous perennial. This tall, common yellow wildflower is a member of the rose family, and its small, brown, hooked fruits catch easily

on clothing or fur. Its basal leaves consist of several leaflets arrayed along a common stem, with a larger one at the end. Usually found in wet meadows and shrub-scrub wetlands, it may also be seen in moist open forests and along streambanks. Various Northwest tribes made poultices of the leaves for boils.

Baneberry, Western Red *(Actaea rubra)*

Native herbaceous perennial. This tall member of the buttercup family has white flowers and shiny, red or white berries. It grows in moist shady forests and clearings, and on streambanks. The berries, foliage, and roots of the baneberry are all highly poisonous; its name comes from the Anglo-Saxon word *bana* meaning 'murderous.' Eating the berries can induce vomiting, bloody diarrhea, and respiratory paralysis. Various Northwest tribes chewed the leaves and spat them on wounds.

Bedstraw *(Galium* species*)*

Native herbaceous perennial and introduced annual. This weak-stemmed plant has tiny white flowers, and stems and burs that cling to clothing. It is found in shady, moist open coniferous or mixed forests, wet clearings, and along streambanks. Bedstraw is a member of the madder family (the source

Western red baneberry bears poisonous berries.

of coffee, gardenias and quinine), and has been used as a caffeine-free coffee substitute. According to Quileute tradition, if a woman wished to attract a particular man, she would collect a bit of his hair and weave it together with her own hair and some bedstraw. This was said to ensure that the man would stick to her as tightly as the hairs to the bedstraw.

Bleeding Heart, Pacific or Western *(Dicentra formosa)*

Native herbaceous perennial. This delicate wildflower has fringed, fern-like leaves and dangling pink, heart-shaped flowers that allow entry to bumble-bees but not honeybees. A common plant, it grows in moist open forests and on streambanks. Ants carry off the seeds, eat the oily, attached food part, then leave the seed to germinate far from the parent plant. All parts of this plant contain the toxic alkaloid *isoquinoline:* cattle have died from eating it, and it can cause contact dermatitis in some people. The Skagit used it as a shampoo, boiled the pounded root of this plant for worm medicine, and chewed the roots for toothache relief.

Bulrush, Small-fruited *(Scirpus microcarpus)*

Native perennial. This common plant, despite its name, is a member of the sedge family, as its triangular stems indicate (remember the saying, "sedges have edges but rushes are round"). A wetland indicator plant, it is found in marshes and forested wetlands. It is an important source of food for wildlife: geese eat the shoots, underground stems, and leaves; muskrats eat the seeds. Various Northwest tribes used these plants to weave light-duty baskets, and as an ornamental trim on hide clothing. The leaves were also used to steam food.

Buttercup, Creeping *(Ranunculus repens)*

Non-native herbaceous perennial introduced from Europe. It grows in wet meadows, disturbed sites, and ditches, crowding out grasses and other native plants. This plant, like all species of buttercup, is poisonous when raw, and can cause inflammation of tissues of the mouth, throat and digestive tract when swallowed. It also contains the chemical protoanemonin, which can cause severe irritation and blistering of skin upon contact. Various Northwest tribes ate roots of native species of *Ranunculus* as winter food or made a poultice from the mashed leaves.

Candyflower *(Montia sibirica* or *Claytonia sibirica)*

Native herbaceous annual/perennial. Also know as Siberian miner's lettuce, this dainty wildflower, a member of the purslane family, has white-to-pink flowers. It grows in moist sites in forests and meadows, and on streambanks. The plant was eaten by Siberian miners to prevent scurvy. Various Northwest tribes chewed the plant during pregnancy so the baby would be soft when born, drank a tea as a general tonic for ailments such as sore throats, or used the crushed stems as a hair rinse.

Cattail, Common *(Typha latifolia)*

Native herbaceous perennial. This classic marsh plant has sausage-shaped brown clusters of tiny female flowers. Geese, beavers, muskrats and other wildlife eat the underground stems (rhizomes) of cattails, while marsh wrens and red-winged blackbirds nest in their stalks. Most tribes in western Washington used the cattail. The stalks were woven into mats for bedding, kneeling pads in canoes, insulation for winter homes, and clothing. Cattail seed fluff was used as stuffing for pillows and mattresses, as a wound dressing, and for diapers. String was made from the leaves, and the rhizomes were eaten raw or baked.

Chicory *(Cichorium intybus)*

Non-native herbaceous perennial. This Eurasian import with striking blue daisy-like flowers can be found in fields and along roadsides. The plant is related to Belgian endive, whose leaves are eaten as a salad green, and the leaves of chicory are high in vitamin C, potassium, phosphorus, and calcium. The chicory taproots can be roasted, ground and used as a coffee substitute.

Duckweed *(Lemna minor)*

Native perennial. This aquatic herb is found on the quiet surface of shallow ponds, marshes, and small creeks. Each tiny "leaf" (called a thallus) is a single flowering plant which functions as leaf, stem, and flower. This primitive plant, as its name suggests, is eaten by ducks and other waterfowl and shorebirds. Generally, the presence of the green scum of duckweed indicates a healthy aquatic environment.

Fireweed *(Epilobium angustifolium)*

Native herbaceous perennial. This tall plant has beautiful spikes of rose-purple flowers. A pioneer plant in recently burned areas (hence its name) it can grow in moist to fairly dry disturbed areas, including meadows, thickets, logged clearings, and roadsides. It is a favorite forage plant for deer and elk. Various Northwest tribes combined the seed fluff with dog hair, mountain-goat wool, or duck feathers and wove the mixture into blankets and clothing. They ate the pith in the stalks, ate the shoots as a laxative, and boiled the roots and drank the liquid as a remedy for sore throat or tuberculosis. The leaves are rich in vitamin C and can be used to make a tea.

Foamflower *(Tiarella trifoliata)*

Native herbaceous perennial. This member of the saxifrage family has mostly basal leaves with tiny white flowers at the end of long stalks. It prefers moist, shady coniferous forests, streambanks, and clearings. The tiny flowers appear like specks of foam, hence the plant's common name. Its unusually shaped, opened seed capsules resemble tiny sugar scoops.

Fringecup *(Tellima grandiflora)*

Native herbaceous perennial. This plant has heart-shaped leaves at the base of the plant, with tall spikes of small fragrant flowers on top of hairy stems. It grows in moist coniferous forests, thickets, and shady streambanks. The Skagit pounded fringecup, boiled it, and drank the tea for any kind of sickness, especially lack of appetite.

Grass, Reed Canary *(Phalarus arundinacea)*

Non-native perennial. This invasive tall grass has round hollow stems and spreads by sprouting from seed or from creeping underground rhizomes. It has invaded wetland areas, growing on muddy shores and in the shallow waters of ponds, lakes, sloughs, streams, and ditches, and is especially common in disturbed sites. The plant provides food, cover, and nesting habitat for birds and other animals, but crowds out other plant species and is very difficult to eradicate.

Hedgenettle, Cooley's *(Stachys cooleyae)*

Native herbaceous perennial. A member of the mint family, its leaves resemble those of stinging nettle, but its four-sided stems, pungent odor, and spectacular spikes of showy magenta flowers make it easy to identify in summer. The leaves occur in pairs, each pair set at right angles to the ones above and below. This plant is common in forested wetlands and along lakeshores and streambanks. Rufous hummingbirds favor the flowers. Various Northwest tribes used the plant in a steam bath to cure rheumatism, to treat boils, or for a spring tonic.

Yellow Iris *(Iris pseudacorus)*

Non-native herbaceous perennial. Also known as yellow flag, this invasive European garden escapee forms tall dense clumps in marshes. Its long, flat, sword-shaped leaves somewhat resemble those of cattails when its bright yellow flowers aren't in bloom, but the overlap of stems at the base of the plant is distinctive. Muskrats are fond of the plant's rhizomes.

Ivy, English *(Hedera helix)*

Non-native evergreen perennial. This European ornamental was spread to local forests when birds dispersed its seeds. An invasive vine, it takes over from native groundcovers and attaches to trees by means of holdfasts on the stems. The plant provides food and shelter to birds and late fall nectar to bees. Although ivy is not a parasite, it causes serious problems by adding weight and bulk to trees, making them vulnerable to storm winds. The entire plant is considered poisonous.

Loosestrife, Purple *(Lythrum salicaria)*

Non-native herbaceous perennial. This tall Eurasian import has four-sided stems and lance-shaped leaves. It bears gorgeous, elongated clusters of magenta flowers that brighten marshes. It can dissuade nesting birds, muskrats, and fish from the area, and take over the habitat of cattails and other native plants. Volunteer efforts in parks often concentrate on the careful removal of this highly invasive plant, which must be pulled up whole and burned.

Milfoil, European Water *(Myriophyllum spicatum)*

Non-native perennial. This Eurasian invader is an aggressive aquatic weed, with feathery leaves suspended just below the surface of the water that spread rapidly to form dense tangles. Efforts are underway to discourage milfoil growth in lakes, reservoirs and sloughs, where its dense mats obstruct swimmers, boaters, and even fish, and can fill a pond in a few seasons. The plant is spread from boats used in affected lakes, so boaters must take care to thoroughly clean their boats after each use.

Nettle, Stinging *(Urtica dioica)*

Native herbaceous perennial. This plant thrives in a wide range of habitats, but often indicates moist, poorly drained soil in meadows, thickets, streambanks, open forests, disturbed sites, and roadsides. Touch it and you will feel a burning sensation that may last for hours. The leaves and stems contain formic acid, the same substance injected by bees, wasps, and biting ants. For an antidote, if you have the nerve, pick up a slug—its slime is said to help neutralize the acid. Crushed red elderberry, bracken fern, or thimbleberry are other natural remedies, or when you get home, apply a paste made out of meat tenderizer or baking soda and water.

Various Northwest tribes used nettles to make rope and fishnets and as a treatment for colds, rheumatism, paralysis, and labor pain. In some native cultures, those who handled corpses would rub nettles on their own bodies afterward for purification.

Nightshade, Climbing or European Bittersweet *(Solanum dulcamara)*

Non-native herbaceous perennial. The leaves and fruit of this Eurasian import are moderately poisonous to people and livestock. The vine-like plant has bright red oblong berries, and lavender flowers with yellow centers that resemble shooting stars. This nightshade can be found in marshes, along roadsides, and in open forests and thickets.

Nightshade, Enchanter's *(Circaea alpina)*

Native herbaceous perennial. This member of the evening primrose family has tiny white flowers and fruits covered with hooked bristles. It is found in damp shady forests and other moist sites such as streambanks and floodplains.

Parsley, Water *(Oenanthe sarmentosa)*

Native herbaceous perennial. This aquatic plant has parsley-like leaflets and white flowers. It is found in shallow standing water in marshes and wet meadows. Sources disagree on whether the plant is poisonous. Various Northwest tribes ate the young stems, put warmed parsley leaves on sore limbs, pounded the root to use as a potent laxative, or cut the mature stalks for children's whistles.

Piggyback Plant (see *Youth-on-age*)

Pond Lily, Yellow *(Nuphar polysepalum)*

Native perennial. This native water lily features yellow blooms that beautify marshes. The large, leathery leaves of this aquatic plant play an important role in lake ecology—they keep the water from getting too warm in summer, provide a place for insects and amphibians to lay their eggs underneath the leaves, and create a protective habitat for young fish. However, once rooted, this plant can dominate and crowd out other plants. Many waterfowl eat the seeds and some eat the rhizomes. Deer eat the leaves, stems, stalks, and flowers; beavers and bears eat the rhizomes; and muskrats eat many parts of the plant. Various Northwest tribes made use of the seeds for food, either grinding them to make flour or roasting them like popcorn. The huge rhizomes were an important source of food and medicine, and were eaten raw, boiled, or roasted.

Queen Anne's Lace *(Daucus carota)*

Non-native herbaceous biennial. Also known as wild carrot, this tall Eurasian immigrant is the wild plant from which the garden carrot was developed. Its lacy pattern is formed by flat clusters of tiny white flowers; within the center of some clusters, there may be a single pink, brown, or purple flower that perhaps serves as a bull's eye for insects. It thrives in disturbed areas like meadows and along roadsides, and the wet leaves may cause an allergic reaction in some people.

Rush, Common *(Juncus effusus)*

Native perennial. This wetland plant forms clumps of round, hollow, dark-green grasslike stems that taper to a sharp point. (Remember the adage, "sedges have edges, but rushes are round.") Common rush is found in standing water in shallow marshes and wet meadows, and it often indicates disturbance. Various Northwest tribes used rushes to tie things together, or ate the early shoots of the larger plants.

Skunk Cabbage, Yellow *(Lysichitum americanum)*

Native perennial. A freshwater wetland indicator, it is found in forested wetland communities. The small greenish flowers grow tightly clustered on a stalk called a spadix, set within a showy yellow modified leaf called a spathe, and appear as early as February, when little else blooms. When bruised, the leaves exude a rank odor, which attracts pollinating insects. Muskrats eat the stems, bears consume the whole plant, and deer browse the leaves. The

The lovely white flowers of western trillium age to pink, then deep rose.

entire plant contains calcium oxalate crystals, which can temporarily paralyze the salivary glands and cause the throat and tongue to swell and constrict breathing.

Various Northwest tribes used the huge leaves as platters, to line berry baskets and steaming pits, to store dried berries, and as poultices for cuts, swellings, headaches, chest pains, and fevers. The root was brewed into tea to relieve respiratory ailments, urinary obstruction, scurvy, and venereal disease. The plant was also used in various ways for contraception, abortion, and to facilitate childbirth. Skunk cabbage was only eaten as a famine food in spring, with the hot peppery roots cooked or roasted, or dried and ground into flour for emergency use.

Starflower *(Trientalis latifolia)*

Native herbaceous perennial. This delicate member of the primrose family has pale pink flowers. Its thin stem holds its leaves and flowers aloft above the forest floor, suspending the flowers in the air like tiny stars. It grows in moist areas in open forests, thickets, and meadows. Various Northwest tribes dug the tubers for food (also known as "Indian potato") or used the crushed plant mixed with water as an eye wash.

Trillium, Western *(Trillium ovatum)*

Native herbaceous perennial. White trillium flowers, among the first wildflowers to bloom, age to pink, then deep rose. These wildflowers grow in moist to wet coniferous or mixed forests, in shaded open areas, and on streambanks. Its leaves, petals, and sepals normally occur in threes (hence its name). Ants carry off the seeds to feast on their oily coating, and disperse the plant through the forest. Various Northwest tribes used the juice of the bulb as eye drops, to bring boils to a head, and as a love potion. The soaked roots were also used as an eye wash.

Vanilla Leaf *(Achlys triphylla)*

Native herbaceous perennial. The plant's distinctive leaf has three triangular leaflets arranged in a horizontal whorl at the end of a wiry stem. A spike of tiny white flowers rises above the leaf on a second stalk that pokes up between the leaflets. Groups of vanilla leaf plants are common in moist, shady forests, in openings, and along streambanks. When dried, the leaves have a mild vanilla-like fragrance. Various Northwest tribes dried the leaves and hung them in houses as an insect repellent, and used the leaves as a remedy for tuberculosis, to induce vomiting, and as a shampoo.

Violet, Marsh or Swamp *(Viola palustris)*

Native herbaceous perennial. This low-growing plant is restricted to peaty soils in marshes, forested wetlands, the edges of bogs, and along streambanks. Both the glossy, kidney- or heart-shaped leaves and the white to lavender flowering stems grow directly from a rhizome, or creeping stem.

Watercress *(Rorippa nasturtium-aquaticum)*

Non-native aquatic herbaceous perennial introduced from Europe. The creeping stems of this plant are rooted in mud, but its leaves and tiny white

The dried leaves of the vanilla leaf herb give off a pleasant fragrance.

flowers float on top of clear running streams or springs, or along the edges of marshes. Although muskrats and ducks eat the leaves, watercress can quickly and completely choke shallow ponds and streams. A common, nutritious salad green, the watercress in local parks is unfit for consumption due to pollution from coliform bacteria from leaking septic tanks and animal waste.

Waterleaf, Pacific *(Hydrophyllum tenuipes)*

Native herbaceous perennial. This herb grows in moist forests, and has hairy stems and leaves, and clusters of tiny greenish-white or lavender flowers. Various Northwest tribes ate the roots.

Water Lily, White *(Nymphaea odorata)*

Non-native perennial. This introduced plant is found in lakes, ponds, and deep marshes. Its white flowers open in the mornings and evenings and remain closed in the heat of the afternoon. The water lily obtains some of its oxygen directly from the air through microscopic openings on the tops of its leaves. Oxygen is transported down the stems to the roots, which are anchored in the lake muck.

Yarrow *(Achillea millefolium)*

Native herbaceous perennial. Rounded clusters of yellow central-disk flowers surrounded by pink ray flowers top the tall stems of the yarrow. Its fringed leaves resemble ferns. It grows in many habitats, from dry to moist soils, in meadows and clearings, in open forests and thickets, and along roadsides. Various Northwest tribes used yarrow as an aromatic herb for therapeutic baths. It was also used in childbirth; women ate the leaves to induce sweating during delivery and drank yarrow tea to heal the uterus afterward. The tea was a remedy for numerous other ailments, including intestinal troubles caused by eating raw meat.

Youth-on-age *(Tolmiea menziesii)*

Native herbaceous perennial. Also known as piggyback plant, this hairy herb grows new leaves from the bases of older ones. Withering old leaves drop to the ground, allowing the new leaves to root. It has tiny brownish-purple flowers on long stems, and grows in moist forests and on streambanks. Various Northwest tribes ate the young sprouts and applied the leaves to boils.

Nonflowering Plants

Fern, Bracken *(Pteridium aquilinum)*

Native deciduous fern. This large fern occurs in a wide variety of habitats, such as meadows, clearings, dry to wet forests, acidic sites such as lakeshores and bogs, and in sterile sandy soils. It is especially common on open and disturbed sites, such as burn areas, where it colonizes disturbed ground. Various Northwest tribes burned wooded areas to lure elk and deer to feed on the young fern shoots, or fiddleheads. The leaves were used in lining cooking pits, and for wiping fish. However, recent research has tied this fern to stomach cancer and chromosome damage.

White water lilies were introduced to the Seattle area.

Deer fern is a favorite forage plant for deer and elk.

Fern, Deer *(Blechnum spicant)*

Native evergreen fern. This fern has two types of fronds: sterile, evergreen ones that lie flat on the ground, and fertile, spore-bearing deciduous ones that grow upright from the center of the clump. The deer fern grows in shady, moist woods, on streambanks and in marshes, and is an important winter food for deer and elk. Various Northwest tribes ate the leaves to prevent thirst when traveling, and as a treatment for lung trouble or stomach distress; they also used them topically to treat paralysis.

Fern, Lady *(Athyrium filix-femina)*
Native deciduous fern. This fern tolerates a wide range of light conditions, from full sun to full shade, but requires a reliable supply of water throughout the growing season. It occurs in moist-to-wet forests, marshes, meadows and clearings, and on streambanks. Various Northwest tribes used its fronds to lay out or cover food; boiled the stems in a tea to ease labor; ate the young fiddleheads boiled, baked, or eaten raw with grease; and ate the baked and peeled rhizomes, sometimes with oil or dried salmon eggs.

Fern, Licorice *(Polypodium glycyrrhiza)*
Native evergreen fern. This fern grows in moss on the trunks of deciduous trees, usually bigleaf maples, or on logs and rocks. However, the licorice fern is not a parasite; it relies on its host tree for physical support, not for nutrients, which it extracts from the air. This fern withers in hot, dry, summer weather, then revives when the rains return in fall. The plant was named for the flavor and scent of its rhizome, or root, that contains the same chemical that gives licorice its flavor. Various Northwest tribes chewed the raw or roasted rhizomes for colds, sore throats or coughs, or boiled them and drank the liquid as a tonic for measles.

Fern, Maidenhair *(Adiantum pedatum)*
Native deciduous fern. This delicate fern thrives in shady, damp, mossy areas near streams and waterfalls, where summer humidity is high. Various Northwest tribes used the strong, shiny brownish-black stems in basketry. The leaves were soaked in water and used as a hair rinse, or were burned and the ashes rubbed into the hair. The leaves were also chewed for sore chest and stomach troubles; to check internal hemorrhages from wounds; and to increase strength and endurance.

Fern, Sword *(Polystichum munitum)*
Native evergreen fern. This is the most common fern in the Northwest, where it covers entire slopes in forests. An indicator of well-drained soils on moist slopes, it requires less water than some ferns but rarely grows in sunny places. Various Northwest tribes used the leaves as flooring and bedding; to line pit ovens, food storage boxes, and baskets; and on berry-drying racks. Rhizomes were dug and eaten roasted or steamed as a starvation food in the spring, or to cure diarrhea. The roots were also boiled and the liquid used to treat dandruff. The young leaves were chewed for sore throat and to facilitate childbirth, or placed on sores and boils.

Fern, Wood *(Dryopteris austriaca)*
Native evergreen fern. This fern is visible year-round; it grows on the dead wood of stumps or logs and prefers damp shady areas in forests and openings. Various Northwest tribes ate the rhizomes for food, gathering them in the fall and winter. Because the rhizomes are a laxative, the native people also ate them after consuming poisonous plants or red-tide shellfish. The pounded root pulp was put on cuts, or the leaves soaked for a hair wash.

Wood ferns remain green year-round.

Horsetail, Common *(Equisetum arvense)*

Native herbaceous perennial. This primitive plant is a remnant from the time of the dinosaurs, when it was much more prevalent and grew as tall as 50 feet. It grows in groups in wet meadows and forested wetlands. The horsetail produces two kinds of stems: bright green, sterile stems with wire-like branches, and whitish fertile stems with terminal spore-producing cones, which turn brownish just before withering.

Uncooked horsetail is poisonous—horses have died from eating it and children have been poisoned by using the stems for whistles or blowguns.

Various Northwest tribes used the plants as scouring pads and to start hand-drilled fires; ate the young fertile shoots as a cure for diarrhea; ate the rhizomes roasted or pressed the juice out of them as a wash for sore eyes; or boiled the stems with willow leaves for irregular periods.

Animals

Birds

Birds are the most abundant and visible wildlife in local parks. Over two hundred species of birds visit or live in the Puget Sound region, and recognizing them can sometimes seem overwhelming. To learn to identify birds, begin with just a few species. Ducks are a great place to start—they're large and numerous, and they stay put for a while on the surface of the water. Invest in a pair of binoculars and a good bird guide (or enlist the help of a more experienced birder), and in a short time, you will be able to recognize the difference between a gadwall, a bufflehead, and a northern shoveler. Or start in your own backyard; set up a bird feeder or plant shrubs and trees that attract birds, and you will soon have your own visiting menagerie.

Be aware of the habitat and the time of year when identifying birds. You will not see a duck in a forest, nor a woodpecker on Lake Washington. Also, while some birds live in the Puget Sound region year-round, others only visit during certain seasons. Because of our mild weather, many birds, especially

The Arboretum Waterfront Trail is a popular promenade for viewing waterfowl.

ducks, winter in the area, making this a prime birding region. Three local chapters of the Audubon Society offer field trips, programs and camaraderie to help you learn to recognize local species. See Appendix B for telephone numbers.

The following list provides general information about the time of year common species can be seen in the Seattle area, and the habitat in which they can usually be found (common birds such as crows, robins, and starlings are excluded).

Auklet, Rhinoceros *(Cerorhinca monocerata)*
Visits in fall and winter. This stocky seabird lives in open bays and on rocky islands in Puget Sound.

Bittern, American *(Botaurus lentiginosus)*
Uncommon resident. Nests here. This secretive heron can be found in marshes and wet meadows. It often freezes with neck and bill pointed upward, presumably to blend in with the surrounding cattails.

Blackbird, Brewer's *(Euphagus cyanocephalus)*
Resident. Nests here. This small blackbird jerks its head as it walks, and forages in large flocks with other blackbirds. It is common in open habitats such as fields.

Blackbird, Red-winged *(Agelaius phoeniceus)*
Resident. Nests here. This polygamous marsh dweller nests in large colonies among cattails, rushes, sedges, and other marsh plants. During the nesting season, squadrons of male birds will fiercely chase away hawks and other predators.

Brant *(Branta bernicla)*
Visits in spring. This small dark marine goose passes through the area on its way north along the coast to Alaska. Local eelgrass beds near exposed bars and sandflats in Puget Sound offer food and resting spots.

Bufflehead *(Bucephala albeola)*
Visits in fall and winter, although some may nest here and remain all summer. This small fluffy duck with a white head patch is an expert diver, and can be found on most lakes, ponds, and wetlands in the region.

Bushtit *(Psaltriparus minimus)*
Resident. Nests here. One of the region's smallest birds, it lives among shrubs in deciduous forests.

Canvasback *(Aythya valisineria)*
Visits in fall and winter. This white-backed duck with a sleek profile dives to eat lake vegetation, and is found on saltwater bays or deep freshwater lakes such as Lake Washington.

Chickadee, Black-capped *(Parus atricapillus)*
Resident. Nests here. This bird searches for insects among the lower foliage of maples, alders, cottonwoods, and other deciduous trees.

Chickadee, Chestnut-backed *(Parus rufescens)*
Resident. Nests here. This type of chickadee prefers dark, humid coniferous forests, where it searches for insects among the higher parts of trees.

Coot, American *(Fulica americana)*
Resident, less common in summer. Nests here. This black bird with a distinctive call often swims with ducks, but is actually a cousin of the rail. It nests among marsh cattails in summer, and moves into the open water of lakes during the winter.

Cormorant, Double-crested *(Phalacrocorax auritus)*
Resident, rare in summer. The only cormorant found inland, this large black fish-eater is seen on both freshwater and saltwater bays. Lacking a waterproof coating on its wings (to better swim underwater), it is often seen perched on pilings or rocks with its wings spread out to dry its feathers after each dive.

Cowbird, Brown-headed *(Molothrus ater)*
Visits in spring and summer. Nests here. This bird is notorious for laying its eggs in the nests of songbirds, such as song sparrows, and letting them raise its young. It frequents deciduous forest edges, open fields, and shorelines.

Creeper, Brown *(Certhia americana)*
Resident. Nests here. This inconspicuous bird lives in coniferous or mixed forests. To feed, it starts at the base of a tree, then spirals upward, probing the bark for insects.

Dipper, American *(Cinclus mexicanus)*
Resident. Nests here. This bird frequents fast-flowing streams, where it perches on rocks or walks in the stream to hunt for insects.

Duck, Ring-necked *(Aythaya collaris)*
Visits in fall and winter. This duck prefers lakes and ponds with muddy bottoms bordered by marshes, where it dives for vegetation and invertebrates.

Duck, Ruddy *(Oxyura jamaicensis)*
Visits in fall and winter, some remain in summer and nest here. This animated white-cheeked duck dives in freshwater marshes and lakes.

Duck, Wood *(Aix sponsa)*
Resident. Some nest here. This rare, colorful duck lives in small marshy ponds or slow-moving streams.

Dunlin *(Calidris alpina)*
Visits in fall and winter. This common shorebird can be seen along both fresh- and saltwater marsh shorelines, and in wet meadows.

Eagle, Bald *(Haliaeetus leucocephalus)*
Resident, more common in winter and spring. Nests here. This majestic bird perches in tall snags near large bodies of water, where it hunts for fish.

Falcon, Peregrine *(Falco peregrinus)*
Resident, rare. Nests here. An extraordinary hunter, this bird is one of the fastest animals in the world. It prefers rocky shorelines, and has built nests atop skyscrapers in downtown Seattle.

Finch, House *(Carpodacus mexicanus)*
Resident. Nests here. This common bird frequents open fields and local feeders.

Finch, Purple *(Carpodacus purpureus)*
Resident. This less common finch favors heavily forested areas of mixed coniferous and deciduous trees.

Flicker, Northern or Red-shafted *(Colaptes auratus)*
Resident. Nests here. This common woodpecker spends more time feeding on the ground than other woodpeckers, and lives in open coniferous or mixed forests.

Flycatcher, Olive-sided *(Contopus borealis)*
Visits in spring and summer. Nests here. This bird prefers coniferous forests, where it usually feeds above the forest canopy.

Flycatcher, Pacific-slope or Western *(Empidonax difficilis)*
Visits in spring and summer. Nests here. This bird lives in moist, shaded coniferous or mixed forests, and the genus name, appropriately enough, means "lord of the mosquitoes."

Flycatcher, Willow *(Empidonax traillii)*
Visits in spring and summer. Nests here. This bird is usually found in brushy areas adjacent to open fields or marshes.

Gadwall *(Anas strepera)*
Resident. Nests here. This unassuming duck frequents shallow, slow-moving streams and marshy ponds.

Goldeneye, Barrow's *(Bucephala islandica)*
Visits fall through spring. This duck nests in trees, and its ducklings must jump down to the ground when only a few days old. It is found in saltwater bays around the Puget Sound area.

Goldeneye, Common *(Bucephala clangula)*
Visits fall through spring. This common duck frequents large bodies of freshwater or saltwater.

Goldfinch, American *(Carduelis tristis)*
Resident, more common in spring and summer. Nests here. This Washington state bird frequents weedy fields and deciduous forests.

Goose, Canada *(Branta canadensis)*
Both resident and migratory. Nests here. The residents in this area were introduced from the eastern part of the state, but are joined during spring and fall by migrating geese from other regions. This bird frequents shorelines, marshes, and open fields.

Grebe, Horned *(Podiceps auritus)*
Visits in fall and winter. This bird leaps up before diving into the water, and is abundant in shallow, protected fresh- and saltwater bays.

Grebe, Pied-billed *(Podilymbus podiceps)*
Resident. Nests here. This reclusive bird can be seen in small lakes surrounded by marshes.

Grebe, Red-necked *(Podiceps grisegena)*
Visits in fall and winter. This bird dives for aquatic animals in saltwater bays and estuaries.

Grebe, Western *(Aechmophorus occidentalis)*
Visits in fall and winter. The largest grebe, this bird has a graceful, swan-like neck and is common on fresh- or saltwater bays.

Grosbeak, Black-headed *(Pheucticus melanocephalus)*
Visits in spring and summer. Nests here. This bird prefers deciduous forests near water.

Grosbeak, Evening *(Coccothraustes vespertinus)*
Resident, more common spring through fall. Nests here. This bird frequents coniferous or deciduous forests, and passes through this region on the way to more mountainous areas in summer and winter.

Grouse, Ruffed *(Bonasa umbellus)*
Resident. Nests here. This bird prefers open deciduous and mixed forests.

Guillemot, Pigeon *(Cepphus columba)*
Resident. Nests here. This common seabird nests under piers and on rocky cliffs (such as Magnolia Bluff) around the waters of Puget Sound.

Gull, Bonaparte's *(Larus philadelphia)*
Visits fall through spring. This bird leaves the area in the summer to nest in spruce trees in the northern forests. During the other three seasons, look for it on the bays of Puget Sound.

Gull, California *(Larus californicus)*
Visits in fall, with a few remaining in winter and spring. This large gull is an opportunistic feeder, and is seen in urban areas, on Puget Sound, and feeding in pastures and on park lawns.

Gull, Glaucous-winged *(Larus glaucescens)*
Resident. Nests here. This common bird appears in large flocks on saltwater bays, estuaries, and lakes.

Gull, Mew *(Larus canus)*
Visits in fall and winter. This small gull prefers natural food rather than handouts. It is seen on Puget Sound, and feeding in pastures and on park lawns during heavy winter rains.

Gull, Ring-billed *(Larus delawarensis)*
Visits in fall and winter. This gull has a black band around its bill. It can be seen on lakes and on the shores of Puget Sound, in pastures, and in urban areas.

Harrier, Northern *(Circus cyaneus)*
Resident. Nests here. This marsh hawk flies in low, zigzag patterns over fields, searching for prey.

Hawk, Cooper's *(Accipiter cooperii)*
Resident. Nests here. This hawk has a long rounded tail and short stubby wings, and rarely soars. It can be found in a wide variety of habitats, including forests and fields.

Hawk, Red-tailed *(Buteo jamaicensis)*
Resident. Nests here. This common hawk frequents open fields and marshes, often perching on telephone poles.

Hawk, Sharp-shinned *(Accipiter striatus)*
Visits in fall and winter. This hawk hunts in fields and bordering forests. Its short wings enable it to maneuver between trees and fly fast enough to run down any small songbird.

Heron, Great Blue *(Ardea herodias)*
Resident. Nests here. This easily recognized hunter fishes in marshes and nests high in large deciduous trees.

Heron, Green *(Butorides striatus)*
Resident, more common in spring and summer. Nests here. This reclusive marsh bird hunts in wetlands at the edges of lakes and rivers, nests in small trees, and is the Seattle area's smallest heron.

Hummingbird, Anna's *(Calypte anna)*
Visits in spring and summer, some reside year-round near feeders. Nests here. This tiny energetic bird lives in open woods, shrubs, and gardens.

Hummingbird, Rufous *(Selasphorus rufus)*
Visits in spring and summer. Nests here. This hummingbird lives in meadows and brush near coniferous or deciduous forests.

Jay, Steller's *(Cyanocitta stelleri)*
Resident. Nests here. This large noisy (except during the nesting season) bird prefers coniferous forests.

Junco, Dark-eyed or Oregon *(Junco hyemalis)*
Resident, more common in fall and winter. A few nest here. This ground dweller lives in undergrowth in fields or open coniferous and mixed forests.

Kestrel, American *(Falco sparverius)*
Resident. Nests here. This uncommon falcon frequents farming areas, where it perches on utility poles to scan fields for prey.

Killdeer *(Charadrius vociferus)*
Resident. Nests here. This shorebird nests in pastures and gravelly freshwater shorelines, and lures predators away from its young by dramatically feigning an injury.

Kingfisher, Belted *(Ceryle alcyon)*
Resident. Nests here. This bird hunts in calm waters, either fresh- or saltwater, and is never far from shore. It builds its nest near the end of a long tunnel excavated a few feet into sandy or dirt banks.

Kinglet, Golden-crowned *(Regulus satrapa)*
Resident. Nests here. This tiny energetic bird lives high in the boughs of conifer forests, or among willows in river bottoms.

Kinglet, Ruby-crowned *(Regulus calendula)*
Visits in fall through spring. This bird prefers mixed coniferous and deciduous thickets and forests, and feeds lower in the conifer canopy than golden-crowned kinglets.

Loon, Common *(Gavia immer)*
Visits in fall and winter. This diving bird spends the winters on Puget Sound, or on freshwater lakes and rivers.

Mallard *(Anas platyrhynchos)*
Resident. Nests here. This common duck lives on small lakes, in marshes, and on shallow, usually freshwater, bays. Several times a year, the males lose their dramatic green head feathers due to molting, but can be recognized by their bright yellow beaks.

Meadowlark, Western *(Sturnella neglecta)*
Some residents, more common in fall and winter. A few nest here. This bird lives in open fields and adjacent brushy areas.

Merganser, Common *(Mergus merganser)*
Resident, less common spring through fall. A few nest here. This swift-flying duck prefers to live on large lakes and rivers.

Merganser, Hooded *(Lophodytes cucullatus)*
Some residents, more common in fall and winter. Some nest here. This dramatic-crested duck nests in woodpecker cavities in trees, and its young must leap down to seek the nearest freshwater wetland. It prefers woodland ponds, and sheltered backwaters of rivers.

Merganser, Red-breasted *(Mergus serrator)*
Visits in fall and winter. A few nest here. This large fish-hunting duck is found mainly on the saltwater bays and estuaries of Puget Sound.

Merlin *(Falco columbarius)*
Resident. Nests here. This small falcon preys on songbirds in the Seattle area and frequents coniferous forests, open fields, and shorelines.

Murre, Common *(Uria aalge)*
Visits fall through spring. This large bird has tiny wings, which causes it to veer from side to side when flying. It can be seen on the waters of Puget Sound.

Murrelet, Marbled *(Brachyramphus marmoratus)*
Visits in fall and winter. This stubby bird can be seen on the waters of Puget Sound in bays and estuaries.

Nuthatch, Red-breasted *(Sitta canadensis)*
Resident. Nests here. This bird forages in coniferous and mixed forests, where it walks headfirst down tree trunks searching for seeds and insects.

Oriole, Bullock's *(Icterus bullockii)*
Visits in spring and summer. Nests here. This striking common bird spends its time in tall deciduous trees near rivers.

Osprey *(Pandion haliaetus)*
Visits in spring and summer. Nests here. This long-winged hawk is often mistaken for an eagle as it hunts for fish in saltwater bays, large lakes, and rivers.

Owl, Barn *(Tyto alba)*
Resident. Nests here. This owl hunts in fields and roosts in old buildings.

Owl, Great-horned *(Bubo virginianus)*
Resident. Nests here. This owl lives in both fields and deciduous and coniferous forests.

Owl, Northern Saw-whet *(Aegolius acadicus)*
Resident. Nests here. This small owl lives in deciduous and coniferous forests.

Owl, Western-screech *(Otus kennicottii)*
Resident. Nests here. This owl lives in deciduous and coniferous forests.

Pheasant, Ring-necked *(Phasianus colchicus)*
Resident. Nests here. This non-native bird frequents dense weedy fields.

Pigeon, Band-tailed *(Columba fasciata)*
Resident, more common in spring and summer. Nests here. This secretive bird prefers coniferous forests, where it builds its nests among the upper branches of Douglas-firs. It frequents nearby open areas and deciduous trees to hunt berries.

Pintail, Northern *(Anas acuta)*
Visits in fall and winter. A few nest here. This elegant duck lives on small lakes, in marshes, and on shallow (usually freshwater) bays.

Pipit, American or Water *(Anthus spinoletta)*
Visits in spring and fall. This bird feeds on insects in open fields.

Quail, California *(Callipepla californica)*
Resident. Nests here. This introduced bird lives in fields near brush, and unlike other quail, roosts at night in trees or thick brush.

Rail, Virginia *(Rallus limicola)*
Resident. Nests here. This reclusive bird resides in marshes and rarely leaves heavy cover.

Sanderling *(Calidris alba)*
Visits in fall and winter. This tiny sandpiper chases the surf along sandy saltwater beaches to pick up invertebrates stirred up by wave action.

Sandpiper, Spotted *(Actitis macularia)*
Resident, more common in spring and summer. Nests here. This common shorebird constantly bobs up and down as it walks along the shores of large lakes and rivers. In winter, it can be found on the shores of Puget Sound.

Sapsucker, Red-breasted *(Sphyrapicus ruber)*
Resident. Nests here. This secretive woodpecker drills lines of parallel holes in coniferous and deciduous trees (it prefers black cottonwoods and red alders), then returns later to drink the running sap and eat attracted insects.

Scaup, Greater *(Aythya marila)*
Visits in fall and winter. This diving duck prefers deep open water in saltwater bays, estuaries and lakes.

Scaup, Lesser *(Aythya affinis)*
Visits in fall and winter. A few may nest here. This diving duck prefers sheltered lakes and freshwater bays and inlets, but can also be seen on saltwater.

Scoter, Surf *(Melanitta perspicillata)*
Visits in fall and winter. This large deep-sea diving duck wrenches shellfish from rocks and forms large rafts of birds in Puget Sound.

Scoter, White-winged *(Melanitta fusca)*
Visits in fall and winter. This heavy-bodied duck dives for hard-shell

invertebrates, which it swallows whole. Scoters fish together in rafts on the
waters of Puget Sound.

Shoveler, Northern *(Anas clypeata)*
Resident. More common fall through spring. A few nest here. This duck
has a large, shovel-like bill and prefers shallow freshwater ponds.

Siskin, Pine *(Carduelis pinus)*
Resident. Nests here. This gregarious bird is found in moist coniferous
forests, among red alders, or in shrubby areas.

Snipe, Common *(Gallinago gallinago)*
Resident. A few nest here. This secretive shorebird frequents grassy
marshes and wet meadows.

Sora *(Porzna carolina)*
Visits in summer and fall. Nests here. A type of rail, this reclusive bird
frequents marshes.

Sparrow, Fox *(Passerella iliaca)*
Resident, more common fall through spring. Nests here. This bird frequents thickets and brambles, and scratches for food on the ground, flipping
up leaves behind it.

Sparrow, Golden-crowned *(Zonotrichia atricapilla)*
Visits fall through spring. This ground feeder prefers meadows and low
shrubs, with nearby thickets for cover.

Sparrow, Savannah *(Passerculus sandwichensis)*
Visits in spring and summer, some reside year-round. Nests here. This
sparrow frequents grassy fields, and prefers to run through the long grass rather
than fly.

Sparrow, Song *(Melospiza melodia)*
Resident. Nests here. This ground feeder is found in weedy fields, thickets, marshes, and on the edges of deciduous forests.

Sparrow, White-crowned *(Zonotrichia leucophrys)*
Resident, more common spring and summer. Nests here. This bird prefers meadows and low shrubs, with nearby thickets for cover.

Swallow, Barn *(Hirundo rustica)*
Visits in spring and summer. Nests here. This bird nests inside barns and
on bridge beams near fields. It forages close to the water or ground for flying
insects, and its deeply forked tail makes it among the most acrobatic of fliers.

Swallow, Cliff *(Hirundo pyrrhonota)*
Visits in spring and summer. Nests here. This swallow likes open areas
near fresh water, and nests under bridges or piers, or on rocky cliffs.

Swallow, Tree *(Tachycineta bicolor)*
Visits in spring and summer. Nests here. This swallow nests in abandoned
woodpecker cavities or in nest boxes, and frequents open fields and freshwater wetlands.

Swallow, Violet-green *(Tachycineta thalassina)*
Visits in spring and summer. Nests here. This bird often nests under eaves
of houses and frequents open fields, freshwater wetlands, and open forests.

Tanager, Western *(Piranga ludoviciana)*
Visits in spring and summer. Nests here. This brightly colored bird spends its time high in the canopy of both coniferous and mixed forests, catching flying insects.

Teal, Blue-winged *(Anas discors)*
Uncommon spring visitor. Nests here. This small, fast-flying duck whistles rather than quacks, and stays with other teals among grassy marshes on lakes and ponds.

Teal, Cinnamon *(Anas cyanoptera)*
Uncommon spring visitor. Nests here. This small, fast-flying duck whistles rather than quacks, and stays with other teals among grassy marshes on lakes and ponds.

Teal, Green-winged *(Anas crecca)*
Resident, more common fall through spring. A few nest here. This small, fast-flying duck whistles rather than quacks, stays with other teals among grassy marshes on lakes and ponds, and may visit coastal mudflats.

Thrush, Hermit *(Catharus guttatus)*
Visits in spring and summer. This bird prefers mixed deciduous and coniferous brush and forests.

Thrush, Swainson's *(Catharus ustulatus)*
Visits in spring and summer. Nests here. This bird prefers mixed deciduous and coniferous brush and forests, especially black cottonwoods.

Thrush, Varied *(Ixoreus naevius)*
Resident, more common in winter. Nests here. This shy bird prefers dark, damp, coniferous forests, moving upland into dense forests in summer to breed.

Towhee, Spotted or Rufous-sided *(Pipilo maculatus)*
Resident. Nests here. This large member of the sparrow family frequents shrubs and brush, where it scratches for food in the ground litter.

Vireo, Hutton's *(Vireo huttoni)*
Resident. Nests here. This bird frequents dense thickets and the canopy of deciduous and mixed forests.

Vireo, Red-eyed *(Vireo olivaceus)*
Visits in spring and summer. Nests here. This bird is found in thick brush, and forages in the tops of deciduous trees along streams.

Vireo, Solitary *(Vireo solitarius)*
Visits in spring and summer. Nests here. This bird frequents dense brush and the canopy of deciduous or mixed forests.

Vireo, Warbling *(Vireo gilvus)*
Visits in spring and summer. Nests here. This common songbird forages for insects in the upper branches of red alders, black cottonwoods, willows, and other deciduous trees.

Warbler, Black-throated Gray *(Dendroica nigrescens)*
Visits in spring and summer. Nests here. This bird is usually found in the

brushy areas of open coniferous and mixed forests near streams.

Warbler, Orange-crowned *(Vermivora celata)*
Visits in spring and summer, some winter here. Nests here. This bird nests and feeds in shrubby thickets at the edges of deciduous forests.

Warbler, Townsend's *(Dendroica townsendi)*
Resident, more common in spring and summer. Nests here. This warbler forages in the upper canopy of coniferous forests.

Warbler, Wilson's *(Wilsonia pusilla)*
Visits in spring and summer. Nests here. This warbler prefers dense brush in moist deciduous forests.

Warbler, Yellow *(Dendroica petechia)*
Visits in spring and summer. Nests here. This warbler is common in shrubby areas and groves of willows and black cottonwoods in open deciduous or mixed forests.

Warbler, Yellow-rumped *(Dendroica coronata)*
Resident. Nests here. This bird prefers open coniferous forests, where it retires to the treetops during breeding season.

Waxwing, Cedar *(Bombycilla cedrorum)*
Resident, more common in spring and summer. Nests here. This bird is found in open brush and in deciduous and coniferous forests.

Wigeon, American *(Anas americana)*
Visits fall through spring, some reside year-round. Nests here. This abundant duck frequents fields and the shallow marshes and shorelines of lakes and saltwater bays. The male's call sounds like a squeezed rubber ducky.

Wigeon, Eurasian *(Anas penelope)*
Visits fall through spring. This bird often appears singly in flocks of American wigeons, and frequents fields and the shallow marshes and shorelines of lakes and saltwater bays.

Woodpecker, Downy *(Picoides pubescens)*
Resident. Nests here. The region's smallest woodpecker, this bird is common in deciduous forests, especially among riverside willows and black cottonwoods.

Woodpecker, Hairy *(Picoides villosus)*
Resident. Nests here. This woodpecker prefers coniferous forests.

Woodpecker, Pileated *(Dryocopus pileatus)*
Resident. Nests here. The area's largest woodpecker, this bird lives in mostly coniferous or mixed forests with large mature trees and dead snags. The elliptical holes it leaves in trees are often the only evidence that these birds are in the area.

Wood-pewee, Western *(Contopus sordidulus)*
Resident. Visits spring and summer. Nests here. This flycatcher prefers open woods and streamside trees.

Wren, Bewick's *(Thryomanes bewickii)*
Resident. Nests here. This common wren prefers shrubby areas.

Wren, Marsh *(Cistothorus palustris)*

Resident. Nests here. This bird frequents marshes and wet meadows bordered by willows. Its globular nest is often seen when vegetation dies back, lashed to cattail stalks 1 or 2 feet above the ground or water.

Wren, Winter *(Troglodytes troglodytes)*

Resident. Nests here. This tiny lively bird favors underbrush in mature coniferous forests.

Yellowthroat, Common *(Geothylpis trichas)*

Visits in spring and summer. Nests here. This warbler lives in marshes and wet meadows bordering freshwater bodies of water.

Amphibians and Mammals

Since the weather in the Pacific Northwest is mild, almost all animals remain active during the winter months. Most animals are spotted during the twilight periods of dawn or dusk, but since they are elusive or difficult to see, the best way to tell if they're in an area is to learn to recognize their tracks and scat.

Bat, Big Brown *(Eptesicus fuscus)*

Native mammal. This larger bat feeds on insects high above the ground along the treetops, sometimes with swallows and swifts. Nocturnal, this flying mammal roosts in trees during the day.

Bat, Little Brown *(Myotis lucifugus)*

Native mammal. This small bat can be seen feeding on insects at dawn and dusk over open areas, sometimes with swallows and swifts. Nocturnal, it roosts in trees during the day, and migrates out of the area or hibernates under roofs during winter.

Bear, Black *(Ursus americanus)*

Native mammal. This animal (often brown) lives in forests, and although nocturnal, can be seen at any time of day. An omnivore, it turns over logs or stones for insects, tears apart decayed stumps or logs for grubs, rips up the ground for roots, anthills, or rodents, tears up berry patches, and eats the outer tissue of trees. It can reach speeds of up to 30 miles per hour and can climb trees for protection or food.

Beaver *(Castor canadensis)*

Native mammal. The largest rodent in North America, this animal builds its massive stick lodges in marshes along lakes, ponds, and streams. Its preferred food and construction materials are black cottonwoods, willows, maples, red alders and birches; it can cut down a 5-inch-thick willow in three minutes. Look for gnawed tree stumps around the shores of Lake Washington and Lake Union.

Beaver, Mountain *(Aplodontia rufa)*

Native mammal. Unique to the Northwest, this mostly nocturnal rodent is not a beaver nor does it prefer a mountainous habitat. The mountain beaver feeds on grasses, wildflowers, bracken fern shoots, salal, and the tender young shoots and bark of shrubs and trees in moist thickets and red alder forests, usually near water. Its burrow system is usually shallow, near cover, and used by many other animals.

Bobcat *(Felis rufus)*

Native mammal. Found only in North America, this spotted wildcat is found in scrubby areas in open forests, marshes, and meadows. During the day it hides in thickets or trees, then emerges to hunt rabbits, mice, and squirrels.

Chickaree (see *Squirrel, Douglas*)

Chipmunk, Townsend's *(Eutamias townsendii)*

Native mammal. The only chipmunk found in the lowland forests of western Washington, it is the region's only true hibernator. This reclusive rodent lives in underground tunnels and forages in undergrowth for a variety of seeds, nuts, and berries.

Cottontail, Eastern *(Sylvilagus floridanus)*

Non-native mammal. This import is now well-established in the Puget Sound area. It grazes in open areas, and among shrubs, where it finds cover. Its chief predators are coyotes, foxes, bobcats, and great horned owls.

Cougar *(Felis concolor)*

Native mammal. Also known as the puma or mountain lion, this carnivore prefers deer, but also eats skunks, porcupines, beavers, coyotes, mice, raccoons, rabbits and birds. It requires more isolated forested areas rich with game, and unlike other cats, may be active by day. It is a good climber and excellent jumper.

Coyote *(Canis latrans)*

Native mammal. The numbers and range of this highly intelligent animal continue to grow, with little competition from other large canine predators. Coyotes offer no danger to humans, and will eat just about anything, including birds, rodents, small mammals like voles, insects, fruits, carrion, garbage, and unfortunately, small roaming house pets.

Deer, Columbia Black-tailed *(Odocoileus hemionus)*

Native mammal. This variety of mule deer is adapted to living in the humid coastal zone of the Pacific Northwest. Common in forests, brushy areas and clearings, it browses on a wide variety of grasses, sedges, fungi, mosses, and lichens, and most herbs and shrubs. It also eats the foliage of trees, such as vine maple, Pacific dogwood, red alder, Douglas-fir and western red cedar.

Elk *(Cervus elaphus)*

Native mammal. Uncommon in the Puget Sound lowlands, some elk live along the drainages of the Green and White Rivers, and in the Cedar River watershed near North Bend. Like deer, they thrive on the shrubs that grow in clearings on logged or recently burned land.

Ensatina *(Ensatina eschscholtzii oregonensis)*

Native amphibian. This common but seldom seen lungless salamander "breathes" by means of gas exchange through its thin moist skin. Rarely found in water except to breed, it is active above ground under leaf litter, rocks, logs, and loose bark, mainly in spring and fall, when the earth is damp and the weather is mild. During cold or warm, dry weather, it retreats to underground holes or rodent burrows, the interior of logs or stumps, or moist crevices in bark, rocks, or decaying wood.

Fox, Red *(Vulpes fulva)*

Non-native mammal. This intelligent animal is seldom seen, since it is shy, nocturnal, and its keen senses of smell, sight, and hearing help it elude people. An omnivore, it eats small mammals, birds, amphibians, reptiles, insects, worms, and a wide variety of fruits and nuts. A fox can live in almost any habitat, and can run so fast that it can go straight up a tree.

Frog, Red-legged *(Rana aurora)*

Native amphibian. This frog breeds in ponds and marshes, but spends most of its adult life out of water. It prefers streams, ponds, and marshes that lie in wooded areas, where it often sits on the bank, just one leap away from water. It makes only a weak, frightened squeak or "pip," and has a very characteristic odor, similar to that of a wet rubber balloon.

Mink *(Mustela vision)*

Native mammal. This animal is essentially a large aquatic weasel. It is an excellent swimmer and forms dens in the banks of streams, ponds, lakes and marshes, but can roam far from water to hunt. A fierce predator, it eats fish, snakes, frogs, birds, rabbits, muskrats, and small rodents.

Mole, Townsend's *(Scapanus townsendii)*

Native mammal. The largest mole in North America, this insectivore burrows just under the surface in fields and lawns. Mole burrows are indicated by raised earth and occasional volcano-like piles of soil.

Mole, Coast *(Scapanus orarius)*

Native mammal. This reclusive mole spends most of its life burrowing through soil searching for worms, sowbugs, insects, and other small creatures. Though nearly blind, the mole is able to sense the location of prey through its sensitive snout whiskers and excellent hearing. It has relatively large forepaws, attached at right angles to the body for more effective digging, and a streamlined profile ideal for scooting down narrow tunnels.

Mouse, Deer *(Peromyscus maniculatus)*

Native mammal. Also known as the white-footed mouse, this rodent is probably the area's most abundant mammal. Mostly nocturnal, it nests in holes in trees, beneath logs and stumps, or amid dense shrubbery. It eats insects, and a wide variety of plant material, especially conifer seeds. Owls, weasels, coyotes, bobcats, and foxes help keep this promiscuous mouse in check.

Muskrat *(Ondatra zibethicus)*

Native mammal. This superb swimmer lives in marshes, where it eats cattails and uses them as a primary material for constructing their large, dome-shaped lodges. It eats sedges, rushes, water lilies, and other aquatic plants, as well as fish, frogs, and crayfish. This animal is primarily nocturnal, but can occasionally be seen during the day.

Newt, Rough-skinned *(Taricha granulosa)*

Native amphibian. This common forest amphibian spends a lot of time in water, where it lives in marshes, ponds, and lakes long after the breeding season has ended. It is the only salamander in our region that is active in the open during daylight, and eats amphibian eggs and larvae, aquatic invertebrates, worms, and small slugs. Its skin glands carry deadly poison that deters almost all predators—the poison on one adult newt is enough to kill 25,000 mice. It is said that some Pacific Northwest Indians used newts to poison their enemies—if you handle one, wash your hands afterwards.

Opossum, American *(Didelphis marsupialis virginiana)*

Non-native mammal. This import from the southeastern United States competes with native animals. A marsupial, its underdeveloped young are born and then crawl up into a fur-lined abdominal pouch to nurse and finish developing for a few more weeks. An opossum will eat almost anything, including fruit, insects, other mammals, eggs, and young birds.

Otter, River *(Lutra canadensis)*

Native mammal. This playful animal is found in or near the shores of bays, lakes, and streams. Normally active by day, it swims rapidly both underwater and on the surface with astonishing grace and power, treading water and raising its head to check out its surroundings. It digs a den in banks, and feeds mainly on fish, but also eats mice and terrestrial invertebrates.

Raccoon *(Procyon lotor)*

Native mammal. This intelligent animal will eat almost anything, including fish, frogs, crabs, reptiles, birds, eggs, snails, fruit, and garbage. During the day, it rests high in trees, in holes in the trunks or on broad limbs, and descends at dusk to prowl for food.

Salamander, Long-toed *(Ambystoma macrodactylum)*

Native amphibian. This common amphibian lives on land from spring until fall, and can be found under logs in wooded areas as long as the forest remains moist. During drier summer and early fall weather, it must find a hole for shelter.

Salamander, Oregon (see *Ensatina*)

Shrew, Trowbridge *(Sorex trowbridgii)*

Native mammal. This insectivore is common, but seldom seen because of its small size. Its metabolism is so high that it must eat insects, worms, and Douglas-fir seeds almost constantly to stay alive. It is hunted by owls, weasels, and other predators.

Shrew-mole, American *(Neurotrichus gibbsii)*

Native mammal. This small insectivore is unique to the Northwest, and prefers shaded ravines of red alders and bigleaf maples. It digs tunnels that resemble moles' with its distinctive shovel-like front feet. This animal forages beneath the forest humus, but emerges above ground to hunt for spiders, worms, and insects.

Slug, Banana *(Ariolimax columbianus)*

Native invertebrate. Unlike the invasive black slug, this slug causes little garden damage. An effective composter, it recycles the leaf debris on the floors of damp forests, and also eats mushrooms, fallen fruits, animal matter, and dung.

Snake, Northwest Garter *(Thamnophis ordinoides)*

Native amphibian. This is the most common snake in the area, found in gardens, fields, meadows, thickets, and sometimes in woods. Its diet is slugs, earthworms, frogs, and salamanders. When handled, it seldom bites, but may defecate or discharge a foul-smelling secretion from its anal glands.

Squirrel, Douglas *(Tamiasciurus douglasii)*

Native mammal. Also known as the chickaree, this small squirrel is found in conifer forests in the Puget Sound area. It eats a variety of plant material, especially cones and berries, and lines its nests in dead trees with moss and strips of cedar bark.

Squirrel, Eastern Gray *(Sciurus carolinensis)*

Non-native mammal. Introduced to the area in the 1920s, this rodent is the squirrel most commonly seen in local parks and backyards. It usually nests in holes in trees, and its habitat has increased with the widespread replacement of conifers with deciduous trees. It eats a wide variety of plant material, including hazelnuts and the seeds of maples and horsechestnuts.

Squirrel, Northern Flying *(Glaucomys sabrinus)*

Native mammal. Unlike other squirrels, this type is almost completely nocturnal and somewhat carnivorous, occasionally eating bird eggs. Though seldom seen, it can be heard chirping in the forest canopy at night, its body slapping against tree trunks as it leaps from tree to tree.

Treefrog, Pacific *(Hyla* or *Psendacris regilla)*

Native amphibian. Also known as the Pacific chorus frog, this frog is by far the most abundant tail-less amphibian in this region. These small frogs gather in early spring to breed in open ponds and swamps, and the loud croaking of the males fills the air for weeks during the night. Tadpoles hatch from little clusters of eggs on sticks or grass stems in shallow water, then leave for the woods in late summer or early fall as young frogs.

Vole, Townsend's *(Microtus townsendii)*

Native mammal. This field mouse lives in underground burrows in open, grassy areas or under fallen logs. It eats stems, roots, bulbs, and tubers, especially grasses and sedges. Weasels, owls, garter snakes, and coyotes feed on voles.

Appendix A:

Selected Reading

Field Guides

The following books are recommended to readers who wish to identify the plants and animals mentioned in *Nature Walks In and Around Seattle*.

General

Kozloff, Eugene N. *Plants and Animals of the Pacific Northwest: An Illustrated Guide to the Natural History of Western Oregon, Washington and British Columbia*. Seattle: University of Washington Press, 1976.

Ransom, J.R., ed. *Harper & Row's Complete Field Guide to North American Wildlife, Western Edition*. New York: Harper & Row, 1981.

Whitney, Stephen R. *Western Forests*. New York: Knopf, 1994.

Plants

Crawford, Victoria. *Wetland Plants of King County and the Puget Sound Lowlands*. King County, Wash., 1981.

Guard, B. Jennifer. *Wetland Plants of Oregon and Washington*. Redmond, Wash.: Lone Pine, 1995.

Little, Elbert, L. *The Audubon Society Field Guide to North American Trees*. New York: Knopf, 1980.

Lyons, Chess P., and Bill Merilees. *Trees, Shrubs and Flowers to Know in Washington and British Columbia*. Redmond, Wash.: Lone Pine, 1995.

McKenny, Margaret (revised by Daniel E. Stuntz). *The Savory Wild Mushroom*. Seattle: University of Washington Press, 1971.

McMinn, Howard H. and Evelyn Maino. *An Illustrated Manual of Pacific Coast Trees*. Berkeley: University of California Press, 1967.

Pojar, Jim and Andy MacKinnon. *Plants of the Pacific Northwest Coast: Washington, Oregon, British Columbia and Alaska*. Redmond, Wash.: Lone Pine, 1994.

Schalkwijk-Barendsen, Helene M. E. *Mushrooms of Northwest North America*. Redmond, Wash.: Lone Pine, 1988.

Strickler, Dr. Dee. *Wayside Wildflowers of the Pacific Northwest.* Columbia Falls, Mont.: Flower Press, 1993.

Taylor, Ronald J. *Northwest Weeds: The Ugly and Beautiful Villains of Fields, Gardens and Roadsides.* Missoula, Mont.: Mountain Press, 1990.

Vitt, Dale H., Janet E. Marsh and Robin B. Bovey. *Mosses, Lichens and Ferns of Northwest North America.* Redmond, Wash.: Lone Pine, 1991.

Watts, Tom. *Pacific Coast Tree Finder.* Rochester, NY: Nature Study Guide, 1973.

Animals

BIRDS

Field Guide to the Birds of North America. 2d ed. National Geographic Society, 1987.

Peterson, Roger Tory. *A Field Guide to Western Birds.* 3d ed. Boston: Houghton Mifflin, 1990.

Robbins, Chandler S., Betel Bruun, and Herbert S. Zim. *Birds of North America: A Guide to Field Identification.* Rev. ed. New York: Golden Press, 1983.

Stokes, Donald and Lillian. *Stokes' Field Guide to Birds, Western Region.* New York: Little, Brown, & Co., 1996.

MAMMALS

Burt, William H. and Richard P. *A Field Guide to the Mammals.* Boston: Houghton Mifflin, 1964.

Murie, Olaus J. *A Field Guide to Animal Tracks.* Boston: Houghton Mifflin, 1954.

Pendall, Karen and Chris Stall. *Animal Tracks of the Pacific Northwest.* Seattle: The Mountaineers, 1981.

Whittaker, John O., Jr. *The Audubon Society Field Guide to the Animals of North America.* New York: Knopf, 1980.

REPTILES AND AMPHIBIANS

Corkran, Charlotte C., and Chris Thoms. *Amphibians of Oregon, Washington and British Columbia: A Field Identification Guide.* Redmond, Wash.: Lone Pine, 1996.

Leonard, William P., Herbert A. Brown, Lawrence L. C. Jones, Kelly R. McAllister and Robert M. Storm. *Amphibians of Washington and Oregon.* Seattle: Seattle Audubon Society, 1993.

Nussbaum, Ronald A., Edmund D. Brodie, Jr., and Robert M. Storm. *Amphibians and Reptiles of the Pacific Northwest.* Moscow, Idaho: University Press of Idaho, 1983.

Regional Interest

Alt, David, and Donald W. Hyndman. *Northwest Exposures: A Geologic Story of the Northwest.* Missoula, Mont.: The Mountain Press, 1995.

Arno, Stephen F., and Ramona P. Hammerly. *Northwest Trees.* Seattle: The Mountaineers, 1977.

Churney, Marie and Susan Williams. *Bogs, Meadows, Marshes, and Swamps: A Guide to 25 Wetland Sites of Washington State.* Seattle: The Mountaineers, 1996.

Clark, Lewis J. *Wild Flowers of the Pacific Northwest.* Sidney, B.C.: Gray's Publishing, 1976.

Fisher, Chris C. *Birds of Seattle and Puget Sound.* Redmond, Wash.: Lone Pine, 1996.

Hunn, Eugene S. *Birding in Seattle and King County: Site Guide and Annotated List.* Seattle: Seattle Audubon Society, 1982. (Somewhat outdated but useful.)

Jacobson, Arthur Lee. *Trees of Seattle: The Complete Tree-finder's Guide to the City's 740 Varieties.* Seattle: Sasquatch Books, 1989.

Kruckeberg, Arthur R. *The Natural History of Puget Sound Country.* Seattle: University of Washington Press, 1991.

Manning, Harvey and Penny. *Walks and Hikes in the Foothills and Lowlands Around Puget Sound.* Seattle: The Mountaineers, 1995.

Manning, Harvey and Penny. *Walks and Hikes on the Beaches Around Puget Sound.* Seattle: The Mountaineers, 1995.

McKee, Bates. *Cascadia: The Geologic Evolution of the Pacific Northwest.* New York: McGraw-Hill, 1972. (Outdated but classic text.)

Morgan, Brandt. *Enjoying Seattle's Parks.* Seattle: Greenwood Publications, 1979.

Mueller, Marge and Ted. *Washington State Parks: A Complete Recreation Guide.* Seattle: The Mountaineers, 1993.

Nehls, Harry B. *Familiar Birds of the Northwest.* 3d ed. Portland: Portland Audubon Society, 1989.

Orr, Elizabeth L. and William N. *Geology of the Pacific Northwest.* New York: McGraw-Hill, 1996.

Schwartz, Susan. *Nature in the Northwest.* Englewood Cliffs, N.J.: Prentice-Hall, 1983.

Turner, Nancy. *Food Plants of Coastal First Peoples.* Vancouver, B.C.: University of British Columbia Press in association with Royal British Columbia Museum, 1995.

Wahl, Terence R., and Dennis R. Paulson. *A Guide to Bird Finding in Washington.* Lynden, Wash.: Print Stop Press, 1994.

Appendix B:

Useful TelephoneNumbers

Parks

Bellevue Botanical Gardens/Wilburton Hill Park: (425) 452-2750

Bloedel Reserve: (206) 842-7631

Bridle Trails State Park: Washington State Parks (425) 649-4276 or (800) 233-0321

Burton Acres: Vashon Park District (206) 463-9602; Vashon Island Kayak Company (206) 463-9257

Camp Long: Park lodge (206) 684-7434; Longfellow Creek Watershed Educator (206) 233-2046

Carkeek Park: Environmental Education Center (206) 684-0877

Coal Creek Canyon Park: King County Parks (206) 296-4171

Cougar Mountain Regional Wildland Park: King County Parks (206) 296-4171

Discovery Park: Visitor Center (206) 386-4236

Ed Munro/Seahurst Park: City of Burien (206) 244-5662

Farrel-McWhirter Park/Redmond Watershed Preserve: Redmond Parks and Recreation Department (425) 556-2300

Grand Forest: Bainbridge Island Parks and Recreation Department (206) 842-2306

Juanita Bay Park: Kirkland Parks and Recreation Department (425) 828-1218

Kelsey Creek Farm and Community Park: (425) 452-7688

Lake Fenwick Park: Kent Parks and Recreation (253) 859-3300

Lake Hills Park: Bellevue Parks and Recreation (425) 452-7225

Lakemont Trail System: Bellevue Parks and Recreation (425) 452-2752

Marymoor Regional Park: King County Parks (206) 296-4171 or 296-2964; Marymoor Museum (425) 885-3684

Meadowdale Park: Snohomish County Parks and Recreation (425) 339-1208

Mercer Slough/Bellefields Nature Park: Winter's House Visitor Center (425) 452-2752; Pacific Science Center Environmental Education Center (206) 443-2925; Enatai Beach Park (canoe and kayak rentals) (425) 637-8838

Montlake Fill: University of Washington Center for Urban Horticulture (206) 543-8616

North Creek Park: Snohomish County Parks and Recreation (425) 339-1208

O. O. Denny County Park/Big Finn Hill Park: King County Parks (206) 296-4171, (425) 820-2413

Pacific Rim Bonsai Garden: (253) 924-3153

Pioneer Park: Mercer Island Parks and Recreation Department (206) 236-3545

Ravenna Park: Seattle Department of Parks and Recreation (206) 684-4075

Rhododendron Species Botanical Gardens: (253) 661-9377

Saint Edward State Park: Washington State Parks (425) 823-2992

Saltwater State Park: Washington State Parks (800) 233-0321

Schmitz Reserve: Seattle Department of Parks and Recreation (206) 684-4075

Seward Park: Seattle Department of Parks and Recreation (206) 684-4075

Soos Creek County Park: King County Parks (206) 296-4171

Washington Park Arboretum: Visitor Center (206) 543-8800; Japanese Garden (206) 684-4725

West Hylebos State Park: Washington State Parks (800) 233-0321, (253) 874-1194

Transportation

Metro Transit: (206) 553-3000, (800) 542-7876; DART 557-5560

Community Transit: (206) 353-7433, (800) 562-1375

Kitsap Transit: (360) 373-2877, (360) 697-2877, (800) 501-7433

Washington State Ferries: (206) 464-6400, (800) 84-FERRY

Organizations

Seattle Audubon Society: (206) 523-4483

East Lake Washington Audubon Society (ELWAS): (206) 431-3717

Rainier Audubon Society (South King County): (253) 939-6411

Washington Native Plant Society: P.O. Box 576, Woodinville, WA 98072-0576

Cascade/Sammamish Orienteering Club Hotline: (206) 783-3866

Acknowledgments

I want to express my gratitude to all the rangers, naturalists, and managers who assisted in the writing of this book. They cheerfully answered my telephone calls, sent maps and brochures, and reviewed the park chapters. These dedicated folks are true stewards of the lands in their care, in spite of the day-to-day realities of overwork and budget cuts.

Special thanks are due to naturalists Chuck Lennox and Chris Mayo, who oversee the King County Parks, and to Paul West and Robert Wilkens, for coordinating the information from several Seattle parks. Debbie Pettersson and Geoff Bradley with the Bellevue Parks and Community Services were especially helpful, while Bill Karras dispersed information on the two Snohomish County parks included in the book.

Jim Ganley and Hugh Jennings of the East Lake Washington Audubon Society, and Jim Flynn, Thais Bock, and Bruce Harpham of the Rainier Audubon Society assisted with bird lists and/or descriptions. The Cascade and Sammamish Orienteering Clubs graciously let us use their base maps to construct some of those included in this book. I was delighted that we were able to to obtain the mapmaking services of Debbie Newell, who also worked on many of the orienteering clubs' maps.

Special thanks to my editors Uma Kukathas, Susan Hodges, and Cindy Bohn, who managed a fine balance of firmness and flexibility in the editing process. The photographs in the book are the work of Jim Hendrickson, whose cheerful demeanor and gentle sense of humor were welcome accompaniments on our treks to scout out parks.

And finally, my grateful appreciation to Stephen Whitney, for giving me the opportunity to build on his splendid initial work and write the second edition of this book—a perfect excuse to spend a lot of time (but never enough) exploring the fascinating forest and wetland pockets of our region.

—*Cathy M. McDonald*

Index

alder, red 16, 19, 20, 26, 31, 35, 40, 44, 49, 55, 60, 63, 66, 70, 75, 76, 78, 83, 88, 92, 98, 101, 105, 109, 112, 119, 123, 127, 132, 135, 140, 143, 146, 153, 157, 161, 165, 166, 168
amanita, panther 92
anemone, sea 56
aplodontia (*see* mountain beaver)
archeology 53–54, 86
ash: European mountain 55, 143, 161; Oregon 20, 28, 40, 70, 88, 98, 146, 168
auklet, Rhinoceros 198
avens, large-leaved 56, 72, 98, 143, 161, 184

bacteria 49, 168, 176
baneberry, western red 185
bass, large-mouth 41, 67, 137
bat 56, 66, 72, 136, 148, 208
beach 26, 40, 50, 53–56, 59, 61, 62, 67, 69, 72, 73, 77, 129, 133, 137, 141, 142, 164
bear, black 22, 63, 66, 91, 120, 124, 208
beaver 45, 65, 66, 78, 79, 88, 98, 101, 208; mountain 32, 56, 60, 64, 72, 120, 208
bedstraw 56, 72, 75, 105, 132, 161, 185
Big Finn Hill Park 75–76
birch: European white 40, 44, 49, 55; paper 31, 98; swamp 40, 98, 147
bittern, American 41, 45, 198
Black River 140
blackberry: evergreen 28, 50, 60, 83, 88, 110, 124, 161, 175; Himalayan 21, 28, 32, 45, 50, 56, 60, 63, 72, 83, 88, 110, 114, 124, 132, 140, 143, 147, 161, 176; Pacific 55, 75, 83, 98, 105, 147, 157, 161, 176
blackbird: Brewer's 198; red-winged 32, 41, 45, 66, 78, 88, 98, 102, 109, 120, 162, 166, 198
bladderwort 19, 78
bleeding heart, Pacific or western 56, 60, 75, 119, 147, 186
blueberry 97, 108
Blue Heron Marsh 153
bobcat 88, 120, 209
bog 20, 88, 97, 107, 123, 145, 148, 181, 191
brant 60, 133, 144, 198
broom, Scot's 45, 56, 76, 109, 136, 161, 176
bufflehead 28, 45, 78, 98, 102, 133, 141, 147, 162, 166, 198
bulrush, small-fruited 19, 40, 56, 88, 162, 186
bur-reed 19, 78
bushtit 28, 32, 40, 41, 72, 78, 83, 136, 147, 157, 162, 166, 198
buttercup, creeping 28, 40, 49, 56, 60, 63, 66, 78, 83, 98, 109, 114, 124, 136, 140, 143, 147, 162, 186
butterflies 98, 171

candyflower 56, 60, 72, 75, 105, 132, 186
canvasback 28, 78, 98, 198
carp 41
cascara 20, 26, 31, 55, 62, 66, 70, 75, 98, 109, 114, 140, 146, 161, 165, 168

cattail, common 19, 28, 40, 45, 56, 66, 78, 88, 98, 109, 136, 140, 161, 166, 186
cedar, incense 31, 42; western red 16, 20, 25, 26, 29, 31, 35, 40, 49, 55, 59, 60, 62, 63, 65, 66, 69, 70, 75, 76, 83, 92, 96–98, 105, 109, 114, 119, 124, 127, 129, 132, 135, 140, 143, 146, 152, 157, 161, 165, 169
cherry, bitter 26, 49, 55, 92, 98, 109, 146, 161, 170
chickadee: black-capped 28, 32, 35, 40, 72, 75, 78, 83, 105, 120, 124, 147, 153, 157, 162, 166, 198; chestnut-backed 28, 32, 35, 40, 75, 78, 92, 120, 124, 136, 147, 153, 166, 198
chicory 45, 187
chipmunk, Townsend's 32, 56, 136, 144, 162, 209
cicely, sweet 56, 132
cinquefoil, marsh 19, 78
clam 54, 59, 62, 131, 133, 142, 156
climate 14–16, 112, 119, 123, 127
coal 14, 87, 91, 108, 115, 116, 118, 119, 121–123
Coal Creek 120–123
coot, American 28, 41, 45, 78, 88, 98, 141, 199
cormorant, double-crested 28, 41, 45, 78, 98, 147, 158, 199
cottontail, eastern 56, 120, 144, 162, 209
cottonwood, black 20, 21, 28, 31, 40, 44, 45, 60, 63, 70, 71, 75, 78, 83, 88, 92, 98, 105, 114, 123, 140, 161, 170
cougar 22, 91, 120, 124, 209
cowbird, brown-headed 136, 199
coyote 32, 56, 60, 64, 66, 72, 75, 78, 83, 88, 92, 94, 98, 109, 115, 120, 124, 136, 140, 148, 162, 209
crab 56, 133
crabapple, Pacific or Oregon 20, 26, 31, 40, 55, 60, 98, 146, 170
cranberry, wild 20, 162
creeper, brown 28, 32, 35, 72, 75, 92, 105, 120, 124, 153, 157, 166, 199
currant: red-flowering 119, 132, 157, 176; stink 75, 114, 132, 147, 176

deer, Columbia black-tailed 64, 66, 78, 83, 88, 98, 115, 120, 124, 127, 140, 162, 209
devil's club 20, 72, 92, 114, 127, 176
dipper, American 60, 63, 120, 199
dogwood: Pacific 31, 40, 49, 55, 70, 127, 146, 152, 165; red-osier 20, 66, 88, 98, 105, 109, 136, 147, 161, 166, 170, 177
Douglas-fir 16, 24, 25, 26, 31, 35, 40, 49, 55, 60, 62, 63, 66, 70, 72, 75, 76, 78, 83, 92, 98, 101, 105, 109, 114, 119, 124, 127, 129, 131, 132, 135, 140, 143, 152, 157, 161, 165, 171
drumlin 148
duck: ring-necked 78, 98, 109, 141, 147, 199; ruddy 45, 78, 98, 199; wood 98, 120, 136, 141, 147, 162, 166, 199
duckweed 19, 32, 78, 136, 147, 161, 187
dunlin 88, 199
Duwamish River 140

eagle, bald 22, 28, 41, 45, 56, 63, 66, 78, 88, 98, 115, 120, 133, 136, 144, 162, 166, 199
elderberry, coast red 20, 26, 35, 55, 60, 72, 83, 88, 114, 119, 127, 132, 136, 140, 143, 147, 157, 161, 177, 189
elk 209
ensatina 32, 133, 209
ethnobotany 168–197

falcon, peregrine 40, 199
fern: bracken 26, 56, 75, 83, 92, 119, 127, 136, 147, 157, 161, 189, 193; deer 20, 35, 56, 140, 147, 161, 194; lady 20, 26, 31, 35, 56, 60, 72, 75, 78, 83, 98, 105, 112, 119, 127, 132, 136, 144, 147, 157, 161, 195; licorice 26, 31, 35, 49, 56, 60, 72, 75, 83, 92, 105, 112, 119, 127, 131, 132, 136, 140, 144, 147, 157, 161, 195; maidenhair 56, 72, 112, 127, 132, 144, 195; sword 15, 26, 31, 35, 40, 49, 56, 60, 63, 72, 75, 83, 88, 92, 98, 105, 112, 119, 124, 127, 132, 136, 140, 144, 157, 161, 195; wood 56, 60, 112, 127, 132, 144, 147, 161, 195, 196
finch: house 72, 144, 166, 199; purple 28, 32, 78, 144, 162, 166, 200
fir, grand 26, 40, 60, 75, 109, 165
fire 35, 75, 119, 122, 123
fireweed 56, 98, 136, 161, 187
flicker, northern or red-shafted 32, 63, 66, 72, 102, 105, 136, 157, 166, 200
flycatcher: 32, 92, 98, 162, 166; olive-sided 28, 200; Pacific-slope or Western 72, 75, 200; willow 78, 136, 200
foamflower 20, 56, 75, 161, 187
Forbes Creek 78
forest: old-growth 16, 21, 33, 59, 119, 127, 132; sunken 70, 126
fox, red 32, 56, 98, 105, 162, 210
fringecup 28, 56, 60, 72, 75, 105, 144, 187
frog 78, 120, 162; Pacific chorus (*see* Pacific treefrog; red-legged 136, 210
fungus 18, 33, 147

gadwall 41, 45, 98, 109, 200
geology 14, 15, 49, 54, 55, 87, 119, 123, 139, 140, 145, 147
gingko 147
glacier 14, 15, 55
goldeneye: Barrow's 41, 98, 133, 144, 147, 158, 200; common 28, 98, 133, 147, 200
goldfinch, American 41, 88, 98, 157, 162, 166, 200
goose, Canada 41, 45, 200
gooseberry: straggly or black 98, 105, 147, 177; swamp or wild 55, 98, 119, 177
grape, Oregon 28, 32, 40, 49, 55, 60, 63, 72, 75, 92, 98, 101, 114, 119, 124, 127, 132, 136, 140, 144, 152, 157, 161, 165, 178, 179
grass, reed canary 19, 40, 78, 98, 109, 136, 162, 187
grebe 60, 133, 158; eared 28; horned 144, 200; pied-billed 41, 45, 78, 98, 109, 141, 200; red-necked 200; western 28, 201
Green River 135, 139, 140
grosbeak 28, 50, 78, 98, 127, 157, 162, 201
grouse, ruffed 72, 98, 120, 127, 136, 162, 201

guillemot, pigeon 144, 158, 201
gull 60, 133, 144; Bonaparte's 201; California 201; glaucous-winged 201; mew 201; ring-billed 201

hardhack 19, 20, 40, 65, 66, 88, 98, 109, 136, 147, 162, 166, 179
harrier, northern 45, 88, 201
hawk 75, 78, 98, 120, 136; Cooper's 32, 88, 201; red-tailed 32, 45, 63, 66, 72, 83, 88, 92, 105, 115, 162; sharp-shinned 166, 202
hazelnut, California 26, 31, 35, 40, 49, 55, 72, 75, 92, 98, 105, 114, 157, 161, 179, 180
hedgenettle, Cooley's 35, 56, 72, 105, 147, 188
hemlock, western 16, 20, 26, 31, 35, 40, 49, 55, 59, 60, 62, 63, 70, 75, 76, 83, 88, 92, 109, 114, 119, 124, 127, 132, 135, 140, 143, 146, 152, 157, 161, 165, 172
heron: great blue 32, 36, 41, 45, 63, 66, 78, 94, 98, 105, 109, 120, 136, 141, 147, 153, 158, 162, 166, 202; green 41, 45, 78, 88, 98, 162, 202
holly, English 21, 28, 32, 35, 50, 55, 56, 60, 63, 72, 83, 109, 132, 140, 143, 157, 173
honeysuckle, orange 72, 179
horsechestnut 31, 49, 55
horsetail, common 19, 32, 40, 56, 72, 78, 127, 136, 143, 147, 162, 166, 196
huckleberry, evergreen 35, 40, 157, 179; red 28, 32, 35, 40, 49, 55, 72, 75, 83, 92, 105, 114, 119, 127, 132, 147, 152, 157, 161, 166, 179
hummingbird: Anna's 88, 127, 202; rufous 32, 72, 78, 98, 127, 153, 162, 166, 202
Hylebos Creek 145

Ice Sheet, Vashon 14, 15, 49, 55, 112, 148
Indian plum 26, 40, 49, 55, 60, 72, 75, 83, 88, 92, 98, 105, 143, 147, 161, 166, 181
interpretive programs 24, 28, 29, 32, 36, 50, 52, 57, 60, 61, 67, 76, 80, 84, 94, 97, 99, 102, 107–110, 115, 120, 133, 141, 145, 148
Iris, yellow 19, 40, 78, 88, 140, 188
Island Crest Park 128
Issei Creek 161
Issaquah Alps 14, 22, 72, 112, 119
Ivy, English 28, 32, 50, 56, 60, 63, 72, 109, 140, 143, 157, 188

jay, Steller's 35, 40, 78, 83, 98, 102, 105, 144, 147, 202
Judd Creek 156
junco, dark-eyed or Oregon 32, 78, 83, 88, 162, 202

Kelsey Creek 103–105, 108
kestrel, American 88, 202
killdeer 32, 45, 78, 88, 98, 109, 136, 202
kingfisher, belted 32, 41, 63, 66, 78, 88, 98, 133, 136, 144, 158, 162, 166, 202
kinglet 40, 78, 98; golden-crowned 28, 32, 63, 75, 83, 105, 120, 124, 127, 153, 162, 166, 202; ruby-crowned 28, 32, 147, 162, 166, 202
knotweed 78

Labrador tea 20, 98, 147, 181
landslides 14, 15, 52, 54, 70, 126
laurel: Portuguese 56; swamp or bog 20, 147

Lewis Creek 111–112
lichens 18
limpet 56
lion, sea 56
liverwort 19, 147
Locks, Hiram M. Chittenden 40
logging 16, 21, 35, 40, 49, 55, 59, 60, 62, 63, 65,
    70, 73, 82, 87, 91, 92, 101, 104, 112, 127, 129,
    134, 142, 145, 156, 161, 164
Longfellow Creek 31
loon, common 28, 60, 133, 144, 158, 202
loosestrife, purple 40, 45, 78, 98, 188

Mackey Creek 83
madrone, Pacific 26, 31, 32, 40, 49, 55, 70, 76, 92,
    127, 143, 152, 157, 161, 165, 173
mallard 28, 32, 45, 141, 147, 203
maple: bigleaf 16, 20, 26, 29, 31, 35, 40, 49, 50, 55,
    60, 63, 66, 70, 75, 76, 78, 83, 92, 97, 98, 101,
    105, 112, 119, 123, 127, 132, 135, 140, 143,
    146, 152, 157, 161, 165, 174; vine 20, 26, 40,
    55, 66, 83, 92, 98, 105, 114, 140, 143, 146,
    152, 165, 166, 174
marsh 19, 21, 28, 39, 40–42, 48, 65, 66, 77, 78, 85,
    86, 88, 92, 97, 133, 134, 137, 153
McSorleys Creek 142–143
meadowlark, western 203
merganser 41, 78, 98; common 203; hooded 45,
    88, 109, 120, 162, 203; red-breasted 203
merlin 203
milfoil, European water 19, 40, 78, 88, 136, 188
mink 98, 162, 210
mole 32, 56, 72, 88, 210
monkey flower, yellow 19, 78, 162
moss 18, 20, 33, 147, 166
Mountains: Cascade 14, 16, 22, 40, 110, 112, 116,
    119, 124, 152, 162; Olympic 14, 50, 52, 56, 59,
    62, 119, 129, 141
mouse, deer 33, 56, 78, 87, 88, 92, 136, 162, 210
murre, common 203
murrelet, marbled 203
mushrooms 18, 35, 75, 82, 92, 112, 119, 147
muskrat 21, 45, 56, 66, 72, 78, 88, 98, 109, 140, 210
mussel 56, 98, 133

native peoples 20, 21, 25, 48, 53–55, 59, 62, 77, 86,
    87, 94, 101, 108, 116, 125, 131, 134, 139, 142,
    155, 159, 164
nettle, stinging 11, 28, 31, 56, 60, 72, 83, 98, 105,
    119, 136, 147, 157, 161, 177, 189
newt, rough-skinned 211
nightshade: climbing 78, 136, 184; enchanters 56,
    98, 105, 144, 184
ninebark, Pacific 66, 98, 136, 181
North Creek 64–65
nurse log 16, 33, 119, 133, 152
nuthatch, red-breasted 28, 32, 35, 40, 75, 83, 98,
    102, 105, 120, 124, 157, 162, 166, 203

oak: Garry 26; Oregon white 165; poison 177
ocean spray 28, 32, 60, 72, 127, 157, 181
opossum 32, 56, 78, 162, 211
orca 56

oriole, Bullocks 41, 78, 98, 141, 162, 203
osprey 28, 41, 78, 98, 115, 166, 203
otter, river 56, 64, 98, 140, 162, 211
owl 40, 45, 60, 63, 78, 98, 115, 120, 136; barn 66,
    72, 203; great-horned 28, 32, 35, 66, 92, 105,
    162, 203; northern saw-whet 28, 204; western-
    screech 28, 32, 35, 204

parsley, water 19, 20, 35, 56, 75, 78, 88, 98, 105,
    140, 147, 189
peat 40, 88, 108, 148
periwinkle 56
pheasant, ring-necked 43, 45, 78, 88, 98, 115, 136,
    162, 204
pigeon, band-tailed 32, 40, 78, 98, 120, 124, 127,
    141, 162, 166, 204
piggyback plant (see youth-on-age)
pintail, northern 78, 88, 98, 204
Pipers Creek 57–60
pipit, water or American 45, 98, 204
plantain, water 78
pond lily, yellow 19, 32, 88, 140, 189
pondweed 19, 78
pool, tidal 52, 56, 59, 133
poplar 28, 31, 49, 55, 88
porcupines 98, 120
porpoise 56
Puget Sound 14, 42, 50, 52, 55, 56, 59, 61, 62,
    129, 141, 142, 162

quail, California 45, 98, 115, 120, 136, 162, 204
Queen Anne's lace 45, 190

raccoon 32, 45, 56, 60, 78, 83, 88, 98, 105, 120,
    140, 144, 162, 211
rail, Virginia 41, 45, 78, 98, 120, 136, 162, 204
Rainier, Mount 24, 50, 52, 110, 112, 134, 139
Ravenna Creek 48
redwood: coast 46, 49, 140, 147, 153; dawn 47
Redmond Watershed Preserve 83–84
rhododendron 38, 97, 100, 102, 165; Pacific 152,
    182; species 150, 152
road, skid 56, 59, 70, 91, 127
rose: baldhip 55, 75, 182; little wild 157, 161, 182;
    Nootka 98, 136, 147, 182
rush, common 19, 40, 66, 78, 87, 98, 127, 136,
    148, 161, 162, 190

salal 28, 32, 35, 40, 49, 55, 63, 71, 72, 75, 83, 92,
    98, 101, 114, 119, 127, 132, 140, 144, 152,
    157, 161, 165, 183
salamander 78, 98, 162; long-toed 32, 211;
    northwestern 32, 66; western redbacked 32
salmon 12, 22, 31, 41, 56, 59, 60, 62, 64, 65, 67,
    78, 80, 83, 87, 105, 135, 140, 143, 161
salmonberry 20, 26, 32, 35, 40, 49, 55, 60, 63, 72,
    75, 78, 83, 88, 92, 105, 114, 119, 124, 127,
    132, 136, 143, 147, 157, 161, 165, 183
Sammamish River 85–87
Sammamish, Lake 14, 86, 88, 94, 100, 104, 108,
    110, 112
sanderling 204
sandpiper, spotted 45, 60, 63, 78, 109, 204

sapsucker, red-breasted 32, 50, 136, 157, 204
scaup 41; greater 98, 204; lesser 78, 98, 204
school trust lands 91, 159, 161
scoter 133, 144, 158, 204
seal 56, 64, 133
sedges 19, 56, 66, 78, 88, 127, 148, 161, 162, 166
Seidel Creek 83
serviceberry, western 184
settlers 16, 20, 21, 55, 59, 62, 65, 82, 87, 97, 101, 104, 108, 112, 126, 132, 134, 139, 156
Ship Canal, Lake Washington 21, 26, 41, 42, 77, 97, 101
shoveler, northern 41, 45, 88, 98, 205
shrew, Trowbridge 32, 56, 88, 136, 162, 211
shrew-mole 56, 60, 211
sisken, pine 78, 98, 102, 136, 147, 162, 166, 205
skunk 78, 144, 162
skunk cabbage, yellow 20, 35, 56, 72, 75, 78, 88, 98, 105, 127, 136, 147, 162, 165, 166, 190
slug 189, 212
snag 16, 22, 118, 119, 133
snail (*Allogona townsendia*) 105
snake, Northwest garter 72, 78, 94, 136, 148, 162, 212
snipe, common 45, 78, 98, 162, 205
snowberry, common 26, 32, 40, 49, 55, 98, 119, 124, 136, 140, 157, 161, 184
soil 14–16, 19, 21, 127, 140
Solomons seal, false 75, 143, 161
Soos Creek 134, 135
sora 45, 78, 98, 205
sparrow 78, 88, 98, 120, 124, 136, 157, 166; fox 28, 162, 205; golden-crowned 28, 115, 162, 205; savannah 45, 88, 205; song 32, 35, 41, 45, 60, 83, 102, 105, 133, 141, 144, 162, 205; white-crowned 115, 153, 162, 205
speedwell, marsh 19, 20, 78, 161
spruce, Sitka 20, 55, 63, 66, 105, 119, 135, 146, 161
squirrel 56, 60, 75, 83, 92, 98, 144; Douglas 148, 162, 212; eastern gray 32, 212; northern flying 120, 148, 212
star, sea 56, 133
starflower 56, 92, 144, 191
stickleback fish 66
stump 35, 83, 92, 119, 127, 132, 152, 157, 165, 166
sundew 20
sunfish, pumpkinseed 41, 66
swallow 32, 45, 66, 78, 98, 144, 162, 166; barn 72, 83, 205; cliff 72, 98, 205; tree 45, 136, 141, 205; violet-green 72, 136, 205

tanager, western 28, 32, 35, 72, 75, 98, 127, 162, 206
teal 41, 78, 98; blue-winged 45, 206; cinnamon 45, 206; green-winged 45, 88, 206
thimbleberry 26, 35, 40, 63, 72, 105, 114, 136, 157, 161, 184, 189
thrush 98; hermit 120, 124, 157, 206; Swainsons 32, 35, 75, 78, 83, 88, 120, 124, 127, 162, 166, 206; varied 28, 35, 72, 92, 120, 124, 133, 162, 166, 206
towhee, spotted (rufous-sided) 28, 32, 35, 60, 72, 75, 78, 83, 98, 102, 105, 120, 124, 133, 144, 147, 157, 162, 166, 206

treefrog, Pacific 32, 50, 66, 98, 105, 148, 212
trillium, western 35, 56, 72, 92, 132, 144, 147, 161, 165, 166, 191
trout 67; cutthroat 41, 66, 78, 143; steelhead 41, 143
twinberry, black 26, 98, 147, 184
twinflower 56, 127

Union Bay 36, 38–42, 48, 49
urchin, sea 56

vanilla leaf 72, 75, 157, 161, 191, 192
violet, marsh or swamp 147, 191
vireo 105, 127, 157; Huttons 28, 32, 75, 120, 124, 162, 206; red-eyed 98, 120, 124, 136, 206; solitary 206; warbling 162, 206
vole, Townsends 56, 66, 78, 88, 162, 212

wapato 21, 77, 97
warbler 28, 32, 78, 98, 105, 120, 124, 127, 144, 157, 162, 166; black-throated gray 35, 75, 206; orange-crowned 136, 207; Townsend's 207; Wilson's 60, 207; yellow 41, 207; yellow-rumped 162, 207
Washington, Lake 14, 24–26, 40–44, 65, 67, 70, 72, 73, 76, 78, 87, 94, 97, 100, 104, 108, 110, 112, 125, 140
Washington, University of 38–42, 86, 142, 164
water hemlock, poison 50
water lily, white 40, 78, 98, 192
watercress 49, 191
waterfall 112, 121
waterleaf, Pacific 56, 60, 75, 144, 147, 192
watershed 19, 29, 80, 83
waxwing, cedar 28, 32, 78, 98, 115, 120, 124, 133, 136, 162, 166, 207
weasel, long-tailed 56, 98, 120, 139, 140, 144
wetland 19, 20, 36, 39, 52, 64–66, 76–78, 88, 94, 100–102, 107, 115, 134, 136, 144–146, 148, 158, 163
widgeon: American 41, 63, 78, 88, 98, 105, 109, 166, 207; Eurasian 41, 45, 63, 98, 105, 109, 158, 207
willow 19–21, 35, 40, 63, 66, 7, 88, 92, 98, 105, 109, 136, 140, 157, 161, 166, 174; Pacific 40, 55, 60, 70, 87; Pipers 174; Scoulers 31, 40, 45, 55, 174; Sitka 28, 66; weeping 28, 55
wind 14, 75, 146
woodpecker 32, 40, 60, 69, 78, 92, 98, 119, 162; downy 83, 105, 115, 136, 147, 207; hairy 63, 72, 83, 136, 166, 207; pileated 22, 27, 28, 32, 34, 35, 63, 72, 75, 120, 124, 136, 165, 166, 207
wood-pewee, western 207
wren 32, 41, 45, 66, 78, 98, 136, 144, 157, 166; Bewicks 28, 60, 78, 102, 147, 207; marsh 88, 98, 120, 136, 141, 162, 208; winter 28, 72, 75, 83, 105, 133, 136, 162, 166, 208

yarrow 83, 120, 193
yellowthroat, common 45, 78, 88, 98, 109, 162, 208
yew, Pacific 26, 31, 35, 49, 55, 66, 70, 157, 165, 174, 175
youth-on-age 28, 56, 60, 63, 72, 75, 105, 114, 119, 124, 127, 132, 140, 144, 147, 193

About the Authors

Cathy M. McDonald
A background in geology led Cathy to a career as a freelance science and nature writer. Covering such interwoven subjects as geology, oceanography, meteorology, botany, and biology, she has written for video, *Earth* magazine, *The Seattle Times*, CD-ROM, and Web sites. Her particular focus is on the Cascadia region (both onshore and offshore). A main goal is to make science and nature accessible and exciting to "real" people, and she enjoys working with scientists to translate discoveries into language non-scientists can understand. She lives in the Seattle area.

Stephen R. Whitney
Steve is the author of seven books on natural history and outdoor recreation, including *A Field Guide to the Cascades and Olympics*, *A Field Guide to the Grand Canyon*, *A Sierra Club Naturalist's Guide: The Pacific Northwest*, and *Western Forests*. He is a former managing editor of the *Sierra Club Bulletin*, now *Sierra*, associate editor of *The Mother Earth News*, and contributing editor of *Backpacker*. In addition, Whitney was editorial manager of The Mountaineers Books for six years. He lives in Seattle.

James R. Hendrickson
Jim Hendrickson is a freelance photographer who also works for a professional photography lab. A Seattle native, he enjoys experimenting with alternative photo processes, gardening, and, of course, hiking. He lives in Seattle with his wife and daughter.

THE MOUNTAINEERS, founded in 1906, is a nonprofit outdoor activity and conservation club, whose mission is "to explore, study, preserve, and enjoy the natural beauty of the outdoors. . . ." Based in Seattle, Washington, the club is now the third-largest such organization in the United States, with 15,000 members and five branches throughout Washington State.

The Mountaineers sponsors both classes and year-round outdoor activities in the Pacific Northwest, which include hiking, mountain climbing, ski-touring, snowshoeing, bicycling, camping, kayaking and canoeing, nature study, sailing, and adventure travel. The club's conservation division supports environmental causes through educational activities, sponsoring legislation, and presenting informational programs. All club activities are led by skilled, experienced volunteers, who are dedicated to promoting safe and responsible enjoyment and preservation of the outdoors.

If you would like to participate in these organized outdoor activities or the club's programs, consider a membership in The Mountaineers. For information and an application, write or call The Mountaineers, Club Headquarters, 300 Third Avenue West, Seattle, Washington 98119; (206) 284-6310.

The Mountaineers Books, an active, nonprofit publishing program of the club, produces guidebooks, instructional texts, historical works, natural history guides, and works on environmental conservation. All books produced by The Mountaineers are aimed at fulfilling the club's mission.

Send or call for our catalog of more than 300 outdoor titles:

The Mountaineers Books
1001 SW Klickitat Way, Suite 201
Seattle, WA 98134
1-800-553-4453 / e-mail: mbooks@mountaineers.org